Issues in Monetary Policy

Issues in Monetary Policy

The Relationship between Money and the Financial Markets

Edited by

Kent Matthews

Philip Booth

John Wiley & Sons, Ltd

Other Wiley Editorial Offices

Wiley have other editorial offices in the USA, Germany, Australia, Singapore and Canada

Wiley also publishes its books in a variety of electronic formats. Some content that appears
in print may not be available in electronic books.

Library of Congress Cataloging-in-Publication Data

Issues in monetary policy : the relationship between money and the financial
   markets / edited by Kent Matthews, Philip Booth.
     p. cm.
   Includes bibliographical references and index.
   ISBN-13: 978-0-470-01819-4 (cloth : alk. paper)
   ISBN-10: 0-470-01819-4 (cloth : alk. paper)
  1. Monetary policy.   I. Matthews, Kent.   II. Booth, P. (Philip), 1964-
   HG230.3.I86 2006
   339.5'3—dc22   2005034996

British Library Cataloguing in Publication Data

A catalogue record for this book is available from the British Library

ISBN 13 978-0-470-01819-4 (HB)
ISBN 10 0-470-01819-4 (HB)

Typeset in 10/12pt Times by TechBooks, New Delhi, India
Printed and bound in Great Britain by Antony Rowe Ltd, Chippenham, Wiltshire
This book is printed on acid-free paper responsibly manufactured from sustainable forestry
in which at least two trees are planted for each one used for paper production.

To Alan Walters from whom we all learned so much and to whom the IEA is grateful for his contribution to the development of the Shadow Monetary Policy Committee

Contents

List of Contributors

Philip Booth
Institute of Economic Affairs, 2 Lord North Street, London, SW1P 3LB

Philip Booth BA, PhD, FIA, FSS is Editorial and Programme Director at the Institute of Economic Affairs and Professor of Insurance and Risk Management at Cass Business School, City University. He has previously worked as a special advisor on financial stability issues for the Bank of England. Philip Booth is editor of the journal *Economic Affairs* and associate editor of the *British Actuarial Journal*. He is a Fellow of the Institute of Actuaries and of the Royal Statistical Society. Amongst previous books he has written are *Investment Mathematics* (Wiley), *Modern Actuarial Theory and Practice* (CRC/Chapman Hall) and *The Way Out of the Pensions Quagmire* (Institute of Economic Affairs). He teaches, researches and writes in the areas of finance, investment and social insurance.

Forrest Capie
Bank of England, Threadneedle Street, London, EC2R 8AH

Forrest Capie has been Professor of Economic History at Cass Business School, City University, since the 1980s. He previously taught at the universities of Warwick and Leeds. He has been a British Academy Overseas Fellow at the National Bureau, New York, a visiting professor at the University of Aix-Marseille, and the London School of Economics, and a Visiting Scholar at the IMF. He has written widely on the history of money, banking and trade and commercial policy. He was editor of the Economic History Review, 1993–99 and is currently on the Academic Advisory Council of the Institute of Economic Affairs.

Tim Congdon
Huntley Manor, Huntley, Gloucestershire, GL19 3HQ

Professor Tim Congdon is an economist and businessman. He was a member of the Treasury Panel of Independent Forecasters (the so-called 'wise men') between 1992 and 1997, which advised the Chancellor of the Exchequer on economic policy. He founded Lombard Street Research, one of the City of London's leading economic research consultancies, in 1989, and was its Managing Director from 1989 to 2001 and its Chief Economist from 2001 to 2005. He has been a visiting professor at the Cardiff Business School and the City University Business

School (now the Cass Business School).He was awarded the CBE for services to economic debate in 1997.

Kevin Dowd

Centre for Risk and Insurance Studies, Nottingham University Business School, Jubilee Campus, Nottingham NG8 1BB

Kevin Dowd is professor of financial risk management and works in the Centre for Risk and Insurance Studies at Nottingham University Business School. He writes on a number of different research and policy areas, including those in financial risk management, financial economics, macroeconomics and monetary economics. He is the author of *Competition and Finance: A New Interpretation of Financial and Monetary Economics* (Macmillan, 1996), *Beyond Value at Risk* (Wiley, 1998) and most recently, the second edition of *Measuring Market Risk* (Wiley, 2005).

Milton Friedman

Milton Friedman is Senior Research Fellow at the Hoover Institution of Stanford University, California, and Paul Snowden Russell Distinguished Service Professor Emeritus of Economics at the University of Chicago. He has taught at universities throughout the world, from Cambridge to Tokyo. Since 1946 he has also been on the research staff of the National Bureau of Economic Research. He is the acknowledged head of the 'Chicago School' which specialises in the empirical testing of policy propositions derived from market analysis. Professor Friedman was awarded the 1976 Nobel Prize in Economic Sciences. He was awarded the Presidential Medal of Freedom in 1988 and received the National Medal of Science the same year and is a past President of the American Economic Association. He has also written a number of books and papers over the years.

John Greenwood

Chief Economist, INVESCO Global, 30 Finsbury Square, London, EC2A 1AG

John Greenwood OBE is Chief Economist of AMVESCAP plc, which includes INVESCO and AIM. A graduate of Edinburgh University, he did economic research at Tokyo University and was a visiting research fellow at the Bank of Japan. In 1983 he proposed a currency board scheme for stabilising the Hong Kong dollar that is still in operation today. Previously an economic adviser to the Hong Kong Government (1992–93), he is currently a member of the Committee on Currency Board Operations of the Hong Kong Monetary Authority. He is also a member of the IEA-sponsored Shadow Monetary Policy Committee in the UK.

Mervyn King

Governor, Bank of England, Threadneedle St., London, EC2R 8AH

Mervyn King is Governor of the Bank of England and is Chairman of the Monetary Policy Committee. He was previously Deputy Governor from 1998 to 2003, and Chief Economist and Executive Director from 1991. Mervyn King was a non-executive director of the Bank from 1990 to 1991. He studied at King's College, Cambridge, and Harvard (as a Kennedy Scholar) and taught at Cambridge and Birmingham Universities before spells as Visiting Professor at both Harvard University and MIT. From October 1984 he was Professor of Economics at the London School of Economics where he founded the Financial Markets Group.

Andrew Lilico

Europe Economics, Chancery House, 53-64 Chancery Lane, London, WC2A 1QU

Dr Andrew Lilico works for Europe Economics, particularly on impacts of financial regulation and issues relating to the cost of debt, the cost of equity, and the impact of real options. Commenting on his March 2004 critique of the Treasury-sponsored Barker Review of Housing Supply, Simon Jenkins wrote in the Evening Standard: 'I have rarely read such a devastating demolition job'. He has written a number of papers on the impact of differing monetary policy regimes on incentives for investment, and on the consequences of limited foresight for financial regulation and monetary policy-making. He has also lectured at UCL on Corporate Finance, on Macroeconomics, and on Money and Banking.

Kent Matthews

Sir Julian Hodge Prof of Banking & Finance, Cardiff University Business School, Colum Drive, Cardiff, CF1 3EU

Kent Matthews is the Julian Hodge Professor of Banking and Finance at Cardiff University. He trained at the London School of Economics, Birkbeck College and Liverpool University and has held previous academic positions at Liverpool University, Liverpool Business School. He has held visiting posts at the Catholic University of Leuven Belgium, Humbolt University, Berlin and University of Western Ontario, Canada as well as professional posts at the National Institute of Economic & Social Research, the Bank of England and Lombard Street Research Ltd.

Patrick Minford

Professor of Applied Economics, Cardiff University Business School, Aberconway Building, Colum Drive, Cardiff, Wales, CF10 3EU

Patrick Minford has been Professor of Economics at Cardiff Business School, Cardiff University since October 1997. He is a member of Monopolies and Mergers Commission 1990–96, one of the HM Treasury's Panel of Forecasters (the '6 Wise Men') between January 1993-December 1996 and received a CBE for services to economics, 1996. He is author of numerous books, articles and journalism on exchange rates, unemployment, housing and macroeconomics. He founded and directs the Liverpool Research Group in Macroeconomics, which has published forecasts based on the Liverpool Model of the UK since 1979.

Michael J. Oliver

École Supérieure de Commerce de Rennes, 2, rue Robert d'Arbrissel, CS 76522, 35065 Rennes, FRANCE
UPC, Jersey (Highlands College), PO Box 1000, St Saviour, JE4 9QA, Jersey, Channel Isles

Michael J. Oliver is currently Professor of Economics at the École Supérieure de Commerce de Rennes and University of Plymouth Colleges, Jersey and a Director of Lombard Street Associates. He is a recognised authority in teaching on monetary policy, exchange rate regimes and financial markets and institutions. His research interests include monetary policy, policy learning and behavioural finance. He has written numerous academic articles and has had several books published on monetary economics and economic history. His latest book with Gordon T. Pepper, *The Liquidity Theory of Asset Prices*, will be published by Wiley in 2006.

Gordon T. Pepper
Lombard Street Research, 30 Watling Street, London, EC4M 9BR

He was essentially a practitioner, who turned academic to pass on what he had learnt. Gordon Pepper is partner of W. Greenwell & Co from 1962–86 where he co-founded their prestigious gilt-edged business and was the principal author of Greenwell's Monetary Bulletin, which became one of the most widely read monetary economic publications produced in the UK in the 1970s and 1980s. Since leaving the City he has been an Honorary Visiting Professor at Sir John Cass Business School. He is currently chairman of Lombard Street Research. A forthcoming publication (with Michael J. Oliver) is *The Liquidity Theory of Asset Prices* (Wiley).

Keith Pilbeam
Dept. of Economics, City University, Northampton Sq., London, EC1V 0HB

Keith Pilbeam is Professor of International Economics and Finance at City University, London. He teaches on the international programmes of Boston University and has been Visiting Professor at the European University Institute in Florence. He has worked for NatWest and the Royal Bank of Scotland and consults for a number of City financial institutions. He also advises the UK Foreign Office on international economic issues. President of the International Economics and Finance Society (UK) he is author of three books, *Finance and Financial Markets*, *International Finance* and *Exchange Rate Management* (all published by Palgrave Macmillan).

David B. Smith
Chief Economist, Williams de Broë plc, PO Box 515, 6 Broadgate, London, EC2M 2RP

David B Smith studied Economics at Trinity College, Cambridge, and the University of Essex in the 1960s. He has since been employed at the Bank of England, Royal Bank of Scotland, National Westminster Bank, Cambridge Econometrics and the London Business School. He joined London stockbrokers Williams de Broë plc as its Chief Economist in 1982. David is currently Chairman of the Shadow Monetary Policy Committee run by the Institute for Economic Affairs (IEA), is a visiting lecturer at the Cardiff University Business School, and was a member of the Economics Board of the Council for National Academic Awards in the late 1970s and early 1980s. He is best known for his analyses of the effects of government spending on economic performance and his forecasting work performed using his own quarterly monetary model of the international and UK economies, developed from the early 1980s onwards.

Peter Warburton
Rhombus Research Ltd, 35 Castlebar Road, Ealing, London, W5 2DJ

Dr Peter Warburton is a director of Rhombus Research and Halkin Services and economic adviser to Ruffer LLP. He spent 15 years in the City as economic adviser and UK economist for the investment bank Robert Fleming and at Lehman. Previously, he was an economic researcher, forecaster and lecturer at the London Business School and City University Business School (now Cass Business School). He is a member of the IEA's Shadow Monetary Policy Committee. He published *Debt and Delusion* in 1999 and edited the *IEA Yearbook of Government Economic*

Performance 2002/03. He is a contributor to the *Practical History of Financial Markets* course at Edinburgh Business School.

Geoffrey Wood

Cass Business School, City University, 106 Bunhill Row, London, EC1Y 8TZ

Geoffrey Wood is Professor of Economics at Cass Business School in London. He is a graduate of Aberdeen and of Essex Universities, and has worked in the Federal Reserve System, the Bank of England, and at several universities in Britain and overseas. He has authored, co-authored, or edited over 20 books, and has published over 100 academic papers. His fields of interest are monetary economics, monetary history, and financial regulation.

Issues in Monetary Policy

Kent Matthews and Philip Booth

1.1 INTRODUCTION

Financial innovation and other developments in an advanced monetary economy will add to the many routes by which monetary policy influences financial assets and the real economy. However, the transmission mechanism of monetary policy is something that is well understood by the undergraduate economics student. The mechanism by which money influences the economy is through two principal routes. These are known as the 'direct mechanism' and the 'indirect mechanism'. The direct mechanism is what is familiarly known as the 'real balance effect', whereby an excess holding of money by firms and households is diminished through a spending mechanism. Households and firms purchase goods and assets until the desired holding of money comes into line with the actual amount of money held. The indirect effect is the effect money has on interest rates, asset prices and the exchange rate, which in turn affects the real economy through changes in consumer spending, investment and trade. The impact of the indirect effect depends on how sharply interest rates and asset prices react to the initial monetary shock – the liquidity effect, and subsequently how fast interest rates and asset prices respond to expectations of future monetary policy – the expectations channel. The complex route by which the indirect effect of monetary policy develops in a financially advanced economy was anticipated in Friedman's Counter-Revolution in Monetary Theory (see appendix 2). Keynesians of all descriptions concentrated on the minutia of the transmission mechanism, denying the existence of one particular route or arguing the weakness of another.[1] In contrast, the Monetarists led by Friedman argued that the channels by which money influences the economy are many, in continuous change and results in impact lags that may be 'long and variable'. The response of an economy to monetary shocks depends on the speed at which expectations adjust to these shocks.

1.2 THE MONETARIST COUNTER-REVOLUTION

Expectations are the key to understanding the short run trade-off between the real sector (real GDP, unemployment, etc.) and the nominal sector (nominal GDP, inflation etc). The conclusions of the Monetarist counter revolution led by Friedman (see appendix 1) are now part of mainstream thinking. Basically, there is no long run trade-of between nominal and real variables. The supposed trade-off between inflation and unemployment, which was the mainstay of British economic policy in the 1960s and mid-70s, was in reality a trade-off

---

[1] Even modern day New Keynesian models, while accepting the framework of the New Classical rational expectations school, pay little attention to the direct mechanism. See for example the Bank of England Quarterly Model in Harrison *et al.* (2005).

Issues in Monetary Policy. Edited by K. Matthews and P. Booth.
© 2006 John Wiley & Sons, Ltd.

between *unexpected* inflation and unemployment. There is no central bank today that does not recognise the importance of market expectations in setting monetary policy. The effectiveness of monetary policy depends in part on the state of expectations. An expansionary monetary shock is likely to have a stronger impact on the economy if it was *unexpected* than if it was *expected*. The speed of adjustment of an economy to a monetary shock and decomposition of the growth in nominal GDP into real GDP growth and inflation depends on inflation expectations and the expectations generating mechanism. The insights of Friedman (1970), Walters (1971), and Lucas (1972) are now safely part of mainstream economic thinking. Theory has firmly grounded the view that rules dominate discretion.

While accepting the implications of the Monetarist and New Classical theories by the world's central banks, the policy debate has shifted towards the anchoring of expectations. In the UK the question of instrument of control was largely by-passed[2] and the focus of debate was principally about the intermediate target or simple rules that hinged on the path of nominal variables. The unhappy experience of monetary policy in the 1980s in the UK saw broad money targets being superseded by narrow money targets and ultimately, exchange rate targets. The collapse of the ERM and the observed instability of the velocity money in the 1980s in the UK and other advanced economies swung the academic and policy debate towards the targeting of alternative nominal variables as a means of anchoring inflation expectations.

1.3   PRACTICE AHEAD OF THEORY

The Monetarist counter revolution was theory that explained the failure of demand management policies and the inability to exploit the fictional trade-off between inflation and unemployment. The near universal acceptance of the key tenets of the Monetarist message by central banks represents the victory of theory over practice. In contrast, the success of inflation targeting by central banks, according to Mervyn King the Governor of the Bank of England (chapter 1), represents the success of practice over theory. Indeed inflation targeting has been viewed by many as an apparent success for central bank policy.[3] But it can be argued that this success has been because of the return of a type of discretion in the setting of interest rates. Central bankers take in a wide range of information in deciding monetary policy[4] which has elevated the basis of their judgement to an 'art' form that eschews the simple monetary target rules of the Monetarists. This is the challenge the Governor has made in the first essay of this book. Much of the remaining essays in the book take up the challenge.

According to King, inflation targeting avoids the one extreme of sticking to a rigid monetary rule or the other extreme of generating fixed reaction functions derived from an optimising framework. By avoiding rigid rules or 'learnable' reaction functions and being flexible (read discretion), the central bank has a better chance of meeting its stated aim. Influencing expectations is one way, of making the market do the work of the central bank. The Governor's articulation of the 'Maradona theory of interest rates' is an example of how the target can be reached without changing monetary policy. This of course will work only if the Bank of England is correct and the market is wrong. However, King is clear that the market cannot be systematically wrong, in the same way that Maradona cannot always score by running in a straight line. The problem is that the market does not have a learnable rule or reaction function

---

[2] The Treasury Green Paper on Monetary Control (1980) came out against monetary base control on pragmatic grounds and had even won over some of its most powerful supporters – see Walters (1984).

[3] See for example Svensson (2000).

[4] See Bernanke *et al.* (1999).

to converge on and like the Monetary Policy Committee of the Bank of England it also looks at everything to try and second guess monetary policy.

The success of inflation targeting is not measured simply in terms of the target but also in terms of financial stability and inflation volatility. Based on the record, the Governor would appear to be correct. But has this simply been luck? Should the Bank be targeting other variables? Should it pay more attention to the monetary aggregates and introduce new or reintroduce hastily discarded other instruments of control? What lessons can be gleaned for monetary policy in general and what lessons can be learned from the experience of other central banks? These questions and others (but not necessarily answers) can be found in the following essays.

1.4   THE DANGERS OF PRACTICE WITHOUT THEORY

David Smith questions the effectiveness of depending on a single instrument of control and takes aim at the new Bank of England macroeconomic model. His chapter argues that the history of monetary policy errors since the 1960s have stemmed from the failure to control the supply of broad money. Other instruments that could be used to control broad money growth have either been removed from the Bank (funding policy, currency intervention) or are not part of the remit of the MPC (reserve requirements, special deposit calls). He takes aim at the new macroeconomic model used by the Bank and argues that because its New-Keynesian (NK) structure offers no role for broad money or credit, the model constrains the monetary debate. To be fair, the constraint is not due to the lack of a role for money. Money is implicit in the Bank model but because it assumes continuous equilibrium in the market for money the 'LM' curve could be validly replaced by an interest rate function. The problem occurs if we think of money as a 'buffer stock', which raises the possibility of aggregate disequilibrium between money demand and money supply. If this possibility is accepted, then measures of broad money must play an explicit role in the macroeconomic model.

Andrew Lilico argues that price level targeting offers several advantages over inflation targeting. In principle, price level targeting could produce higher economic growth, less need for fine tuning, results in a lower average rate of inflation or even deflation, and offers a superior way of dealing with deflationary depression. The chapter distinguishes between inflation volatility and inflation uncertainty. A credible price level targeting policy means that any deviation from the target results in a predictable movement back to the target, therefore lowering inflation uncertainty, reducing the inflation risk premium and creating higher growth through marginal investment. A credible price level target also generates self-regulating actions by the market to reinforce the target, lessening the need for fine tuning and eliminating a liquidity trap situation. However, one problem Lilico recognises is that the central bank has to identify changes in the price level caused by temporary demand shocks and permanent supply shocks. The outcome is a trade-off between short-run and long-run price level volatility.

Keith Pilbeam takes up the issue of supply versus demand-based shocks to the price level within the framework of an open economy theoretical macroeconomic model. The analysis extends the seminal work of Poole (1970) to ask the question, when is a price level target most appropriate. It turns out that a price level target is output stabilising when the economy is hit by money demand shocks and aggregate demand shocks but not when it is hit by supply side shocks. In the wake of rising oil prices and the aftermath of hurricane Katrina in 2005, this issue has a contemporary resonance. Pilbeam argues that in the case of negative supply shocks, some flexibility to the price level target is necessary. The problem for the central bank is trying to distinguish between the different types of shocks. Forward looking asset market variables such as the rate of interest and the exchange rate reflect market expectations of shocks to the economy. However, the central bank may fail to distinguish between different types of shocks particularly when they result in the same qualitative response from forward looking asset market variables. This is a classic 'signal extraction' problem. In a rational expectations framework, it is not just the central bank but also all economic agents that are trying to extract information from the observed forward-looking variables. In this case it is not clear what the optimal policy response should be.[5]

Patrick Minford squares up to the challenge of practice over theory made by King. In his essay the economy is modelled in a general equilibrium representative agent framework. The representative agent is assumed to be liquidity constrained, is risk averse and aims to smooth consumption. Expectations are rational. The utility of the representative agent is maximised when the variance of the real wage is minimised. Faced with different types of shocks, agents chose a wage contract that is fixed, indexed to the price level (or auction wage) or some combination of both (endogenous). The economy is assumed to be hit by monetary shocks and productivity shocks. These shocks cannot be neatly separated in demand and supply influences. In keeping with the general equilibrium nature of the model, the productivity shocks also affect demand through its effect on the return on capital and investment decisions. Using stochastic simulation, several policy questions are posed. Interest rate control is compared with money supply control. Under interest rate control shoe-leather costs are minimised but the variance of unemployment is higher compared with money supply control. Money or price-level targeting produces different results on the volatility of real wages and unemployment. Under money supply targeting, prices are less stable and therefore real wages and consumption of the employed are less stable. However, the volatility of unemployment is minimised under price level targeting. The welfare implication for the economy depends on the relative weighting of the various elements. The policy maker is faced with the choice of weights that maximise the welfare of the representative agent and in this result we may have a clue to the success of the Bank of England. It could be said that the Bank of England has been lucky so far with a benign period for the experiment of inflation targeting. It was period of relative calm. However, as the global economy enters a new phase of high oil prices and potential for supply-side shocks the Monetary Policy Committee may be faced with some real choices and trade-offs.

Dowd takes aim at the Bank of England's inflation fan charts. The Bank has for some-time been forecasting both inflation and the density function of the forecast, which gives the probability of inflation being above or below the mean or mode. The fan chart is a measure of inflation uncertainty. While the Bank has been assiduous in assessing its performance in relation to the point forecast, Dowd shows that the density forecasts have been biased. The fan charts reveal that the Bank thought that there was a significant probability that inflation would not remain at the point forecast but rise over time. This outcome has not materialised and the Bank appears to have failed to learn from its mistakes. In essence it has exaggerated the risk of medium term inflation. But does this matter? The Bank has a good record on its point forecast of inflation and has a successful track record of steering the economy based on the point forecast. In which case Dowd asks, why do they forecast the density?

The financial crisis created by the collapse of LTCM highlighted the fact that banks are not the exclusive foci of a modern financial system. In a rapidly developing financial world, where

---

[5] Minford and Peel (1983) show that the minimum output variance outcome is a monetary policy rule that minimises the variance of monetary policy shocks.

disintermediation and capital market transactions dominate, non-bank financial corporations are as much the attention of central banks and regulatory authorities as the banks. Forrest Capie and Geoffrey Wood re-examine the role of the central bank within the modern financial system. The role of the central bank is to maintain financial stability. The question Capie and Wood pose is that given that the central bank has to act as a crisis manager, should the Lender of Last Resort (LOLR) function be extended to non-bank financial institutions. What should be the central bank response to unstable asset prices? In situations of financial crisis the line between insolvency and illiquidity is not easy to draw. With the aim of ensuring financial stability it is hard to avoid an implicit Too-Big-To-Fail (TBTF) policy. They conclude that it is not the business of central banks to stabilise asset prices but to be prepared to act as LOLR only if the financial system is threatened.

Tim Congdon traces the monetary transmission mechanism from its roots in Irving Fisher, through Milton Friedman and to Patinkin's well-known 'Real Balance Effect'. The principal theme is the emphasis on the stability of the desired ratio of money to expenditure. The key distinction is the adjustment of the individual's holding of money relative to his desired holding and the adjustment of the economy as a whole between actual and desired money balances. Where an individual can adjust their actual holdings of money to disequilibrium between actual and desired, the adjustment for the economy as a whole is more complicated. For example, an excess supply of money leads to an excess demand in all other markets al la Patinkin. Everyone tries to get rid of their excess money by acquiring goods and assets. The resulting excess demand in all other markets brings about changes to variables such as asset prices and goods prices that feedback on to the level of desired money balances. Ultimately, desired money balances rise to match the actual level of money balances when the price level rises in line with the rise in the money supply. As Yeager (1968) has put it, unwanted money will continue to be passed around until it ceases to be unwanted. In this chapter Congdon also takes a swipe at the Bank of England's view of the transmission mechanism. First, the Bank pays little or no attention to the direct mechanism of the real balance effect and focuses only on the indirect mechanism of the rate of interest. Second, Congdon argues that sector imbalances of money play an important role in the transmission mechanism. An excess of money held by the non-personal sector would be translated into asset demands and asset prices, which eventually feeds into domestic demand. Peter Warburton presents some econometric evidence to support this proposition in an annexe to this chapter.

Empirical evidence is beginning to mount that the Bank of England does implicitly target asset prices.[6] This is something that many economists outside the Bank have suspected but Gordon Pepper and Michael Oliver pose the question, should they? They start with an examination of types of traders in capital markets. Although not using the same language, Pepper and Oliver describe the workings of the stock market in terms of the interactions of 'informed' and 'noise traders' in the sense of Shiller (2005). An implicit monetary loanable funds theory is linked to the disequilibrium money framework of David Smith and Tim Congdon's essays. Expectations are not rational in this world. The players that inhabit the stock market have extrapolative expectations underpinned by sentiment, intuition, inertia and herd behaviour. Fuelled by excess money balances stock market players interact to generate speculative bubbles. Should the central bank target asset prices? Despite the role of money in initiating a speculative bubble Pepper and Oliver conclude that the central bank should not target asset prices but be available to act as LOLR to deal with the consequences of a crash.

---

[6] See Kontonias and Montagnoli (2004) and Allington and McCombie (2005).

The final chapter by John Greenwood traces the monetary policy history of Japan in the last three decades of the 20th century. In particular this chapter focuses on the monetary policy of the Bank of Japan (BOJ), which took Japan from a period that had experienced one of the best monetary policies of the OECD economies to one of the most inept. In this chapter we find relevant lessons for the Bank of England, lest the success of its inflation targeting policy gives rise to complacency. During the golden era (1976–85), the BOJ oversaw a period of low inflation and steady economic growth based on monetary targeting. Monetary policy began to go off the rails in the five years of 1985–89 when the BOJ took their eye off the growth in the money supply so as to pursue external objectives. The result was acceleration in money growth and rapid growth of stock and real estate prices. But what was remarkable about the period was the relative lack of goods price inflation. The pricing of the asset price bubble in 1989–91 had the desired effect but also tipped the economy into recession, the medium term results of which are well known. Greenwood takes the reader through the policy responses (fiscal and monetary) and the failures of monetary policy to deal with medium term deflation. The lesson for the Bank of England is obvious. The BOE has been successful in its inflation targeting policy in delivering low inflation and steady economic growth. But a number of economists would argue that they, like the BOJ, have taken their eye off the monetary ball and with broad money growing in mid 2005 in double digits, the consequences for asset prices have not been appreciated. The question for the Bank is whether it has sufficient instruments of control to buttress a sliding economy if the asset price boom turns into a protracted debt deflation.

This book brings together a collection of essays that picks up the gauntlet thrown down by the Governor of the Bank of England. Even as Pepper and Oliver suggest that there is much that economic theory can learn from the practitioner, the current successful policy of inflation targeting is not a situation of practice ahead of theory. Minford shows that there is no inconsistency between theory and practice and indeed the success of the Bank of England may partly be due to the benign environment it has overseen. The other essays challenge the Bank's view of the transmission mechanism, its over-reliance on the single instrument of control and its role in the monetary system. In particular, in failing to heed the lessons of recent UK monetary history and of the experience of Japan, the Bank is in danger of forgetting the fundamental lessons provided by the Monetarist counter-revolution.

REFERENCES

Allington N.F.B. and McCombie J.S.L. (2005) Measuring the Reaction of United Kingdom Monetary Policy to the Stock Market: A Heteroskedastic Approach, Cambridge Centre for Economic and Public Policy Research, mimeo.

Bernanke, B.S., Laubach, T., Mishkin, F. and Posen, A. (1999) *Inflation Targeting: Lessons from the International Experience*, Princeton: Princeton University Press.

Friedman, M. (1970) A Theoretical Framework for Monetary Analysis, *Journal of Political Economy*, **78**, 193–238.

Harrison, R., Nikolov, K., Quinn, M., Ramsay, G., Scott, A. and Thomas, R. (2005) *The Bank of England Quarterly Model*, London: Bank of England.

Kontonikas, A. and Montagnoli, A. (2004) Has Monetary Policy Reacted to Asset Price Movements? Evidence from the UK, *Ekonomia*, **7**.

Lucas, R.E. (1972) Expectations and the Neutrality of Money, *Journal of Economic Theory*, **4**, 103–124.

Minford, A.P.L. and Peel, D.A. (1983), Some Implications of Partial Current Information Sets in Macroeconomic Models Embodying Rational Expectations, *Manchester School*, Sept, 235–249.

Poole, W. (1970) Optimal Choice of Monetary Policy Instruments in a Simple Stochastic Monetary Model, *Quarterly Journal of Economics*, **84**, 197–216.

Shiller, R.J. (2005) *Irrational Exuberance*, (2nd ed), New Jersey: Princeton University Press.

Svensson, L. (2000) Open Economy Inflation Targeting, *Journal of International Economics*, **50**, 155–183.

Walters, A.A. (1984) The United Kingdom: Political Economy and Macroeconomics, *Carnegie – Rochester Conference Series on Public Policy*, **21**, North-Holland, 259–280.

Walters, A.A. (1971) Consistent Expectations, Distributed Lags and the Quantity Theory, *Economic Journal*, **81**, 322, 273–281.

Yeager, L.B. (1968) Essential Properties of the Medium of Exchange, Kyklos, 1, reprinted in R. Clower (ed) *Monetary Theory*, Harmondsworth: Penguin.

2
Monetary Policy: Practice Ahead of Theory[1]

Mervyn King[2]
Governor of the Bank of England

2.1 INTRODUCTION

Monetary policy is aimed at maintaining price stability. That may seem self-evident. Thirty years ago it was not. From the end of the Second World War until the mid-to-late 1970s, the majority view of academic economists and policy-makers alike was that monetary policy had rather little to do with inflation, and was largely ineffective as an instrument of demand management.[3] The intellectual basis for that view was never clear. And painful experience taught us that price instability led to costly fluctuations in real output and employment. Far from being ineffective, a monetary policy aimed at price stability has proved to be the key to successful management of aggregate demand. Fortunately, the theory and practice of monetary policy in the UK have changed out of all recognition in the past twenty-five years.[4] We have moved from the Great Inflation to the Great Stability.

The story of monetary policy in Britain during the intervening period is told by the Mais Lectures.[5] The first Mais Lecture was delivered by my predecessor, Lord Richardson, in 1978, at a point when monetary policy was emerging as the main tool to deal with inflation. Not before time, you might think, since only two years earlier inflation had reached 27%. In 1981 the Chancellor of the Exchequer, Geoffrey Howe, chose as the title of his Mais Lecture: 'The Fight Against Inflation'. As he said then, with inflation still in double figures, 'squeezing inflation out from an economy which has become accustomed to higher rates over a period of years cannot be an easy or painless task. ... the inflationary mentality must be eradicated. ... When we have done that we will find that low inflation or even price stability need not be painful'. The conquest of inflation was to prove harder than expected. In the decade that followed Geoffrey Howe's lecture, inflation averaged over 7% a year. Only since 1992 has inflation fallen to levels that could be described as price stability.

---

[1] This chapter is reproduced with kind permission of the Bank of England.
[2] This chapter was the Mais Lecture delivered on 17 May 2005 at the Cass Business School, City University, London. I am indebted to James Proudman, Gertjan Vlieghe, Tony Yates and Richard Harrison who have worked closely with me and are effectively co-authors. Alan Mankikar and Tim Taylor provided excellent assistance in preparing the empirical and historical research.
[3] This proposition is documented in detail by Batini *et al.* (2005).
[4] See Capie *et al.* (2001).
[5] The Mais lecture series is a long running series of lectures, held at City University Business School (now Cass Business School) at which senior people involved in the policy process have lectured on issues to do with monetary policy and finance. A record of the Mais lectures can be found in Capie and Wood (2001).

Issues in Monetary Policy. Edited by K. Matthews and P. Booth.

In retrospect, two Mais Lectures seem to have been of particular significance: those by Nigel Lawson in 1984 and by Tony Blair, then Leader of the Opposition, ten years ago this month. Despite clear differences of view, what stand out from those two lectures are their similarities. Both emphasised the need for a medium-term framework for monetary and fiscal policy. Over 25 years we have moved from monetary targets to an inflation target and from a medium term financial strategy to rules for fiscal policy over the cycle. Yet the essential objective of maintaining monetary and fiscal discipline remains the same. All major political parties in the UK now agree that stability is the key to economic success.

We do not know whether the Great Stability will continue, as it has for more than a decade now. In part, it will depend upon whether our framework of inflation targeting can respond to the economic shocks that will undoubtedly be visited upon us in the years ahead. And that is the subject of this chapter. In only fifteen years inflation targeting has taken the central banking world by storm. Table 2.1 shows that there are now twenty-two countries in which monetary policy is based on an inflation targeting regime. So this chapter examines what inflation targeting really means, why it has been successful in Britain and elsewhere, and what challenges it faces in the years ahead.

It tries to answer three questions. First, what can monetary policy do and how has our understanding of that changed over time? Second, what are the challenges for central banks that result from incomplete knowledge of the transmission mechanism of monetary policy?

Table 2.1   Inflation targeting countries

Country	Adoption of Inflation Targeting
New Zealand	Dec. 1989
Chile	Jan. 1991
Canada	Feb. 1991
Israel	Jan. 1992
UK	Oct. 1992
Sweden	Jan. 1993
Finland	Feb. 1993
Australia	Mar. 1993
Spain	Jan. 1995
Czech Republic	Apr. 1998
Korea	Apr. 1998
Poland	Oct. 1998
Mexico	Jan. 1999
Brazil	Jun. 1999
Colombia	Sep. 1999
South Africa	Feb. 2000
Thailand	May 2000
Iceland	Mar. 2001
Norway	Mar. 2001
Hungary	July 2001
Peru	Jan. 2002
Philippines	Jan. 2002

Source: Truman and Edwin (2003), *Inflation Targeting in the World Economy*, Institute for International Economics, Washington DC. The table not only includes current inflation targeting countries, but also Spain and Finland, which have since joined EMU.

Third, is inflation targeting the answer to those challenges? I believe that it is. Inflation targeting, I shall argue, is the natural way to conduct policy when there is a great deal about its effects that we do not understand. The practice of monetary policy must recognise that monetary theory will continue to evolve. That is why the chapter is subtitled: practice ahead of theory.

2.2   WHAT CAN MONETARY POLICY DO?

In practice, monetary policy means setting the level of the official interest rate at which the central bank deals with the banking system.[6] But ideas about how interest rates should be set, and with what objective, have been subject to radical changes since the 1970s. Let me give three examples. None is new; the subject has moved on. I give them to show that monetary policy operates against an ever-changing backdrop of ideas about the way the economy works, a theme that lies at the heart of my lecture.

First, it is now widely accepted that there is no long-run trade-off between output and inflation. Both theory – following Friedman (see the Appendix to this book) and Phelps – and practice – particularly in the 1970s – showed that permanently higher inflation does not bring faster growth or higher employment, and may well reduce both. But in the post-war period views were different. In 1959 the Radcliffe Report on the Workings of the Monetary System seemed to support the idea of a permanent trade-off. The objectives of monetary policy included, it argued, 'a high and stable level of employment' and 'reasonable stability of the internal purchasing power of money'. But it went on, '... there are serious possibilities of conflict between them'.[7]

Second, the rate of inflation in the long run is determined by monetary policy, not by microeconomic factors. Again, that is now taken for granted, but much effort was devoted to the imposition of detailed direct wage and price controls in the 1960s and 1970s. Nicholas Kaldor, adviser to Harold Wilson, wrote in 1971 that 'It is also far more generally acknowledged' – even by Conservative Prime Ministers – that the process of inflation is 'cost-induced' and not 'demand-induced', with the evident implication that it can be tackled only by an incomes policy'.[8] Not many Whitehall advisers would give that answer today.

Third, in the short run monetary policy does affect output and employment and so has the potential to be an effective stabilisation tool. Reflecting a post-war consensus that monetary policy was rather ineffective, however, the Radcliffe Report concluded that '... there can be no reliance on this weapon [interest rate policy] as a major short-term stabiliser of demand'[9] It is now accepted that monetary policy lies at the heart of any attempt to stabilise the economy.

The source of monetary policy's influence over output and employment lies in frictions, which mean that prices and wages do not adjust instantaneously to clear markets whenever demand and supply are out of balance. Firms change prices only irregularly in response to changes in demand; wages adjust only slowly as labour market conditions alter; and expectations are updated only slowly as new information is received. Such frictions generate short-run

---

[6] For many years there was a debate about whether policy was better seen as setting short-term interest rates or determining the monetary base. That is no longer an issue. For some time, the demand for money has been purely demand-determined. As a result, central banks can set the short-term interest rate either to influence real interest rates or to determine the path of the monetary base or a broader monetary aggregate. Money remains at the heart of the transmission mechanism but since its velocity is unstable most central banks use interest rates as their instrument rather than a monetary aggregate.

[7] Radcliffe Report (1959) pp. 18–21.

[8] Kaldor, N. (1971), p. 14.

[9] Radcliffe Report (1959) p. 177.

relationships between money, activity and inflation.[10] The nature of frictions goes right to the heart of the policy debate over inflation targeting. From time to time shocks will move inflation away from its desired long-run level, and the policy question is how quickly it should be brought back to that level. There is no right or wrong answer to that question. Only an analysis of the nature of the relevant frictions tells us what is the 'optimal' monetary policy.

That is why recent academic analysis portrays monetary policy as a 'policy reaction function' which describes the reaction of the official short-term interest rate to any possible configuration of economic shocks that might arise in future. For a given model of frictions it is possible to derive the appropriate policy reaction function which most advances the objectives of the policy-makers. Such a reaction function is a state-contingent monetary policy rule. It describes policy in every situation. There are no exceptions and, by construction, the rule does not change over time.

Monetary policy rules have become a major area of research.[11] Perhaps the most famous is the so-called Taylor rule, named after John Taylor who has just returned to Stanford after serving as Under Secretary at the US Treasury. The Taylor rule implies that interest rates should rise if inflation is above its target and output is above its trend level, and fall when the converse is true. The path along which inflation should return to its desirable long-run level will therefore vary according to the state of the economy.

A key motivation for the study of monetary policy rules was the insight that if economic agents base their decisions on expectations of the future then the way monetary policy is expected to be conducted in the future affects economic outcomes today. Hence it is very important to think about how policy influences the expectations of the private sector. Consider a simple and stark example. Suppose that a central bank managed to control inflation perfectly by responding to all shocks instantaneously. The outcome would be a constant inflation rate. Households and firms would know that potential movements in inflation would never emerge because all future shocks would be instantly offset by changes in interest rates. Interest rates would change with no apparent link to or effect on inflation. To an observer – whether journalist or econometrician – interest rate changes would appear to have little to do with inflation. The central bank would appear to be behaving almost randomly. But that inference would be false. Indeed, if people did expect the central bank to behave randomly, then the behaviour of households and firms would change and inflation would no longer be stable.

This is what I call the 'Maradona theory of interest rates'. The great Argentine footballer, Diego Maradona, is not usually associated with the theory of monetary policy. But his performance against England in the World Cup in Mexico City in June 1986 when he scored twice is a perfect illustration of my point. Maradona's first 'hand of God' goal was an exercise of the old 'mystery and mystique' approach to central banking. His action was unexpected, time-inconsistent and against the rules. He was lucky to get away with it. His second goal, however, was an example of the power of expectations in the modern theory of interest rates. Maradona ran sixty yards from inside his own half beating five players before placing the ball in the English goal. The truly remarkable thing, however, is that Maradona ran virtually in a straight line. How can you beat five players by running in a straight line? The answer is that

---

[10] In a deep sense, only a complete understanding of the nature of the frictions makes it possible to decide on the objectives of monetary policy. Woodford (2003) and others discuss the link between that fundamental analysis and the proposition that monetary policy should aim to stabilise inflation and output.

[11] An excellent example is the recent book by Michael Woodford (2003) which builds on the ideas of the Swedish economist Knut Wicksell one hundred years ago that the key to price stability lies in thinking about the appropriate path for future nominal interest rates.

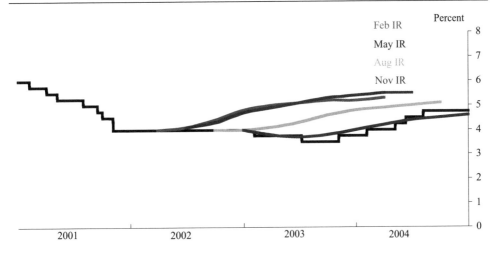

Figure 2.1   The Maradona theory of interest rates in 2002
Note: The black line represents the bank of England official interest rate. The shaded lines represent the market's expectations of future interest rates, as calculated in each of the four *Inflation Reports* published in 2002.

the English defenders reacted to what they expected Maradona to do. Because they expected Maradona to move either left or right, he was able to go straight on.

Monetary policy works in a similar way. Market interest rates react to what the central bank is expected to do. In recent years the Bank of England and other central banks have experienced periods in which they have been able to influence the path of the economy without making large moves in official interest rates. They headed in a straight line for their goals. How was that possible? Because financial markets did not expect interest rates to remain constant. They expected that rates would move either up or down. Those expectations were sufficient – at times – to stabilise private spending while official interest rates in fact moved very little. An example of the Maradona theory of interest rates in action is shown in Figure 2.1. It is a 'porcupine' chart which shows the Bank's official interest rate (the repo rate) as the thick black line together with forward interest rate curves at the time of successive *Inflation Reports* in 2002. Although by no means a perfect measure, the forward interest rate curve provides an idea of market participants' expectations of future policy rates. During 2002 the Bank of England was able to achieve its goal by moving on a straight line with unchanged official interest rates. But, although interest rates scarcely moved, expectations of future interest rates – as embodied in the forward curve – did move around as the economic outlook changed from an expectation of a swift recovery to worries about a protracted slowdown. And in turn those changes in expected future rates affected activity and inflation. In other words, monetary policy was able to respond by less than would otherwise have been necessary because it affected expectations.

That pattern is sometimes described as 'the market doing the work for us'. I prefer a different description. It is the framework of monetary policy doing the work for us. Because inflation expectations matter to the behaviour of households and firms, the critical aspect of monetary policy is how the decisions of the central bank influence those expectations. As Michael Woodford has put it, 'not only do expectations about policy matter, but, at least under current conditions, very little *else* matters'. Indeed, one can argue that the real influence of monetary policy is less the effect of any individual monthly decision on interest rates and more the ability of the framework of policy to condition inflation expectations. The precise 'rule' which central banks follow is less important than their ability to condition expectations. That is a fundamental point on which my later argument will rest.

It should be clear that, just as Maradona could not hope to score in every game by running towards goal in a straight line, so monetary policy cannot hope to meet the inflation target by leaving official interest rates unchanged indefinitely. Rates must always be set in a way that is consistent with the overall strategy of keeping inflation on track to meet the target; sometimes that will imply changes in rates, at other times not.

2.3   LEARNING AND ITS IMPLICATION FOR MONETARY POLICY

The academic literature on monetary policy rules has performed a great service in emphasising the importance of expectations. But there are two basic problems with the use of rules. The first is that the validity of any given rule depends upon the model of the economy that underlies it being true. The second is that the calculation of the rule – or policy reaction function – is extraordinarily complex. Moreover, these two problems interact, in that the complexity of the decision rule is increased enormously when the possibility of learning about the true model is introduced. So although policy rules offer important insights they do not provide a practical guide to decision-making, and it is useful to examine more deeply why that is the case.

No economist can point to a particular model, and in honesty say 'that is how the world works'. A crucial difference between economic and, say, meteorological analysis is that in economics there are no natural constants, not even for the natural rate of unemployment. Our understanding of the economy is incomplete and constantly evolving, sometimes in small steps, sometimes in big leaps. The stock of knowledge is not static. So any monetary policy rule that is judged to be optimal today is likely to be superseded by a new and improved version tomorrow. In other words, there is no time-invariant policy reaction function which could describe the policy intentions of a central bank. Rather, monetary policy in practice is characterised by a continuous process of learning embedded, in the case of the Bank of England, in the rounds of meetings and forecasts that are the daily life of the Monetary Policy Committee.

To convince you of how important learning about key economic relationships is to decisions on monetary policy, let me show you two charts which illustrate some of the challenges facing the Monetary Policy Committee. A basic proposition common to most models of the economy is that if demand exceeds the supply capacity of the economy then there will be upward pressure on wage and price inflation. In the labour market supply capacity is often equated, in the long run, with a particular rate of unemployment. Figure 2.2 plots the unemployment rate against the inflation rate in the UK over the period 1993–2005. It shows the trade off between unemployment and inflation in the short run, also known as the Phillips curve. Unemployment fell from nearly 10% in 1993 to less than 3% in 2004. But – in stark contrast to the earlier post-war period – inflation remained virtually unchanged. How can we explain this phenomenon? Was it because the natural rate of unemployment also fell – perhaps as a result of labour arket reforms enacted in the 1980s and 1990s? Or did the Phillips curve become flatter – perhaps because inflation expectations were anchored on the target so that deviations of unemployment from the natural rate generated less pressure on wages and inflation than before? Or was the outcome the result of a chance sequence of shocks that held inflation down?

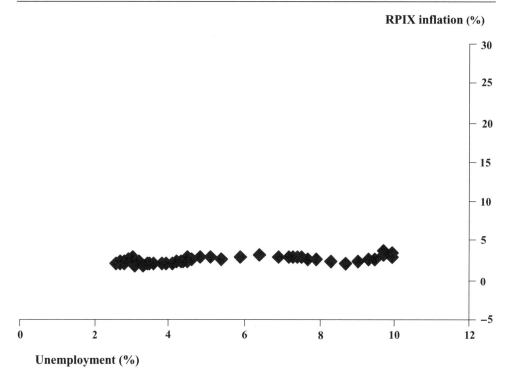

RPIX inflation (%)

Unemployment (%)

Figure 2.2   Inflation and Unemployment 1993–2005
Source: ONS.
Note: The unemployment rate used here is the Claimant Count measure.

Figure 2.3 shows that the slope of the short-run Phillips curve has moved around during the post-war period, apparently in response to changes in the monetary policy regime.

In the 1970s labour market pressure was not offset by tighter monetary policy, leading to a spiral of wage and price inflation. The short-run Phillips curve steepened, with larger inflationary consequences of any deviation from the natural rate of unemployment. As monetary policy became more focused on controlling inflation, the Phillips curve flattened in the latter part of the 1980s and 1990s. Such changes in the monetary policy regime can also be detected in the behaviour of inflation over time. Table 2.2 shows that the persistence of inflation – measured by the estimated explanatory power of past inflation in predicting current inflation – has fallen quite markedly since the inflation target was introduced in 1992. Was this because the failure of monetary policy to react quickly to an inflationary shock in the 1970s meant that inflation remained high for some time? And has the prompt response of monetary policy meant that movements in inflation more recently have proved short-lived?

The answers to these questions matter for monetary policy. But the economy is continually evolving, and we can never definitively conclude that one answer is right and the others wrong. So learning about changes in the structure of the economy lies at the heart of the daily work of central banks. To describe monetary policy in terms of a constant rule derived from a known model of the economy is to ignore this process of learning. So how should central banks behave in the light of their ignorance? Two approaches have been suggested.

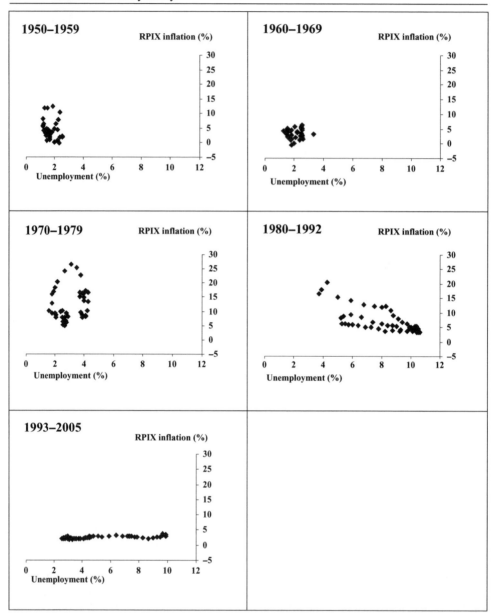

Figure 2.3   Inflation and unemployment by decade
Note: The unemployment rate used here is the Claimant Count measure, published by the ONS from
1971. Unemployment data before 1971 is from Haldane and Quah (1999). The published RPIX series
start in 1976. For observations before 1976, the all-items RPI was used. The RPI series before 1976 did
not include mortgage interest payments.

Interestingly, at one end of the spectrum, both Milton Friedman and Robert Lucas argued
that policy should be based on a simple rule precisely because of our ignorance. Central banks,
in their view, should have limited ambitions and aim simply at steady growth of the money
supply – the so-called *k% rule* under which the money stock rises at a fixed rate, k%, each
year. As Friedman (1968) put it, 'Steady monetary growth would provide a monetary climate

Table 2.2   The persistence of inflation 1950–2005

	Persistence
1950–59	0.5
1960–69	0.3
1970–79	0.7
1980–92	0.8
1993–2005	0.2

Note: Persistence in this table is the sum of the coefficients on lagged inflation in a regression of quarterly inflation on a constant and 4 lags. The measure of inflation is RPI before 1976 and RPIX from 1976, seasonally adjusted.
Source: ONS and Bank of England calculations.

favourable to the operation of those basic forces . . . that are the true springs of economic growth. That is the most that we can ask of monetary policy at our present state of knowledge'.[12] The principle of adopting a strategy that takes into account limits to our knowledge is a sound one. But advocates of a rigid *k% rule* argue that we should ignore all other sources of information (estimates of the output gap, for example) and allow any shocks to the velocity of money to feed through to activity or the price level. In practice, experience in both Europe and the US has shown that velocity shocks can be large and few economists now advocate the use of k% rules. So committing to a wholly inflexible rule is likely to be neither desirable nor credible. Our knowledge is neither complete nor constant.

At the other end of the spectrum, rational optimising behaviour can, in principle, generate a policy reaction function which takes into account uncertainty about the economy and the process of learning about economic relationships. Such a reaction function would describe how a central bank would respond to any conceivable shock in the future, and explain how estimates of parameter values and the weights attached to particular models would be updated. But even in very simple examples the cleverest economists find the solution of those decision problems almost impossibly complicated. Fully rational optimising behaviour is unreasonably demanding. In the words of Gerd Gigerenzer (2001), optimisation is for 'Laplacean demons' not human beings – a reference to an imaginary being that '. . . could condense into a single formula the movement of the greatest bodies of the universe and that of the lightest atom . . .'[13]

Both approaches, for very different reasons, end up with a monetary policy rule. The simple rule is not credible because we do know some things and we can learn from the past. The complicated rule is not feasible because it places unrealistic demands on our ability to process information. Given the lack of further guidance from economists as to how to make decisions, central banks have often retreated to the position that setting interest rates requires the exercise of unfettered discretion. But this has problems of its own. As has long been recognised, pure discretion does not keep private sector expectations of inflation in line with the desired rate of inflation. If we are to find our way through the minefield between rules, on the one hand, and pure discretion, on the other, we need to think more carefully about the nature of decision-making in a complex world where the central bank and economic agents alike are learning about their environment.

---

[12] Friedman (1968).
[13] Laplace (1995 translation).

Human beings, including central bankers, are not 'Laplacean demons'. Given the constraints on their scarce time, observation suggests that people follow simple rules of thumb.[14] These rules of thumb are sometimes described as 'heuristics'. The easiest way to understand a heuristic is to imagine a cricket match. The fielder is standing in the deep when the batsman hits the ball somewhere in his direction – see Figure 2.4. How should the fielder try to catch the ball? One view – the rational optimisation view – is that the fielder either knows, or behaves as if he knows, the laws of physics. Then he could compute the trajectory of the ball, run to the point at which he could catch it (A in Figure 2.4), and wait for the ball to arrive. This theory of decision-making has testable implications. The fielder will run in a straight line (the solid line FA), and will normally be stationary when making the catch. But that is not how fielders behave in practice. Various empirical studies of baseball and cricket players suggest that fielders follow simple heuristics. For example, they keep their eye on the ball, adjusting their running speed so that the angle of the gaze – the angle between the eye and the ball – remains roughly constant.[15] The heuristic will guide the fielder to the point at which he can catch the ball, without a need to acquire information about variables such as wind speed and direction, spin or the other relevant factors, nor perform complex calculations on those data. But it means that the fielder will run in a slight arc (the dotted line FA) and be moving when the ball arrives. What is instructive about this example is the ability to distinguish empirically between a simple heuristic and fully optimising behaviour, and that the evidence favours the former.

A useful heuristic has two characteristics. It should be *fast* to compute and *frugal* in its data requirements. New heuristics can be adopted when needed. We might think of a 'toolbox' of heuristics from which an appropriate choice can be made according to the task that is to be performed. Experimental evidence in laboratory settings shows that some fast and frugal heuristics can be about as accurate as much more data-intensive, optimisation-based methods such as multiple regression.

What are the implications of heuristics for monetary policy? There are two issues. First, although the central bank will try to be as rational as possible in processing all the relevant information, it may well itself use a range of heuristics. For example, in normal circumstances the heuristic 'set interest rates such that expected inflation two years ahead is equal to the target' might serve the Monetary Policy committee well. But in other circumstances, say following a large shock, the heuristic might be 'bring inflation back to target over a period of more than two years and explain carefully why the heuristic has changed'. The central bank can adapt its particular policy-setting heuristic to changing circumstances and evolving knowledge, so that the policy regime as a whole is robust to changing views about how the economy works.

Second, we do not know whether – and, if so, to what extent – people use heuristics to make real economic decisions. But a central bank should be alert to the possibility of their doing so. Given the importance of expectations, the more the central bank can do to behave in a way that makes it easy for the private sector to adopt a simple heuristic to guide expectations the better. A good heuristic from that point of view would be 'expect inflation to be equal to target'. A bad heuristic would be 'if inflation is well away from target expect it to deviate further'. We can encourage people to use the first by announcing targets that are quantitative and useful. We can discourage the second by being open and transparent about the reasons for movements in inflation and decisions on monetary policy. If we have no hidden message, then eventually people will stop looking for it.

---

[14] Todd (2001).
[15] To be precise, the angle of gaze remains within a certain range – reported by Gigerenzer and Selten (2001).

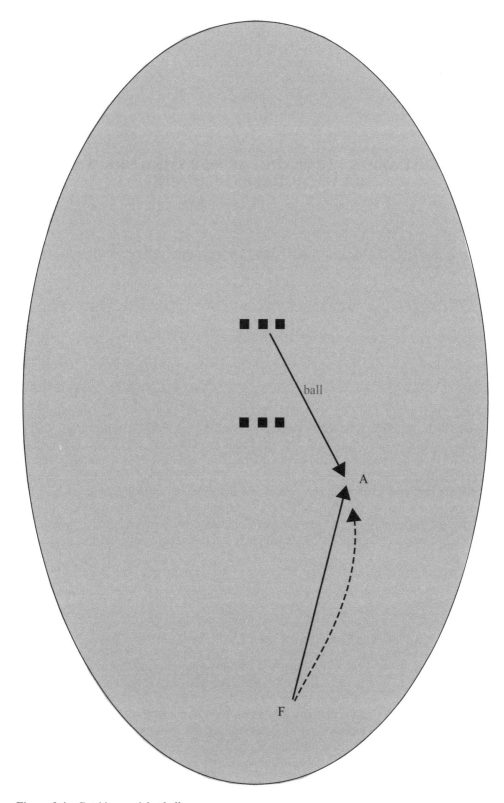

Figure 2.4 Catching a cricket ball

Rational optimising behaviour is in many situations too demanding, and actual decisions may reflect the use of heuristics. That must be taken on board in the choice of monetary policy strategy. In turn the strategy may affect the heuristic chosen by economic agents. And a good strategy will not only help agents choose a heuristic but will be robust with respect to that choice. Does inflation targeting meet those criteria?

2.4   INFLATION TARGETING AS A FRAMEWORK WHICH ACCOMMODATES LEARNING

So far three key points about monetary policy have been emphasised. First, expectations play a fundamental role in the way monetary policy works. As the Maradona theory of interest rates shows, expectations of future monetary policy actions are at least as important as the level at which the official interest rate is set today. Second, our knowledge of the economy is continually evolving. There simply is no unchanging rule, however complex, that can adequately describe the optimal monetary policy strategy. Third, the complexity of optimising behaviour means that central banks need to allow for the possibility that people use simple rules of thumb.

Taken together, these arguments provide a powerful case for inflation targeting. An inflation targeting framework combines two distinct elements: (a) a precise numerical target for inflation in the medium-term and (b) a response to economic shocks in the short term. The inflation target provides a rule-like framework on which the private sector can anchor its expectations about future inflation. As Gordon Brown put it in his Mais Lecture in 1999, 'a credible framework means working within clearly defined long-term policy objectives, maximum openness and transparency, and clear and accountable divisions of responsibility'. It is a natural heuristic around which agents can form their expectations. And the discretion in responding to shocks afforded by inflation targeting allows the central bank to adapt its strategy to new information. That is why inflation targeting is sometimes referred to as a framework of 'constrained discretion'. Following a shock which moves inflation away from target and output from its normal level, there is discretion about the horizon over which inflation is brought back to target. But the exercise of that discretion must be clearly explained and justified in terms of the need, in the words of the remit of the Monetary Policy Committee, to avoid 'undesirable volatility in output'. The great attraction of an inflation target is that it is a framework that does not have to be changed each time we learn about aspects of the economy such as the velocity of money or the underlying rate of productivity growth, as was the case in the past with frameworks based on targets for money aggregates or nominal GDP growth. It is a framework designed for a world of learning.

The empirical evidence suggests that inflation targeting has helped to confer tangible benefits. One test of whether inflation expectations are well-anchored is the volatility of long-term interest rates. Figure 2.5 shows the standard deviation of ten-year forward interest rates in the United Kingdom since 1992 and compares it with the figure for the United States. In both countries, volatility rose in the early 1990s. But whereas volatility has been broadly stable in the United States since the mid-1990s, it has fallen steadily in the United Kingdom. In a comparative study of OECD countries, Levin et al. (2004) found that inflation expectations were better anchored in inflation targeting countries in the sense that movements in actual inflation were less likely to cause inflation expectations to change.The clarity and simplicity of an inflation target mean that a natural heuristic for the private sector is 'expected inflation equals the inflation target'.

Figure 2.5   The variability of expected future interest rates, US and UK
Note: Variability is calculated as the standard deviation of daily changes in the ten year instantaneous nominal forward rate over a yearly window.
Source: Bank of England calculations.

Inflation targeting is a framework for making and communicating decisions. It is not a new theory of the transmission mechanism of monetary policy. It does not reflect a new understanding of the laws of economics. But, by anchoring inflation expectations on the target, it can alter the transmission mechanism by reducing the persistence of inflationary shocks. And it does so without pretending to commit to a rule that is incredible because it is not expected to last.

The implications of an inflation target for central bank communications are natural enough. First, the clarity of the inflation target focuses attention on the case for price stability which must be made continually. Second, each forecast must be accompanied by an explanation of the current thinking behind the MPC's views; in essence the 'model' underlying the MPC's thinking is changing all the time. Third, there is no point trying to communicate a time-invariant policy reaction function when that does not exist. The regular commentary on its thinking published in its Minutes and *Inflation Reports* is part of a process by which the MPC communicates with the general public. A reputation for communicating openly and honestly about the range of possible outcomes matters, because it makes it more likely that people will continue to listen.

What are the main challenges for inflation targeting in the future? The most immediate challenge stems from its very success. Although it is now widely accepted that there is no

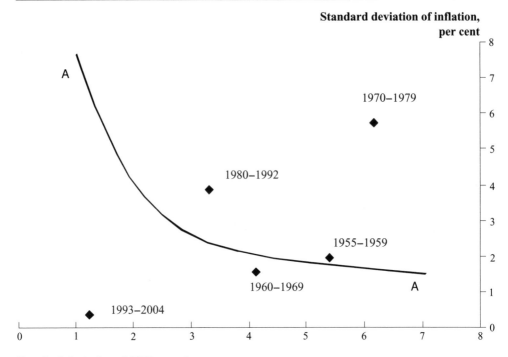

**Standard deviation of GDP growth,
per cent**

Figure 2.6   The variability of inflation and output, 1955–2004
Note: Standard deviation of inflation is calculated from quarterly observations of annual inflation; standard deviation of output growth is calculated using annualised quarterly observations of output growth.
Source: ONS and Bank of England calculations.

long-run trade off between inflation and output, the ability of monetary policy to affect output in the short run means that there is, in principle, a permanent trade off between the **volatility** of inflation and the **volatility** of output, which might be represented by the line AA in Figure 2.6. The choice of a horizon over which to bring inflation back to target is equivalent to choosing a point on this volatility trade off. The striking change, however, is the remarkable improvement in the trade-off that followed the introduction of inflation targeting, as can be seen in Figure 2.6. The volatility of both inflation and output growth were much lower than in earlier periods.

Part of the improvement may lie in the pattern of shocks over the past decade, although the world economy has hardly contributed to that stability. So the challenge ahead is that if a shock, larger than we have experienced recently but not large relative to historical experience, were to move inflation significantly away from target, then inflation expectations might become dislodged from the target. The behaviour of expectations and so the economy as a whole would change. So far there is little sign that the shocks we have experienced have detached inflation expectations from the target, and that is a source of comfort. But the MPC will continue to pay particular attention to the evidence on inflation expectations. Many of the problems of the past resulted from the failure to take action before expectations had started to drift upwards, and the cost of that inaction proved to be high. When the time comes for me to write an open letter to the Chancellor because inflation has deviated by more than one percentage point from target –

and it is very surprising that such a letter has not been required in the eight years since the MPC was set up – I will welcome the opportunity to explain how we expect to bring inflation back to target and over what horizon. Such letters are an integral part of the policy framework, not an indication of its failure.

2.5 CONCLUSION

Three propositions have been advanced. First, expectations are of fundamental importance to monetary policy. Second, the strategy of policy is more important than any of the individual monthly decisions on interest rates. Third, in designing a strategy be aware of the likely role of heuristics in forming expectations, and so keep it simple.

From those perspectives inflation targeting appears a natural way to conduct monetary policy. And experience of inflation targeting suggests that a managed monetary standard can lead to stability – of both inflation and the economy as a whole – without the straitjacket of a gold standard, currency board or rigid fixed exchange rate target. Inflation targeting anchors inflation expectations, yet allows a flexible response to economic shocks.

Is inflation targeting the last word in monetary policy? Almost certainly not. Twenty-five years from now, I am confident that one of my successors will be able to look back and explain the great improvements that took place between 2005 and 2030. But I like to think that the inflation target framework has the ability to serve us well over that period.

Thirty years ago the theory of monetary policy was ahead of its practice, at least in the United Kingdom. Now I hope that the practice has given the theorists something to think about.

REFERENCES

Batini, N. and Nelson, E. (2005) The UK's Rocky Road to Stability, Federal Reserve Bank of St Louis Working Paper, 2005-020A.

Blair, T. (1995) The Economic Framework for New Labour, Mais lecture.

Blinder, A. (1997) Distinguished Lecture on Economics in Government: What Central Bankers Could Learn from Academics – And Vice Versa, *Journal of Economic Perspectives*, 3–19.

Brown, G. (1999), The Conditions for Full Employment, Mais lecture.

Capie, F. and Wood, G. (eds) (2001), *Policy Makers on Policy – The Mais Lectures*, Routledge.

Friedman, M. (1968), The Role of Monetary Policy, *American Economic Review*, **58**, 1–17.

Gigerenzer, G. (2001) The adaptive toolbox in Gigerenzer, and Selten (eds) (2001).

Gigerenzer, G. and Selten, R. (eds) (2001) *Bounded rationality: the adaptive toolbox*, MIT Press.

Gigerenzer, G. and Selten, R. (2001b) Rethinking rationality in Gigerenzer, G. and R. Selten (eds) (2001).

Haldane, A. and Quah D. (1999) UK Phillips Curves and Monetary Policy, *Journal of Monetary Economics*, **44**, 259–278.

Howe, G. (1981) The Fight Against Inflation, Mais lecture.

Kaldor, N. (1971) Conflicts in national economic objectives, *Economic Journal*, **81**, 1–16.

Laplace, P.-S. (1995) *A Philosophical Essay on Probabilities*, Springer Verlag (translated from *Essai philosophique sur les probabilités*, 5th French edition, 1825).

Lawson, N. (1984) The British Experiment, Mais lecture.

Levin, A. Natalucci, Fabio and Piger, Jeremy (2004) The Macroeconomic Effects of Inflation Targeting, *Federal Reserve Bank of St Louis Review*, **86**, 51–80.

Lucas, R.E. Jr (1972), Expectations and the neutrality of money, *Journal of Economic Theory*, 103–124.

McLeod, P., Reed, N. and Dienes, Z. (2003) How fielders arrive in time to catch the ball, *Nature*, **426**, 244–245.

Phelps, E. (1967) Phillips Curves, Expectations of Inflation, and Optimal Unemployment over Time, *Economica*, **34**, 254–281.

Radcliffe Committee Report (1959) Committee on the Working of the Monetary System Report, Cmnd 827, London HMSO.

Richardson, G. (1978) Reflections on the Conduct of Monetary Policy, Mais lecture.

Taylor, J. (1993) Discretion versus policy rules in practice, *Carnegie-Rochester Conference Series on Public Policy*, 195–214.

Todd, P. (2001) Fast and frugal heuristics for boundedly rational minds in Gigerenzer and Selten (Eds) (2001).

Woodford, M. (2003) *Interest and Prices: Foundations of a Theory of Monetary Policy*, Princeton University Press.

3
Are the Structure and Responsibilities of the Bank of England Optimal, and If Not, Does It Matter?

David B. Smith

3.1 INTRODUCTION

The speed with which the Bank of England was granted the operational independence to set interest rates five days after the May 1997 general election, and the abruptness with which its responsibilities for the Gilt-Edged market and financial supervision were removed three weeks later, meant that the new institutional arrangements were little challenged at the time.[1]

This chapter considers the economic justification for the new institutional structure established in May 1997, and whether it can be improved upon. This issue has attracted little attention.[2] One reason is that, after eight years of practical experience, the Monetary Policy Committee (MPC) is widely perceived as having achieved its inflation aims and added to wider economic stability. In addition, major institutional changes are not easily reversed, while British participation in European Monetary Union (EMU) would render current UK arrangements obsolete, even if this looks unlikely in the immediate future.

Many of the issues that arise are not UK specific, but there are intriguing differences between the 'twin pillars' strategy of the European Central Bank (ECB) and the approach adopted in many Anglo-Saxon countries. The varying conceptual frameworks employed by the world's central banks makes an interesting contrast with hard sciences, such as physics, where no one would argue that the laws of nature differ between New York, London and Frankfurt. While perfect policy-making institutions cannot eliminate the hard choices that have to be made by policy makers, there is evidence that well executed non-inflationary monetary policies can improve the short-term trade off between output and inflation and boost the sustainable rate of economic growth.[3] In contrast, ill-designed institutions can induce problems of co-ordination, information gathering, and assessment and lead to sub-optimal policies being pursued that eventually damage the credibility of the monetary authorities.

The next section briefly summarises the current responsibilities of the Bank of England as codified in the 1998 Bank of England Act. This is followed by a discussion of the Conventional Theoretical Macroeconomic Model (CTMM), which is widely employed by central banks

---

[1] This is despite rumours that the then Sir Edward George had been rendered 'volcanic' (Merrell 2003) by the transfer of the Bank's supervisory and regulatory functions to the Financial Services Authority (FSA) and the removal of its responsibility for managing the national debt to the Debt Management Office (DMO).

[2] Except for Gowland (1997) and the Conservative Party's Bank of England Commission (2000).

[3] OECD (2003) Table 2.8 p. 88.

Issues in Monetary Policy. Edited by K. Matthews and P. Booth.
© 2006 John Wiley & Sons, Ltd.

and seems to provide the main intellectual justification for the UK's monetary arrangements. The CTMM is a neat pedagogic device, particularly for those who believe people form their expectations rationally. However, it has limitations as a model of reality. These make it an insecure foundation on which to erect institutional structures and policy advice. The important, if possibly sub-conscious, roles that the CTMM plays in: firstly, the MPC's view of the monetary transmission mechanism; and, second, the Bank's main economic forecasting models are next discussed. The reasons why people who have reservations about the CTMM might prefer a central bank with a wider range of responsibilities are then set out. Finally, a 'potted' UK monetary history of the last four decades brings out the importance of aspects of monetary policy not incorporated in the CTMM and not part of the Bank's current remit. The final section makes some suggestions as to how the current UK arrangements can be improved.

3.2   CURRENT ARRANGEMENTS

An account of the Bank of England's structure and responsibilities can be found on its website (www.bankofengland.co.uk) while further useful background can be found in Bean (2001) and Kohn (2001). Briefly, the Bank of England was founded in 1694, and was privately owned until its nationalisation in 1946, when it was also made subordinate to the Treasury. Today, the Bank has three core responsibilities:

(1) First, to chose and implement the interest rates necessary to meet the inflation target set by the Chancellor of the Exchequer. This includes the work of the MPC (Lambert, 2005), but also covers the Bank's tasks in data collection and economic analysis, and the information provided by the Bank's regional agents. The latter supplements the data supplied by the Office for National Statistics (ONS), whose frequent revisions have lost it credibility.
(2) Second, to maintain the stability of the financial system and to act as the lender of last resort in exceptional circumstances. This task is now shared with HM Treasury and the FSA, with the latter being responsible for individual institutions and the Bank for the system as a whole. The Bank was directly responsible for supervising individual deposit taking institutions before 1997, although it did not supervise Building Societies, whose deposits are also included in M4 broad money.
(3) Third, the Bank also works to ensure that the UK financial system supports the rest of the economy and that the UK remains an attractive location for international financial business. Unfortunately, the Bank is now perceived as being less interested in boosting the City than it was before 1997.[4] There is also widespread concern that the FSA has become an overbearing and unduly risk-averse regulator, when compared with the Bank.[5]

3.3   THE CONVENTIONAL THEORETICAL MACRO MODEL (CTMM)

One reason why it is difficult to be dogmatic about the appropriate range of functions that should be performed by a central bank is the variations in the practices of different countries.[6] This suggests that no one model has an obvious superiority, although history and legal and

---

[4] Corporation of London (2003), p. 19.
[5] Centre for Policy Studies (2005).
[6] All the major central banks can be accessed through the Bank for International Settlements website www.bis.org.

constitutional frameworks have also played important roles. A more fundamental intellectual reason is that there still seems to be little consensus among monetary economists on two issues:

(1) The first is whether it is 'the' rate of interest that determines real activity and the price level – this is the approach associated with today's New Keynesians/Neo-Wicksellians – or whether it is the stocks of money and/or credit that are the most important. The latter will be called the 'monetarist' view.[7] It also will be argued later that broad money monetarists should include the short-term interest rate, as well as broad money balances, in their attempts to explain economic activity, because the payment of interest on bank deposits induces shifts in the demand for money.

(2) The second important divide is whether it is possible for *ex ante* imbalances between the supply of, and the demand for, money, to exist and act as drivers of the real economy. This approach is quite explicit in Robertson (1928) – which is still well worth reading – and is something that old-school Friedmanite 'Monetarism 1' advocates believed, but the rational expectations school generally do not. Recent accounts of the issues can be found in Mayer and Minford (2004) and Meltzer *et al.* (2004). Despite the lack of consensus, it could be argued that the target/threshold monitoring involved in buffer-stock monetarism (or 'Monetarism 3') is not inconsistent with the rational expectations approach. To put it crudely, rational people who based their consumption on their expected life-time wealth should still revise their spending plans if their monthly bank statement unexpectedly revealed that their money balances have fallen to zero, or they have a massive overdraft, because this development suggests that their initial expectations were incorrect.

As a result of these intellectual uncertainties, it seems best to follow the former US Federal Reserve Governor Laurence Meyer (2001) and set out (in words) what seems to be the nearest approximation to the CTMM underlying the approach of the US Federal Reserve and many other 'Anglo-Saxon' central banks, while recognising that this represents a serious over-simplification of the range of competing approaches now existing in theoretical macroeconomics.

The CTMM is typically expressed in terms of three simple forward-looking dynamic equations. These describe the determinants of: (1) the 'output gap', which is usually defined as the percentage point deviations of actual output about its potential long-run supply trend; (2) the rate of inflation; and (3) the nominal rate of interest. The **first equation** in this system relates the present period's output gap to its actual value in the previous period, its expected value in the next period, and negatively to the real rate of interest, defined as the current period's interest rate less the expected inflation rate in the next period. The **second equation** relates the inflation rate to the present period's output gap, and a weighted average of inflation in the previous period and expected inflation in the next period. Finally, and in the **third equation**, the nominal rate of interest is determined by its equilibrium real rate, together with expected inflation in the next period, the previous period's output gap and the deviations of the previous period's inflation rate from the official inflation target.

A few general comments seem appropriate.[8] One is that the CTMM assumes that economic agents form their expectations 'rationally' as if they knew the true underlying model of the economy and had faith in the authority's commitment to anti-inflationary policies. The model

---

[7] Wicksell believed that he was working in the quantity theory tradition. See Amato (2005).
[8] For an elegant account of the CTMM see Meyer (2001).

has less pleasant properties and can simulate 'stagflation', for example, if the expectations of future inflation are formed in another way such as 'adaptive learning'.

3.3.1   Role of Interest Rates in the CTMM

The second set of comments concerns 'the' rate of interest. The first point here is that Central Banks can only set the nominal REPO rate, not the expected real rate that features in the first equation of the CTMM. There may be little difficulty in translating nominal REPO rates into the equivalent real rate when anticipated inflation is low and steady. However, the CTMM could be rendered inoperable if inflationary expectations were high and volatile or were de-stabilised by a switch of inflation targets to a measure that did not carry the confidence of the public. Under these circumstances, the growth of real broad money could be a better guide to the monetary stance than nominal interest rates. This seemed to be the case in the inflationary 1970s, for example, and may explain why so many central banks had adopted money supply targets by the early 1980s.

The second interest-rate point is that even 'the' nominal rate of interest is not always clearly defined in theoretical papers. In practice, central bankers are well aware that there is not one rate of interest – but three, at least – that matter for monetary policy. These are: the rates on overnight money, such as Fed Funds; the three-month interest rate, which influences base borrowing costs; and the government bond yield, which is important for investment. There is also a growing central-bank literature on the 'pass through' problem, that is the limited extent to which changes in REPO rates influence the rates charged by commercial lenders. A failure of low official REPO rates to be reflected in borrowing costs could result from a cartelised banking system. But it could also reflect high levels of bad and doubtful debts leading to credit rationing, in which only the most secure borrowers are given access to credit. However, such real world phenomena have no place in the CTMM.

The concept of multiple interest rates may seem complex to people brought up on economic textbooks, but much of the practical monetary debate in the last century was about these issues, particularly outside Britain. One reason why Continental central bankers liked reserve asset ratio requirements, for example, is that it allowed them to push up overnight rates sharply when confronted with a run on their currencies without unduly raising industry's borrowing costs. The legacy of wartime debt also meant that funding policy was the dominant British monetary concern for much of the last century (Goodhart, 1999). More recently, official debt repurchases have become a fashionable antidote to the real interest rate trap caused by deflation. However, while central banks can see the specific need for an active funding policy in these circumstances, they do not seem to be considering whether there is a general case for resurrecting open market operations. The mainstream econometric forecasting models that prevailed until the 1990s, not only tried to explain the gap between bond yields and short rates, but also modelled how various types of expenditures reacted to different rates of interest. The fact that most British models no longer have these features may partly reflect resource constraints. However, this certainly does not apply to the Bank of England, where a possibly misplaced faith in the CTMM seems a more likely explanation. More detailed models have survived in other countries.

3.3.2   Time series considerations

The third set of comments on the CTMM concerns the time series properties of the variables involved. Thus, in terms of the co-integration literature for which Engle and Granger won

Table 3.1   Time series properties of UK retail prices and associated variables*

	Levels			Yearly Differences			Change in Yearly Differences		
	ADF Test			ADF Test			ADF Test		
	DF Test	1st Order	4th Order	DF Test	1st Order	4th Order	DF Test	1st Order	4th Order
Log Retail Prices Ex. Mortgages (RPIX)	−1.56	−1.10	−1.06	−1.61	−2.48	−1.64	−9.28	−7.43	−6.09
Log RPI Ex. Mortgages & Depreciation	−1.72	−1.18	−1.10	−1.59	−2.46	−1.61	−9.27	−7.42	−6.09
Log M4 Broad Money Supply	−3.15	−1.52	−1.13	−2.10	−2.93	−2.28	−8.92	−6.79	−5.08
Log 'Excess' M4 Broad Money	−2.56	−1.83	−1.44	−2.88	−3.12	−2.39	−11.84	−8.80	−6.37
Log Trade-Weighted Overseas Prices	−4.47	−1.74	−1.91	−1.02	−1.95	−1.42	−7.27	−5.96	−5.77
Log Sterling Index	−2.06	−2.03	−2.01	−4.21	−6.12	−3.42	−9.62	−8.79	−7.29
UK Three-Month Inter-Bank Rate	−2.07	−2.67	−2.46	−4.56	−7.26	−4.38	−9.76	−9.11	−7.01
'Real' Inter-Bank Rate	−2.74	−3.65	−2.73	−4.94	−8.28	−5.03	−9.47	−8.28	−8.94
Real Household Consumption 'Gap'	−1.95	−1.72	−2.23	−5.61	−4.49	−3.65	−18.19	−11.04	−7.85

the 2003 Nobel prize in economics (see: Engle and Granger, 1991), it is generally accepted that, in most countries, the (logarithmic) price level is I(2) – that is it has to be differenced twice, before it becomes a stationary variable with a constant mean and variance. This means that the yearly change in the logarithmic price level – which approximates to annual inflation – is I(1), and the change in inflation is I(0), views which seem to be supported by the UK statistics for the past four decades (Table 3.1 below). The output gap probably ought to be a stationary I(0) variable by construction, even if this may require the removal of more than a simple trend from real output or expenditure, while the real interest rate also seems to be I(0).

Now, one of the essential points of the co-integration approach is that it requires an I(2) variable to 'explain' an I(2) variable and so on. Because both of the true independent variables in the CTMM's equation 2 are probably I(0), the inflation rate is being explained by its own history and expectations of future inflation, leaving it close to a random walk. One way in which econometricians might correspondingly want to estimate equation 2 would be to take the I(0) rate of change of inflation as the dependent variable. This may well be acceptable from the viewpoint of time series estimation, particularly if one fears deterministic breaks, but it has

---

[9] The Dickey-Fuller (DF) and Augmented Dickey-Fuller (ADF) tests are designed to test whether a variable is stationary (ie has a constant mean and variance) or not. A variable is considered stationary if the test value is negative and exceeds the critical value of c2.9 appropriate to the number of observations considered here. A time-series variable is said to be 'integrated of order zero' or I(0) if its level passes the DF or ADF tests, I(1) if it has to be differenced once before doing so, I(2) if it has to be differenced twice, etc. The DF test is performed by regressing the change in the variable on a constant and its level in the previous period and testing whether the coefficient of the lagged level is zero against the alternative that it is negative. The ADF (1) test includes additionally one lagged value of the change in the dependent variable. The ADF (4) test allows for up to four lagged differences and is particularly relevant to quarterly data, where seasonal patterns may be present. 'Excess' M4 is broad money divided by real GDP at basic prices. The household consumption gap represents the deviation of real household consumption about a fitted time trend. 'Log' denotes the natural logarithm of the variable concerned. The database used contained quarterly figures from 1955 Q1 to 2005 Q3 and the tests were performed over the longest period for which data existed. This represented 1965 Q2 to 2005 Q3, at a minimum, but was often longer. Data and further details are available on request.

a serious economic implication. That is that one is throwing away all the information contained in the low-frequency I(2) and, possibly, the I(1) components of the data generating process. However, most economic theories are only concerned with the low frequency equilibrium tendencies in the data, and have little to say about the high-frequency wobbles left after differencing. This means that differencing can mean junking economic theory, at least in its more classical forms.

The (logarithmic) money supply can potentially 'explain' trends in the price level – because it is an I(2) variable – as can overseas prices which might be used in an international-monetarist model of the price level, together with the I(1) exchange rate. However, such variables do not appear in the CTMM. This does not invalidate the CTMM as a logical construct, because the CTMM implicitly applies to closed economies and assumes rational expectations, which rule out the possibility of any low frequency disequilibria. This is one reason why the assumptions underpinning the CTMM seem unappealing to monetarists and old-fashioned Keynesians alike, both of whose theories emphasise the slow and complex process by which equilibrium is restored following an economic shock.

A caricature of the three viewpoints is that: old-school Keynesians would argue that a capitalist economy would never return to equilibrium after a negative output shock without offsetting government intervention; Friedmanite monetarists would argue that the economy would prove self-righting under such circumstances, but that this might require a few years to achieve; while the rational expectations school would argue that the economy would either rapidly return to equilibrium, or could not produce such an irrational collapse in activity in the first place. These different approaches have the modelling implication that: extreme Keynesians would not include stabiliser terms in an Error Correction Model (ECM) – because they know capitalist economies are not self-stabilising – while believers in rational expectations would exclude stabiliser terms on the grounds that people would not slowly move back to equilibrium after a shock but would jump back in the next period. In contrast, Friedmanite monetarism is very largely about the movement towards a new equilibrium in the long run. The stabiliser term in the ECM correspondingly provides a mechanism to bring this about in statistical relationships, although Friedman's re-launch of the quantity theory in the 1950s was two decades ahead of the development of ECM's.

For the empirical pragmatist, of course, there is no need to choose between the estimation of price equations in differences and in levels because both approaches can be encompassed in an ECM framework. In practice, the author has usually found when estimating ECM equations that the long-run 'stabiliser' terms are at least as significant as the output gap, although they should not be regarded as competitors, apart from in one particular sense. That is there is likely to be a high degree of multi-collinearity in a simple monetarist model between capacity utilisation, which is driven by real broad money balances, and the undigested element of excess money that has not yet worked its way through into a higher price level. In this case, the capacity utilisation term in the CTMM may be acting as a proxy for the excluded stabiliser term in a monetarist ECM of the price level, and the power and significance of the output gap term may be overstated as a result. Incidentally, the same argument would hold if one substituted the exchange rate for money, in an international monetarist model of the price level. Unfortunately, there have been few attempts to set up a 'horse race' in which different inflation models are tested against the same data. However, the Reserve Bank of New Zealand did this and found that both money and the real interest rate gap provided more information about future inflation than estimates of the output gap (Razzak, 2002).

3.4 HOW THE BANK'S MAIN MACRO MODEL CONSTRAINED THE MONETARY DEBATE

The logic of the CTMM appears to underlie the present institutional arrangements for the Bank of England, which emphasise its REPO rate setting function, while MPC members often seem to have this framework in mind when discussing monetary policy. The CTMM is also reflected in the Banks' account of the monetary transmission mechanism from which Diagram A (below) has been taken (Bank of England, 1999a) and also in the Bank's Main Macroeconomic forecasting model (or 'MM' in Bank parlance; see Bank of England, 1999b and 2000). The MM was the Bank's main forecasting tool from the early days of the MPC until the autumn of 2003, when the new Bank of England Quarterly Model (BEQM) discussed in the next section took over. The Bank has long employed a suite of some thirty models, not just the MM and the BEQM. However, the MM and its BEQM successor are especially significant because of their central role in the MPC's forecasting process (Pagan, 2003) and the revelatory way in which their structures have progressively eliminated many traditional monetary concerns from consideration.

For example, there was no scope for funding policy to have an effect in the MM for three reasons. One was that the gilts yield was simply assumed to equal the short rate, for simulation purposes. A second reason was the dearth of long-term interest rate effects on real expenditures. Finally, there was the unconventional specification of the demand for money relationship in the MM, which had the opportunity cost of holding M4 represented by the difference between the rate of interest paid on bank deposits and base rate. This was doubly unorthodox because the interest rate paid on bank deposits was driven off base rate, implying that interest rates ultimately have no effect on the money supply, and because the opportunity cost of holding money is usually considered to be the difference between the yield on bonds and the interest rate paid on money. Even so, this did not matter because the money supply did not feed back elsewhere into the MM. The conclusion at the time appeared to be that the limited range of monetary effects considered in the CTMM had been trebly consolidated – once, in the

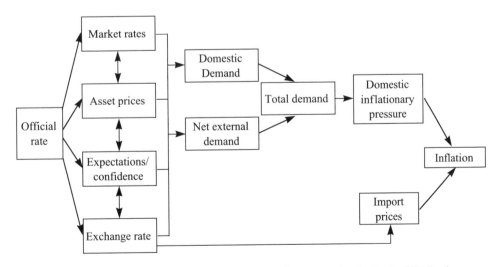

Figure 3.1   The transmission mechanism of monetary policy as seen by the Bank of England

institutional structure of the Bank, again, in its intellectual framework and, finally, in its main forecasting model – and this had precluded any consideration of the intellectual adequacy of the theory concerned.

3.5   THE NEW BANK OF ENGLAND QUARTERLY MODEL

However, if the old MM seemed light in its representation of traditional monetary policy concerns the new BEQM seems to have eliminated them almost entirely. The Bank published an overview of the BEQM in the summer 2004 *Bank of England Quarterly Bulletin* but it was not until January 2005 that a detailed 244-page account of the new model was published (see: Harrison, *et al.*, 2005). The BEQM represents such a massive and complex piece of work that only the aspects most relevant to the present chapter will be touched on here.

The first point about the BEQM is that the model is built in two distinct parts: a theoretical 'core' model with imposed calibrated coefficients and a set of 'non-core' equations that include additional variables and dynamics not formally modelled in the model core. This is analogous at the level of the whole model to the classic co-integration approach, in which the steady state is estimated in stage one and the dynamics in stage two. The stabiliser terms in the BEQM are defined as the difference between the lagged dependent variable and the prediction from the 'core model'. This means that the whole model snaps back very quickly onto its imposed core. This property has led people to question whether the BEQM is unduly stable. A specific concern is that the BEQM seems to be not very sensitive to the REPO rate.

However, there are two differences with the classic co-integration approach in BEQM, which could be regarded as potentially unfortunate. These are that the stage one relationships are not freely estimated – which is alright if the calibrated core is known to be true but could have built-in misleading model properties if not – and there is no third stage, in which the initial stage one estimates are modified to eliminate any bias in the initial long run relationships. It is possible to have reservations about the imposition of the calibrated core in the BEQM, if one suspects that we do not know enough about reality to be confident that the calibrated core is correct. Calibration is a useful tool when laying down the framework of a computerised forecasting system, because getting a rough-and-ready prototype up and running, before improving it with estimated relationships, is usually an efficient way of developing a model in its early stages. However, a personal view – and this is a matter of scientific philosophy rather than economics – is that the calibration approach is essentially anti-empiricist and pre-Galilean in that it relies too much on the 'Papal infallibility' of the assumed theory and too little on empirical observation.

However, this is a digression from the main concern, which is the apparent absence from the BEQM of any measure of broad money or credit, which contrasts with the weight attached to broad money in the twin pillars approach of the ECB (see: Issing, 2004) and Deutsche Bundesbank, 2005). Notes and coin, which are the main element of the monetary base, are included in the BEQM but their role appears to be as an interest-free element of official funding. In addition, the only rate of interest incorporated in the BEQM is the short-term rate, precluding by design any consideration of funding effects on the wider economy. That this may not be just a matter of intellectual conviction, but also a matter of the mandate delivered to the MPC can be seen from the following quotation (Harrison *et al.*, p. 5):

> The Bank of England is mandated by the Chancellor of the Exchequer to aim for an inflation target – at the time of writing, a 2% annual inflation rate of the Consumer Price Index (CPI) – and uses a very short-term nominal interest rate as its instrument to pursue this target.

This is worrying, despite the enormous technical sophistication of the techniques embodied in the BEQM, which clearly represents a major advance in UK forecasting methodology. The UK had a torrid monetary history by international standards in the three decades before the granting of operational independence to the Bank of England. It is an interesting thought experiment to ask whether the framework incorporated in the BEQM would have provided advance warning of some of the great policy fiascos of this period, if it had existed forty years ago. It could not have done so if most such incidents were triggered by factors not represented in the BEQM's framework.

3.6   THE MONETARIST CASE FOR A BIG CENTRAL BANK

It is now appropriate to discuss why broad-money monetarists would prefer a central bank with a wider range of responsibilities over one which only sets REPO rate. There are two arguments here. The first is that monetary policy is a seamless garment so that rending it into separate parts, and giving them to separate institutions makes it impossible to maintain a coherent policy-making framework. The second is that, by using a wide range of monetary tools, it is possible to avoid overstraining the base rate weapon and tackle situations where British monetary conditions appear too loose but sterling seems too high, for example. Since both phenomena are essentially monetary, it is unlikely that the more activist fiscal stance advocated by some commentators as appropriate in these circumstances would be of practical help.

The UK Money Supply Identity

---

a. Public sector net cash requirements (deficit +, surplus −)
    Less
b. public sector net debt sales to M4 private sector
    Less
c. external and foreign currency finance of the public sector
    Equals
d. **Public Sector Contribution**
    Plus
e. MFI lending to the M4 private sector
    Plus
f. external (i.e. with overseas sector) and foreign currency transactions of MFIs (lending +, deposits −)
    Less
g. Net non-deposit sterling liabilities of MFIs
    Equals
    Change in M4

The UK broad money supply identity is set out above. For many years from the late 1960s to mid 1980s, this represented the way in which the authorities thought about the links between fiscal and monetary policy, and figures using this framework continue to be published every month in the Bank's *Monetary and Financial Statistics.* The money supply identity also explains why a central bank that was interested in monetary control, but did not wish to place sole reliance on REPO rate, might wish for wider powers than the Bank of England now has.[10] In particular, the table makes it clear that, in an accounting sense at least, gilt sales or falls in the official reserves reduce the money stock. The identity also explains why other potential instruments, such as reserve ratio requirements or, mandatory increases in bank capital and reserves (which

---

[10] But see Tucker (2004) for the official view.

are included in non-deposit liabilities) can affect the size of the balance sheet of Monetary Financial Institutions (MFIs) or their willingness to create credit.

Such identities do not allow for possible feedbacks between the variables concerned, however, while institutional changes mean that policies that might have worked in the past will not necessarily do so today. Several monetarist commentators suggested in the late 1990s that the appropriate response to the dilemma caused by the combination of a strong pound and rapid M4 growth was to over-fund the Budget deficit through the gilts market. Arithmetically, this makes sense and is a tactic for capping base rates at the expense of higher bond yields.[11]

3.7   LESSONS FROM BRITAIN'S MONETARY HISTORY

The great advantage of the UK money supply identity is that it provides a coherent framework for debates of this sort and it may well come back into fashion if the financial markets become worried by the UK's worsening fiscal position. However, it also provides a useful framework for setting out a list of stylised facts about Britain's turbulent monetary history of the past four decades (see also: Goodhart, 2003). These can be summarised as follows:

(1) Most of the major UK monetary shocks, recorded from the 1960s onwards, were not primarily caused by the authorities misjudgement of the short-term interest rate, which is the only monetary instrument considered in the BEQM. However, political resistance to pre-emptive rate increases often prevented policy being tightened in good time, and this justifies the forward-looking element in the current system of inflation targeting. In the past, rising inflation often meant that real interest rates were falling, even as nominal interest rates rose. This is a potential issue in the BEQM where it is the real short-rate which drives economic behaviour, and the model relies on sticky expectations to convert the nominal interest rate into the real rate perceived by economic agents.

(2) The fact that the most widely used UK broad money definitions, such as the old M3 or present M4, contain many interest-bearing deposits means that the demand for money can react 'perversely' to higher short-term interest rates. This is because short rates largely represent the 'own rate' on money rather than the 'opportunity cost' of holding money. The latter may be best thought of, perhaps, as the difference between gilt yields and money-market interest rates.[12]

(3) The 'own-rate' effect has meant that: (a) broad monetary growth has frequently provided perverse signals when the level or structure of interest rates has been changing, which is why the authorities inadvertently imposed a monetary overkill in the early 1980s; (b) higher base rates squeezed the economy by raising the demand for broad money rather than by cutting its supply; and (c) broad monetary targeting has seemed to be impossible without additional policy instruments, including an active funding policy. An additional important implication is that both the real rate of interest paid on money and real money balances themselves belong in Friedman and Meisleman style money multipliers, which have a real expenditure as the dependent variable, with the negative effects of the rate of

---

[11] One practical objection, however, was that higher gilt yields would attract overseas capital inflows, which would offset the initial gains from over-funding.

[12] In the Williams de Broë forecasting model, for example, the equilibrium demand for real M4 broad money reflects: real household consumption, with an elasticity of unity; the nominal three-month inter-bank rate in natural units with a coefficient of minus 0.0451; and the gap between the twenty year gilt yield and inter-bank rate with a coefficient of minus 0.0597; as well as terms in inflation and real house prices, which will be ignored from now on. The significance of this specification is that putting the terms in the three-month rate and the yield gap together indicates that a 1 percentage point rise in the three-month rate of interest raises the demand for real M4 by some $1^1/_2$ percentage points, *ceteris paribus*.

interest picking up the effect of shifts in the demand for broad money associated with the own rate phenomenon.

(4) The two major money and credit explosions in the post-war period were caused by deregulation. This is true of both the 1970s Heath-Barber boom, which followed a substantial reduction in the banking sector's liquid asset ratio, and the rapid expansion in MFI balance sheets in the 1980s. It is also conceivable that the monetary slowdown of the early 1990s was exacerbated by the re-regulatory shock of the 1988 Basle agreement.

(5) There have been at least two occasions when the authorities lost control of broad money because they attempted to stem the pound's recovery from the oversold positions associated with a sterling crisis. The first was following the UK's 1976 International Monetary Fund (IMF) loan, and may have contributed to the over 20% inflation recorded in the early Thatcher years. The second was after the oil price collapsed in the mid 1980s, when the pound's subsequent recovery was resisted by the then Chancellor of the Exchequer, Nigel Lawson. The loss of reserves associated with ERM withdrawal in September 1992 reduced money growth and helps explain the subsequent diminution of UK inflation.

(6) The Bank of England's operations in the gilt-edged market have also had occasional unintended monetary consequences. The Bank's support of gilts prices following the 1967 devaluation, for example, effectively turned the national debt into money, stimulated home demand, and prevented the balance of payments from improving. It is also possible that the pursuit of the full funding rule during the period of budget surpluses in the late 1980s turned illiquid bonds into base money, and exacerbated the Lawson boom.

One could go on, but the twofold message that emerges is clear. That message is that: (1) most of the major UK monetary shocks since the 1960s have arisen from aspects of monetary policy which are not considered in the BEQM and are not part of the MPC's remit, rather than from misjudged REPO rates; and (2) the clearest sign that something was amiss was provided by broad money and credit and fixed asset prices. It can be argued that the NDO's simple funding remit means that funding policy will do no harm in future, even if it does no good, and that the MFI's are so deregulated that further shocks are unlikely to arise from this source. However, there could still be future regulatory shocks arising from Basle II (Gandy, 2003). Unfortunately, the contractual nature of the current MPC arrangements, under which individual members are responsible for meeting the inflation targets using REPO rate as their sole implement, makes it difficult for the MPC to consider the use of other monetary tools.

3.8 MAIN CONCLUSIONS

This chapter has examined how much light economic arguments can throw on the responsibilities that should be allocated to a central bank, with special reference to the post 1997 arrangements of the Bank of England. There are four main conclusions:

(1) First, institutions, such as central banks, normally grow organically, although the ECB is an interesting exception, which may have a lot to teach central banks that developed in a more evolutionary manner (see: Issing, 2004). Even so, the differing institutional practices found around the globe suggest that there may be no unique correct answer concerning the functions that Central Banks should perform. Not all central banks have regulatory responsibilities, for example. However, the likelihood that a new Central Bank should not be burdened with a particular function does not mean that it is wise to remove these responsibilities from an institution with a long and successful experience in a particular area.

It has recently been revealed that Lord George had been having conversations with Tony Blair and Gordon Brown for two years before 1997, with the then Conservative Chancellor Kenneth Clarke's blessing (George, 2004), and this may explain the Governor's alleged volcanic reaction to the dismemberment of the 'Old Lady of Threadneedle Street'. The transfer of the bank's supervisory responsibilities to the FSA may well have damaged the competitiveness of the UK financial sector and led to a noticeable increase in administrative costs.

(2) Second, different macroeconomic theories imply different functions for the central bank. The post-May 1997 establishment of the Bank of England is sensible from the viewpoint of the CTMM but appears unduly limited in the light of other theoretical approaches. Thus, traditional monetarists could claim that any instrument that might affect either the supply of money, or the demand for money, should be considered for placing under the control of the central bank. In the past, such instruments included official debt sales, currency intervention, reserve ratio requirements, special deposit calls, and credit controls. Unfortunately, poor policy co-ordination has meant that these levers have been inadvertently pulled in opposing directions on occasion.

(3) Third, when Gordon Brown established the MPC he was probably mainly concerned with the Bank's role as guardian of the currency, and how its creditability could be improved in this respect. However, the collapse of Long-Term Capital Management (LTCM) in 1998 subsequently reawakened interest in the role of central banks as lender of last resort. The contrast between the need to issue unlimited liquidity in the face of a financial panic, while maintaining monetary discipline, has been a recognised dilemma for a couple of centuries (Hawtrey, 1932) is still worth reading on this). As a result, there is a well-accepted approach as to how central banks should proceed under these circumstances. The problem facing central bankers is that it is not always clear whether they are facing a genuine financial panic, particularly when dealing with such secretive creatures as hedge funds. Stripping away the Bank's regulatory responsibilities may have initially weakened the Bank's intelligence network, and left it less clear whether it should act as lender of last resort or not. However, the subsequent response has been to recruit more people, leading to some duplication of costs with the FSA.

(4) Finally, all organisations wax and wane over time and the Bank of England has experienced major cutbacks before, such as the closure of its exchange control division in the early 1980s. The weight the MPC now attaches to the data produced by the ONS, when combined with the number of own goals achieved by the ONS in recent years, suggest that data collection and dissemination may be an area where the Bank should increase its responsibilities in the future. The main arguments against seem to be that the inevitable problems of revisions could damage the Bank's credibility in its rate-setting role, and the belief that the target measure of inflation should be produced independently of the body whose duty it was to hit that target. This difficulty might be overcome by privatising the compilation of the RPI and CPI figures; for example, by putting them in the hands of a reputable market research company.

How one regards the removal of the Bank of England's debt management and regulatory responsibilities ultimately depends on one's theoretical perspective. However, even those who adhere to the CTMM and believe that the main role of monetary policy is to set the correct level of REPO rates, might be concerned about the potential loss of market feel that the post-1997 arrangements imply when the Bank has to act as lender of last resort.

The stylised monetary history of the UK suggests that many of the largest shocks have not come from misjudged base rates, however, but from other aspects of monetary policy, such as financial regulation, funding policy and currency intervention. It can be argued also that the sole reliance on REPO rates leaves the authorities helpless when confronted with monetary dilemmas, such as how to set base rates when the currency is overvalued but monetary growth is excessive.

These difficulties might be ameliorated by the introduction of additional monetary instruments. Splitting the monetary remit across several institutions means that such possibilities may not be considered and makes it difficult to run a subtle and effective monetary policy. The dismemberment of the Bank of England was by no means a disaster. Even so, the post-1997 arrangements may still leave room for improvement. It would appear sensible to re-open the debate and consider: (1) re-integrating the DMO into the Bank; (2) restoring the Bank's responsibilities for the supervision of the wholesale markets and the deposit-taking institutions whose liabilities constitute broad money; and (3) making the Bank the main source for compiling and disseminating the UK's macro-economic statistics (possibly, other than the RPI and CPI) while leaving a down-sized ONS to concentrate on population data, regional statistics, and the census.

REFERENCES

Amato, J.D. (2005) The Role of the Natural Rate of Interest in Monetary Policy, Bank for International Settlements BIS Working Paper No. 171, March 2005 (www.bis.org).

Bank of England (1999a) The Transmission Mechanism of Monetary Policy, *Bank of England Quarterly Bulletin*, May 1999.

Bank of England (1999b) *Economic Models at the Bank of England.*

Bank of England (2000) *Economic Models at the Bank of England: September 2000 Update.*

Bank of England (2004) The New Bank of England Quarterly Model, *Bank of England Quarterly Bulletin*, Summer 2004.

Bank of England Commission (2000) *Final Report: 29 March 2000*, London Business School.

Bean, C. (2001) The Formulation of Monetary Policy at the Bank of England, *Bank of England Quarterly Bulletin*, Winter 2001.

Centre for Policy Studies (2005) The Leviathan Is Still at Large: An Open Letter to Mr John Tiner, Chief Executive of the FSA, *Centre for Policy Studies*, 57 Tufton Street, London SW1P 3QL (www.cps.org.uk).

Corporation of London Centre for the Study of Financial Innovation (2003) *Sizing Up the City – London's Ranking as a Financial Centre*, Corporation of London, PO Box 270, Guildhall, London EC2P 2EJ.

Deutsche Bundesbank (2005) The Relationship Between Money and Prices, *Deutsche Bundesbank Monthly Report*, January 2005.

Engle, R.F. and Granger, C.W.J. (1991) *Long-Run Economic Relationships: Readings in Cointegration*, Oxford University Press.

Gandy, A. (2003) A Risky Business? A Survey of Industrial Preparations for Basel II, *Financial World*, September 2003.

George, E. (2004) Lord of the Manor (Interview with Eila Rana), *Financial World*, October 2004.

Goodhart, C.A.E. (1999) Monetary Policy and Debt Management in the United Kingdom: Some Historical Viewpoints in *Government Debt Structure and Monetary Conditions*, Chrystal K.A. (Ed.), Bank of England.

Goodhart, C.A.E. (2003) Money and Monetary Policy, in *The Challenge of Change: Fifty Years of Business Economics*, Hirst J. (Ed.) London: Society of Business Economists & Profile Books Ltd.

Gowland, D. (1997) *Banking on Change: Independence, Regulation and the Bank of England*, Politeia, 22 Charing Cross Road, London WC2H 0HR.

Harrison, R., Nikolov, K., Quinn, M., Ramsay, R., Scott, A. and Thomas, R. (2005) *The Bank of England Quarterly Model*, Bank of England.

Hawtrey, R.G. (2000) The Art of Central Banking, reprinted in *The Development of Monetary Theory 1920s & 1930s*, Capie, F. and Wood, G.E. (eds), Routledge.

Kohn, D. (2001) The Kohn Report on MPC Procedures, *Bank of England Quarterly Bulletin*, Spring 2001.

Issing, O. (2004) *The ECB and the Euro: The First Five Years*, Institute of Economic Affairs, London.

OECD, (2003) *The Sources of Economic Growth in OECD Countries*, Organisation for Economic Co-operation and Development, Paris.

Lambert, R. (2005) Inside the MPC, *Bank of England Quarterly Bulletin*, Spring 2005.

Mayer, M. and Minford, P. (2004) Monetarism: A Retrospective, *World Economics*, Vol. 5 No. 2, April–June.

Meltzer, A., Desai, M., Haldane, A. and Congdon, T. (2004) Responses to 'Monetarism: A Retrospective', *World Economics,* Vol. 5 No. 3, July–September 2004.

Merrell, C. (2003) Exit, Pursued by a Bear, *Financial World*, May 2003.

Meyer, L.H. (2001) Does Money Matter? The 2001 Homer Jones Memorial Lecture, Washington University, St. Louis Missouri, March 28 2001. US Federal Reserve Website (www.federalreserve.gov).

Pagan, A. (2003) Report on Modelling and Forecasting at the Bank of England, *Bank of England Quarterly Bulletin*, Spring 2003.

Razzak, W.A. (2002) *Monetary Policy and Forecasting Inflation With and Without the Output Gap*, Reserve Bank of New Zealand Discussion Paper DP2002/03 (www.rbnz.govt.nz).

Robertson, D.H. (1928) Money, reprinted in *The Development of Monetary Theory 1920s & 1930s*, Capie, F. and Wood, G.E. (Eds), Routledge (2000).

Tucker, P. (2004) Managing the Central Bank's Balance Sheet: Where Monetary Policy Meets Financial Stability, *Bank of England Quarterly Bulletin*, Autumn 2004.

4
Why Price-Level Targeting is better than Inflation Targeting

Andrew Lilico

4.1 INTRODUCTION

Since 1992, UK monetary policy has been based on inflation targeting. Under inflation targeting the Bank of England sets policy to try to achieve a desired annual change in the Consumer Prices Index of 2%, with a tolerance band of 1% either side. One plausible alternative is for monetary policy to be geared, instead, towards meeting a *price-level target*. Price-level targeting is similar to inflation targeting, except that instead of targeting a rate of change in the price level year-by-year, the monetary authority targets a series of price levels. In this chapter I shall explain in more detail how such a system would work, and argue that price-level targeting (which in practice, as we shall see, would actually be 'average inflation targeting' – as explained below) offers considerable advantages over inflation targeting. In particular, price-level targeting:

(1) could lead to higher economic growth;
(2) involves less need for fine-tuning policy interventions;
(3) allows a lower average rate of inflation (or even slight deflation) to be achieved; and
(4) offers a superior way to deal with a deflationary depression.

4.2 HOW DO INFLATION TARGETING AND PRICE-LEVEL TARGETING DIFFER?

4.2.1 Long-term price stability

First we should discuss the basic difference between the two regimes. Targeting a price level does not necessarily mean targeting no change in the price index. If there are good reasons to prefer 2% inflation to 0% inflation, then the price-level that is targeted could rise by 2% each year. However, for simplicity let us initially compare an inflation target of 0% with a price-level target of 100 (defining the starting price index as 100).[1]

Now suppose there are unexpected price rises and actual inflation is 2% for two years, raising the price index to 104.04. In the third year the monetary authority targeting 0% inflation will attempt to keep the price level at 104.04, while the authority targeting a price-level of 100 will attempt to deflate prices back to 100. This is the key difference: under inflation targeting we let bygones be bygones while under price-level targeting we attempt to remedy our past failures.

---

[1] Clearly there are important questions here about how to define the price index – for example whether it should include only consumer prices, how housing costs should be included, how to avoid perverse feedback when interest rates change, and whether geometric or arithmetic inflation measures are to be preferred. However, these are beyond the scope of this chapter.

Issues in Monetary Policy. Edited by K. Matthews and P. Booth.

This means that the long-term price-level (and hence the long-term inflation rate) is more certain under price-level targeting than under inflation targeting (other things being equal). Because of the base slippage caused by the effective price-level target being updated each year, under inflation targeting the price-level wanders around randomly, and after a few years the difference can become quite significant. In the very long term, under inflation targeting, the possible real value of a money contract can vary enormously, since the price level can wander off either towards zero or towards infinity.

4.2.2   Short-term inflation volatility

However, the year-on-year inflation rate may differ more under price-level targeting than under inflation targeting (i.e. short-term price volatility may be higher). This is because unexpected rises in the price-level will be followed by attempted reductions in the price-level (or rises below trend). After a price-level shock inflation will not return to normal, but there will instead be another change in the opposite direction.

This is not always true, though. Under models without commitment and with nominal rigidities in the economy – e.g. if prices are sticky – then short-term volatility can be lower because output shocks have persistent effects. To see why, suppose there is an inflationary demand shock pushing inflation above the target and output above its trend level. However, let us also suppose that the new inflation rate, though above the target, is still within the target band (e.g. the $+/-1\%$ band of the Bank of England). When inflation is within the target band we would expect the monetary authority also to care about output (again, like the Bank of England). That is, after all, why there *is* a target band.

Under this scenario, as the inflation-targeting authority reduces inflation back to the target, it will change the inflation rate in proportion to the output gap (the amount by which output is above trend). In other words, if output is way above trend inflation will be reduced more rapidly than if output is only just above trend. Similarly, the price-level targeting authority will bring down the price-level in proportion to the output gap. If output is way above trend then the price-level will be brought down quicker than if output is only just above trend. But since inflation is the *change* in the price level, under price-level targeting the movements in the inflation rate will be proportional to the *change* in the output gap, rather than the *size* of the output gap.

If there are moderate nominal rigidities in the economy, then when there are output shocks they will tend to be at least moderately persistent. If, for example, some shock raised output by 1.0% compared with trend, under moderate nominal rigidities output might still be, say, 0.8% above trend a year later, and 0.64% above trend a year after that. In such cases the change in the output gap is only 0.2% or so of output – smaller than the size of the output gap. Provided that there are not other regular significant output shocks tending to increase the size of the output gap, this unwinding of previous output shocks will be the main driver of change in output, and since under this scenario the change in the size of output gaps will tend to be lower than their magnitude, changes in the inflation rate (i.e. inflation volatility) will be lower under price-level targeting (when inflation volatility depends on changes in output gaps) than under inflation targeting (when such volatility depend on the size of output gaps).

So, typically, if there are moderate nominal rigidities (so that output shocks are moderately persistent) and significant output shocks are sufficiently rare (so that the unwinding of output shocks is, on average, the main driver of change in output) then the volatility of the short-term inflation rate will be lower under price-level targeting than under inflation targeting.

Furthermore, once people understand the new price-level regime, their behaviour may change. For example, they may sign longer-term contracts, thereby reducing short-term wage and price movements, and since people expect other people's temporary price rises to be reversed, they will react less to them in setting their own prices.

4.2.3 Output volatility

Output might be more volatile under price-level targeting. Consider an earthquake that destroyed 20% of our productive capacity. At least until new imports became available, there would be rises in the prices of food and clothes and other goods, because their supply has become scarce. This is the appropriate response because this sort of supply shock alters the *equilibrium* price level.[2] So sometimes the equilibrium price level will, quite appropriately, rise. But a price-level target might force the monetary authorities to try to return the price-level to its previous level, even though higher prices reflected a new equilibrium, thereby imposing real costs on the economy. For example, in the earthquake case returning prices to their previous level might result in queuing and could delay the new investment required to restore capacity. These real costs would be larger the greater are nominal rigidities, especially in cases where prices would need to fall to maintain the target. (However, as mentioned above, in the case where there are such nominal rigidities then short-term price volatility may be lower.)

Of course under inflation targeting the monetary authority would again be trying to contain the rise in prices, thereby similarly combating the move to a new equilibrium and imposing real costs. The difference is that once the new equilibrium is reached the inflation targeting authority will stop fighting (since prices have stopped rising), whereas the price-level targeting authority will try to take prices back down again.

Thus the case for price-level targeting versus inflation targeting is a judgement about the trade-off of greater certainty about long-term prices (i.e. about long-term inflation) for possibly greater short-term price and output volatility.

4.3 WHAT IS THERE TO GAIN FROM LONG-TERM PRICE STABILITY?

Let us look a little closer at long-term price stability, since this is the main attribute of price-level targeting. Why would we care about this? Suppose an individual lends another £100 today in return for a promise of £120 in five years' time, anticipating that inflation will average 2% during this period. Suppose that actually inflation averages 3%. Even though the annual inflation difference is very slight, it alters this deal from one in which the lender makes about £8.70 (in real terms) to one in which he only makes about £3.50. The return is more than halved. So if the lender thinks that inflation will probably be about 2%, but worries about the risk of it being higher (i.e. if he is 'risk averse'), then he will probably require compensation for this risk through the in the interest rate charges. For example he might be content with £120 in five years' time if he were certain that inflation would be only 2%, but actually charge you £125, to compensate for the real return risk.

---

[2] One can think of the earthquake as having caused a leftwards shift in the aggregate supply curve (because of the loss of productive capacity). If we assume that future profit expectations (and hence investment), expected lifetime wealth (and hence consumption), money supply, import preferences and other demand determinants are unchanged, then with a downward-sloping aggregate demand curve a leftward shift in aggregate supply will cause a rise in the price level.

If interest rates are higher because of uncertainty about inflation, then some investment projects will become unprofitable at the margin. For example, if inflation turns out to be 2%, as expected, this project might be profitable if the interest cost is £20, but not if it is £25.

Thus greater inflation uncertainty renders some investment projects unviable, even though they would be expected to make a profit if we could be sure about inflation. This reduces the growth of the economy and makes us all poorer. Price-level targeting offers greater long-term price certainty than inflation targeting, therefore price-level targeting offers the prospect of greater economic growth and prosperity.

Perhaps, in practice, relatively few investment contracts are secure over a long time-scale. Even with mortgages, many people choose to have variable-rate agreements and thus are affected by year-on-year changes. However, firstly, this behaviour may well reflect a lack of confidence in the long-term price-level. If there were greater confidence about the long-term price-level, optimal contracts, fixed in nominal terms, might change their time-horizon. Second, the degree of indexation resulting from these agreements does not fully capture the variability in inflation. It acts as a form of insurance against large risk, rather than a removal of that risk. Like all insurance, the ability to vary the interest-rate year-on-year and to sell out of one mortgage to buy into another comes at a price. If we did not face that risk, and did not need to pay that insurance, we would be wealthier.

Studies for the US suggest that price-level variability there was small even before the era of inflation targeting. This would mean that explicit price-level targeting there might deliver only small insurance-related gains. Whether this is because of the excellence of US institutions, the virtues of the monetary policies pursued, or perhaps even the presence of an implicit price-level target is beyond the scope of this chapter. However, it is worth noting that, for some countries at least, a switch to price-level targeting would not mean a dramatic change.

4.4   INFLATION VOLATILITY IS NOT SAME THING AS INFLATION UNCERTAINTY

Although (in the absence of significant nominal rigidities) prices are more volatile over the short-term under price-level targeting, that is not because they are more uncertain. Some investment projects need to make a return over a short time-scale – perhaps three or four years, rather than twenty years. Thus it might seem as if short-term volatility presented the same kind of problems we discussed before, only applying to short-term contracts. This is not so. Although prices are more volatile in the short-term, the extra volatility is predictable. For example, suppose that unexpected inflation above trend has occurred. Then under inflation targeting the next expected price movement is with trend, while under price-level targeting the next move will be below trend – a bigger change on the previous year. However, as we have just seen, everyone will *expect* a movement below trend. Thus extra short-term volatility is not the same thing as extra short-term uncertainty.

4.5   PRICE-LEVEL TARGETING GENERATES ITS OWN CREDIBILITY

One classic problem in monetary policy is time-inconsistency. Because, in the short-term, unemployment can be reduced and output raised by creating surprise inflation, a monetary authority that is seeking to maximise the welfare of its citizens will have a permanent incentive to create surprise inflation. Because there is this permanent incentive to create surprise inflation, inflationary expectations will be raised. Even if a monetary authority would prefer not to create inflation, expected inflation will be higher because of the *risk* that it might do so. Thus an inflationary bias is introduced into the system.

The standard idea of how to minimise this inflationary bias is through an independent central bank with a mandate to control inflation and, at most, a lexicographic output rule (i.e. a rule which says something like: 'only if you have succeeded in keeping inflation at 2%, and without reducing your chances of keeping it at 2% in the future, maximise output'). The pros and cons of this arrangement have been discussed extensively elsewhere, and I do not propose to enter this debate here. However, it is worth noting that price-level targeting should, itself, reduce or even eliminate the incentive to create surprise inflation.

To see why, suppose a central bank is considering the merits of surprise inflation, and that it has a long-term price-level target of 100. This year it could create surprise inflation, raising the price-level to, say, 105. This would reduce unemployment and increase output. However, since the price-level target is 100, that would mean that *next* year it would have to *reduce* the price-level again, back to 100. If the previous discussion was correct in suggesting that reducing prices, or raising them below trend, would involve real costs, then surprise inflation today would (insofar as the price level regime was maintained at all) be followed by output losses tomorrow.[3] Since, under price-level targeting, surprise inflation would lead to real costs, it would not be as welfare improving, and the monetary authority would have greater credibility in claiming not to want to generate it. Inflation targeting will also mean that surprise inflation leads to real costs, and hence to increased credibility, but the costs, and hence the credibility gain, would not be as high as with price-level targeting.

If there is still a net gain from surprise inflation, there will still be a credibility problem, but the equilibrium expected inflation associated with it might not be as high as under inflation targeting, or might even take the form of a harmless price-level bias with no average inflation bias at all.

4.6 PRICE-LEVEL TARGETING IS SELF-REGULATING

One interesting feature of price-level targeting is its self-regulating nature. Provided that credibility is maintained, a price-level target tends to be maintained by market forces without much need of intervention.

Consider the following scenario. Suppose that the year 1 price-level is 100 and that the ideal inflation rate is 0%, so that the permanent price-level target is 100. Suppose also that an individual possesses an item worth £100, which he is indifferent between keeping and selling at that price. Then suppose that (without the monetary base having changed) there is some shock to the economy causing deflation of 5%, so the item now becomes worth £95. Suppose that the monetary authority has not yet done anything (e.g. has not yet changed interest rates) but that everyone has full confidence that it will act if necessary. Will the individual sell the item for £95? Well, he knows that the monetary authorities are going to return the price-level to 100, so the item will soon be priced at £100 again. Why should he sell it for only £95? On

---

[3] Clearly there is a possibility that the price-level targeting regime would be abandoned altogether tomorrow, if society preferred not to face the costs of deflating. However, we assume that the costs of abandoning a monetary regime altogether are of a different order from those of deviating within the regime. Under inflation targeting there may still be an inflation bias within the scope for discretion (e.g. within the target band). The point being argued is that there will be less or no *inflation* bias *within* a price-level targeting regime.

the contrary, what the individual should do is to find others foolish enough to sell the same item for £95 and buy those items, making an easy profit.[4]

Since other people will also be doing this, the price of £95 items will be bid up back to £100, quite independently of any policy response. A credible price-level target creates something akin to an arbitrage opportunity if prices deviate from the target, and hence the market will itself tend to keep the price-level at the target with less need of intervention, provided that the monetary authorities really are prepared to intervene if necessary (i.e. provided that credibility is maintained). All that will be required is a steady rise in the monetary base sufficient to permit the economy to grow in the medium term and for the price-level trend-path to meet the target.

4.7   PRICE-LEVEL TARGETING OFFERS ESCAPE FROM A LOW-EMPLOYMENT EQUILIBRIUM

Suppose there is a classical deflationary depression caused, not by incompetence on the part of the monetary authorities, but by some economic shock (the scenario widely feared, though not realised, after the bursting of the 'tech bubble' of the late 1990s). Prices and output fall, and unemployment rises; debts become impossible to service; banks fail; the economy slumps. One merit of inflation targeting is that it will attempt to combat this scenario early, by preventing the initial fall in prices. However, suppose that it fails, and that prices fall. If the economy has extensive nominal rigidities, it is not inconceivable that in extreme circumstances a new low-price-level quasi-'equilibrium' could continue for some time. Then output would not recover quickly, and unemployment would not fall back. For practical purposes, in the short-term the economy could seem to be trapped.

If this happens then inflation targeting will not help us. The price-level might stabilise at the new equilibrium, so that an inflation-targeting authority would take no action, except perhaps to attempt to stifle a recovery in prices if it started. Fiscal action might be taken, but would probably lead to a rise in prices if it were successful.[5] Then the fiscal and monetary authorities would be working against each other. The probable response is that the monetary authority's inflation target would be changed – perhaps increased significantly to aid the recovery in prices. But if this were to occur then it is clear that the variable being targeted here (albeit implicitly) is not the inflation rate, but the price-level. If the price-level were explicitly the target from the start then early action could be taken to aid the recovery in prices, and to work with fiscal measures rather than against them.[6]

Furthermore, because a price-level targeting regime contains within it a recipe for escaping from a liquidity trap should it arise, under a robust and credible price-level targeting regime no liquidity trap should be able to arise. As we have seen above, when a price-level target is

---

[4] Technically-minded readers should note that this discussion glosses over issues of discounting and positive long-term real interest rates. Think of there being no discounting and a zero long-term real interest rate, for simplicity. Then note that since inflation that returns the price level up to 100 will be above-trend (the trend rate being zero), real interest rates during the transition will be necessarily below-trend (i.e. negative). Hence the option to buy the good at £95 and sell later at £100 will deliver strictly superior expected returns to the option to sell today at £95 and invest the proceeds until prices return to 100. The argument could also be run in terms of a non-storable non-durable consumption good.

[5] Note that in the scenario under consideration the quantity of the monetary base is assumed not to have fallen much, so that the fall in prices is associated with a fall in the broad money supply associated with a fall in the money multiplier (e.g. because people become less willing to use money substitutes such as credit cards). But in the medium term the money multiplier must depend on structural features of the economy, rather than ephemeral monetary conditions. An economic recovery will be associated with a return of the money multiplier to its previous levels (approximately), and hence to an expansion of the broad money supply and thence to inflation.

[6] This issue is explored in considerably more detail in Lilico (2002).

credible, market forces themselves return prices to the target level following a shock. In this way price-level targeting allows a liquidity trap to be evaded altogether.

4.8   THE 'COSTS' OF PRICE-LEVEL TARGETING HAVE CORRESPONDING BENEFITS

The main benefit of price-level targeting is greater certainty about long-term inflation, offering the prospect of greater investment in viable projects and hence of higher growth. Furthermore, we have seen that the supposed drawbacks of price-level targeting are easy to overstate. If prices are more volatile in the short-term, that may not matter, as the short-term volatility is largely delivered by market forces and is predictable, because a price-level target is self-regulating and potentially very credible. If there are significant nominal rigidities in the economy, so that price-level targeting leads to greater short-term output volatility, then short-term price-level volatility will be lower, and the economy could be subject to a low-employment equilibrium after a deflationary depression. In this latter scenario inflation targets would probably be revised upwards anyway, reflecting an implicit price-level target, since price-level targeting would offer a superior monetary policy response.

This does not mean that price-level targeting has no disadvantages versus inflation targeting. Long-term price stability is not unambiguously good. As discussed in the earlier earthquake example, sometimes the equilibrium outcome is for the price level change more than had previously been anticipated. Another example would be sudden technological changes reducing production costs. Such technological advances might be expected to be associated with falls in the price-level. A price-level targeting regime would attempt to reverse these equilibrium shifts in the price-level. Under inflation targeting, they would be resisted as they occurred, then accepted. The biggest trade-off from the use of price-level targeting is between the costs and benefits of certainty in the long-term price level.

Arguments along these lines have been used to favour what is called a 'productivity norm', whereby appropriate changes in the price-level are accommodated.[7] The problem with a productivity norm is that it can be very difficult to tell why the general price level is tending to change. Sometimes, for example, it may be falling because of productivity improvements. But at other times it might be falling because of bank failures or some negative economic shock such a collapse in confidence. Similarly, when the price level is tending to rise that may be because of rising imported raw materials costs. But it may be because of increased monopoly power or because of an expansion in the money supply. The central bank will doubtless have an opinion on the source of pressure for the general price level to change. But experience and theory suggests that in many countries it is undesirable to allow the central bank full discretion to decide whether to allow the general price level to rise or fall. If the central bank is granted discretion, there is a tendency for it to be too accommodating which can lead to an upward bias in inflation. Furthermore, there are gains from the certainty of some pre-declared target or target range for monetary policy, since that can enable more efficient planning and more accurate formation of expectations.

Thus monetary policy frameworks around the world have tended to shift towards rules (such as an exchange rate target) or some form of constrained discretion (such as an inflation target or inflation band – or indeed a price-level target). This is not true everywhere, and the US Federal Reserve in particular operates under discretion, so a productivity norm

---

[7] For more on the productivity norm, see Selgin (1997).

may be a useful guide for policy there. But in developed small and medium-size economies which do not use discretion, since there will tend to be cost-reducing innovations that make a small decline in the price-level over time optimal (say, 0.5%–0.75% per annum), a price-level (or average inflation) target with trend deflation will be superior to a productivity norm.[8]

4.9   PRICE-LEVEL TARGETING VS. AVERAGE INFLATION TARGETING

We have argued above that price-level targeting is superior to inflation targeting in many ways. However, it may be difficult to see how a true price-level targeting regime could be implemented in practice. Price-level targeting requires the government to commit to a long-run path for inflation. But how can the government commit to what will happen in ten years' time, when it may be a completely different government in power? In contrast, an inflation target offers politicians the opportunity to be judged on something concrete over a reasonable political timescale. The electorate can decide that it wants to elect a government which will set a higher or lower inflation target, and that will happen. Might not the likelihood that the price-level target would change at some point in the future undermine the credibility of the regime?

Although such a pure price-level targeting regime does not rest easily with certain aspects of a democracy subject to periodic elections, there is something close which is achievable, and which offers much the same opportunity for political accountability. This is called 'average inflation targeting'.

If it supported average inflation targeting, an incoming government would state its target (say 2.0%) for the average inflation rate over the next Parliament. Then, if, in year 1 inflation were too low (say 1.0%), the Bank would aim to achieve above 2.0% (actually, about 3.0%) in the following year, so as to bring the average back to the target. At the end of the Parliament, say after four years, the electorate could decide whether it liked having a 2% average inflation rate, or whether it wanted to change it.

If the electorate always liked the same average inflation target, an average inflation targeting regime would be just like a price-level targeting regime. But, in any event, many of the gains of price-level targeting would still be present under average inflation targeting.

4.10   THE HISTORY OF PRICE-LEVEL TARGETING

The sole example, so far, of a central bank using a price-level target was during the Great Depression. Between 1931 and 1937, after the collapse of the Gold Standard, the Swedish Riksbank used price-level targeting. In that case the main goal was to prevent the fall in prices which blighted so many other countries in this period. There were two main ideas about what an appropriate price-level target should be. Wicksell, in 1898, had argued for a constant price-level. Another Swedish economist of the time, Davidson, had argued that prices should fall at the rate of growth in industrial output productivity (cf. the argument above about technological change and long-term falling prices). The Swedes opted for the Wicksell proposal, and were quite successful in maintaining stable prices (and, incidentally, rather more stable output than

---

[8] For more on this claim, see Lilico (2003).

many other countries of the time) through until 1937, when the pure price-level targeting regime was abandoned.

4.11   CONCLUSION

Price-level targeting offers greater long-term certainty over the price-level than inflation targeting. This could mean that more viable projects obtain investment, and hence that the economy grows more. This greater long-term price-level certainty may come at the price of greater volatility in short-term prices and/or short-term output. However, the volatility in short-term prices will largely be delivered by market forces, since price-level targeting is self-regulating, and hence may be quite benign. Short-term variability in output will be greater if nominal rigidities are greater, but if there are such rigidities then price-level targeting offers a way out of the deflationary depressions which may occur. Price-level targeting was tried in Sweden in the 1930s, and it worked. Price-level targeting is simple, safe and successful. We should be considering its use in the UK.

REFERENCES

Lilico A., (2002) The liquidity trap and price-level targeting, *Economic Affairs* **22(2)**, 47–52.
Lilico, A. (2003) Could deflation be ideal?, *Economic Affairs* **23(1)**, 44–48.
Selgin, G. (1997) Less than Zero – The case for a falling price level in a growing economy, *IEA Hobart Paper No. 132*, London: Institute of Economic Affairs.

5

A Price Targeting Regime Compared to a Non Price Targeting Regime. Is Price Stability a Good Idea?

Keith Pilbeam

5.1 INTRODUCTION

There has been a large move by central banks to inflation targeting as a means of keeping inflation under control in the belief that this will ultimately lead to a better economic performance. In this chapter, we look at the effects of stabilising the price level when the economy is hit by various economic shocks assuming that the country has a flexible exchange rate – we call such a regime a price targeting regime (PTR). Currently the European Central Bank, the Bank of England, the Bank of Japan and the Federal Reserve have varying degrees of commitment to price stability combined with flexible exchange rates. We compare a price targeting regime (PTR) in which the price level is fixed following an economic shock but the exchange rate is left to float freely, with a non price targeting regime (NPTR) whereby both the exchange rate and domestic price level are allowed to find their own levels once the economy is hit by transitory shock. We show that a PTR is the better regime when the economy is hit by transitory money demand and aggregate demand shocks. However, a PTR is not such a good idea when the economy is hit by a transitory aggregate supply shock since a PTR will exacerbate the impact of the economic shock on the level of real output in the economy. The conclusion is simple, that while PTR is a good idea in the face of money demand and aggregate demand shocks some flexibility of the price target may be necessary in the case of a supply side shock.

An important point that follows from the analysis is that it is that to avoid costly policy errors it is necessary for the central bank to distinguish between different types of economic shock that hit the economy. As such, we explore the issue as to whether contemporaneously available financial data might be useful in distinguishing between an inflationary aggregate demand shock and an inflationary aggregate supply shock. The need to distinguish between these two types of shock is important for central banks because while both are inflationary a PTR will lead to a poorer real output performance than a NPTR in the case of an aggregate supply side shock.

5.2 THE ULTIMATE OBJECTIVE OF ECONOMIC POLICY

There are many factors that policy makers have to take into account when designing their policies. Most importantly, they have to decide what their objectives are, the weight to be attached to each of them and then the most efficient means of achieving these aims. Inevitably,

Issues in Monetary Policy. Edited by K. Matthews and P. Booth.
© 2006 John Wiley & Sons, Ltd.

the choice is not easy because policy makers are confronted with a wide range of different and often conflicting economic analysis to choose from and even considerable scepticism as to whether they can influence the economy in a predictable fashion. In this paper, we consider the following objective function O(P, Y):

$$O(P, Y) = w(Y - Y_T)^2 + (1 - w)(P - P_T)^2 \qquad 0 \le w \le 1$$

Where Y is actual real income and Y_T is target real income, P is the actual domestic price level and P_T is the target price level. A value of w = 1 means that the objective involves only domestic income stability, whereas if w = 0 the sole concern is with domestic price stability.

The basis of including the reduction of the variance of the domestic price level in preference to reducing the variance of the output level can be questioned because the price level is only a nominal variable while the output level is a real variable. It can be argued that if a choice has to be made between reducing the variance of a real as opposed to a nominal variable one should always go for the former. For a review of literature on inflation targeting, other monetary rules and nominal GDP targeting, see Svensson (1999). However, most central banks today seek to bring some degree of stability to the price level as in our PTR case, even though there may be a cost in terms of the stability of the real output level of the economy. The intention of this chapter is to explore precisely the likely trade off between price stability and real output stability by comparing a PTR and NPTR in the face of differing economic shocks. As such we do not consider the welfare consequences to private agents of the PTR regime, such an analysis can be found in Lawler (2005).

5.3 MODELING ECONOMIC SHOCKS

In what follows, we use a streamlined macroeconomic model to compare a PTR to a NPTR. The focus of the analysis will be to see which regime best stabilises real economic output when the economy is hit by a shock. The analysis is essentially theoretical but for empirical evidence relating to the Eurozone area, see Coenen and Wieland (2005).

5.3.1 Assumptions of the Model

Before setting out the formal model this section briefly states the assumptions underlying the model:

(1) The economy is subjected to various transitory shocks which have a zero mean and normal distribution.
(2) Three types of shock are considered; money demand, aggregate demand and aggregate supply.
(3) The authorities like private agents only know that the shocks impinging upon the economy are transitory in nature with zero mean and normal distribution.
(4) There is assumed to be perfect capital mobility and perfect substitutability between domestic and foreign bonds, so that the expected yields on domestic and foreign bonds are equalised. This means that under floating exchange rates the positive nominal interest rate differential between domestic and foreign bonds is equal to the expected depreciation of the domestic currency in accordance with the uncovered interest parity condition.
(5) The model permits transitory deviations of the exchange rate from PPP because of imperfect goods arbitrage in the relevant time horizon.

(6) Expectations are rational in that economic agents have imperfect information on the source of any transitory disturbance impinging upon the economy, however, because they know that the shock is only transitory a variable is always expected to revert to its normal/target value.

(7) Labour and employers are locked into contracts which have the effect of keeping nominal wages fixed.

(8) The authorities can change monetary policy costlessly and instantly to stabilise the domestic price level at its target value or allow the economic shock to adjust the price level.

(9) The wage contracts themselves are fairly simple in nature, the wages that are set by employers and workers are those that are expected to achieve full employment in the following period. Workers agree to supply all the labour demanded by employers in the case where following a shock to the economy there is a change in employers' demand for labour.

(10) The foreign economy is assumed to be stable so we do not consider foreign price and output shocks. In addition, the foreign economy is large in the sense that it is not significantly affected by the shock impinging upon the 'small' economy that is the focus of the analysis. Hence, we do not explicitly model the foreign economy and trace through the effects of various shocks to it and the resulting additional effects on the domestic economy.

(11) The domestic interest rate, exchange rate and domestic price level are all contemporaneously observable but domestic output is not. This assumption is not too unrealistic since exchange rates and interest rates are observable instantaneously and the price level is easier for economic agents to observe and is published on a monthly basis while output data is published often with major revisions only quarterly.

(12) The model considers the stabilisation properties of either a PTR regime or a NPTR regime. Under a PTR regime the authorities adjust monetary policy to keep the price level fixed following a shock. Under a NPTR there is no adjustment of monetary policy to the economic shock.

5.4   THE MODEL

The demand for the home country's money is a positive function of the aggregate price index, a positive function of real domestic income and inversely related to the domestic nominal interest rate. In the following all variables except interest rates are expressed in log form. That is:

$$M^d_t = P_{it} + \eta Y_{dt} - \varphi r_t + U_{1t} \qquad (5.1)$$

Where M^d_t is the demand to hold money in current period t, P_{it} is the currently observable aggregate price index made up of a weighted average of the domestic and foreign price levels as set out in equation (5.2) Y^d_t is real domestic income in period t which is not currently observable, r_t is the domestic nominal interest rate in current period t which is a currently observable financial variable. U_{1t} is a stochastic transitory disturbance term with zero mean and normal distribution.

The idea of incorporating the aggregate price index in the demand for money function is derived from the monetarist proposition that the demand to hold money is a demand for real balances related to the purchasing power of money. The aggregate price index is a weighted average of the domestic price level and the domestic price of the imported foreign good, which is equal to the exchange rate times the price of the foreign good. That is:

$$P_{it} = \alpha P_{dt} + (1 - \alpha)(S_t + P_{mt}) \tag{5.2}$$

Where α is the weight of the domestic good in the overall consumption basket, S_t is the exchange rate defined as domestic currency per unit of foreign currency in the current period, P_{dt} is the price of domestic good in the current period and P_{mt} is the price of the imported foreign good in the foreign currency in the current period.

The demand for domestic output is a positive function of the real exchange rate and inversely related to the domestic real interest rate and a positive function of the natural/target level of income. That is:

$$Y^d_t = \Theta(S_t + P_{mt} - P_{dt}) - \beta(r_t + P_{dt} - P_{dt+1/t}) + \pi Y_T + U_{2t} \tag{5.3}$$

Where $P_{dt+1/t}$ is the expected price level in one periods time given the information available in the current, period. Y_T is the normal/target level of output and U_{2t} is a stochastic disturbance term with zero mean and normal distribution.

The real exchange rate is given by the first bracketed expression, an appreciation of the exchange rate would reduce the demand for the domestic good. Similarly, the real domestic interest rate is given by the second bracketed expression and is equivalent to the nominal interest rate minus the expected rate of price inflation. A rise in the real interest rate will act to reduce the current demand for the domestic good.

The supply of domestic output is derived from a fixed capital stock model with variable labour input, for a production function with diminishing returns. The supply of domestic output depends upon the price at which producers are able to sell their output relative to the wage rate that they must pay per unit of labour. That is:

$$Y^s_t = \sigma(P_{dt} - W_t) + U_{3t} \tag{5.4}$$

Where Y^s_t is the supply of the domestic good, and U_{3t} is a stochastic disturbance term with zero mean and normal distribution.

Equation (5.4) says that if the price of the domestic good rises relative to the wage rate domestic producers will increase their output and employment levels as the real wage facing them falls. It is assumed that financial capital is perfectly mobile and that domestic and foreign bonds are perfect substitutes. As a result the uncovered interest parity condition is assumed to hold continuously. That is:

$$r_t = r^*_t + (S_{t+1/t} - S_t) \tag{5.5}$$

where r^* is the foreign interest rate in current period, $S_{t+1/t}$ is the expected exchange rate in period $t + 1$ given information available at time t and the expression $(S_{t+1/t} - S_t)$ gives the expected rate of depreciation of the currency.

Wage contracts have a duration of one period and establish a nominal base wage W^*_t. The contracts for the current period t are written at the end of period $(t - 1)$ so that W^*_t is set with imperfect information concerning the stochastic shocks likely to occur in period t. It is assumed that the base wage W^*_t is set at the level required to generate an expected level of output at the natural level Y_n, which is also the target level of the authorities.

If we set Y^s_t equal to Y_n and W_t to W^*_t in equation (5.4) and use the fact that $P_{dt+1/t} = P_{dt/t-1}$ and rearrange terms we obtain:

$$W^*_t = P_{dt/t-1} - Y_n/\sigma \tag{5.6}$$

Where $P_{dt/t-1}$ is the expected domestic price level at time t given information at time $(t - 1)$. Thus, workers and firms attempt when setting W^*_t to ensure full employment in each subsequent period.

The wage rate actually faced by producers in period t will be the base wage that is:

$$W_t = W_{t^*} \tag{5.7}$$

To close the model we require the simultaneous fulfillment of the following two equations: That money demand in the current period (M^d_t) equal the current money supply (M^s_t) and that current aggregate supply equal current aggregate demand. That is:

$$M^s_t = M^d_t \tag{5.8}$$

and

$$Y^s_t = Y^d_t \tag{5.9}$$

Under a NPTR the money supply is exogenously determined and the domestic price level, output level, interest rate and exchange rate are endogenously determined. While under a PTR the price level is stabilised at its initial price level prior to the introduction of an economic shock by the authorities altering the money stock to achieve the desired price target and the output level, interest rate and exchange rate adjust to the values necessary to keep the price level stable. We now set out the model using a diagrammatic exposition.

5.5   DETERMINING EQUILIBRIUM

We use for exposition purposes aggregate supply and demand schedules defined by equations (5.3) and (5.4) respectively and also make use of the money market curve as set out by equation (5.1). Initial equilibrium is found where all three schedules intersect as depicted in Figure 5.1.

The aggregate demand schedule is given by Y^d_1 and is derived from equation (5.3), it is downward sloping because a rise in the domestic price level leads to a fall in aggregate demand for the domestic good ceteris paribus for two reasons: Firstly, by inducing a decline in net exports and secondly since any rise in the domestic price level leads to a future expected return of the price to its target level (P_T), the expected rate of price inflation will be negative which raises the real interest rate.[1]

M^d_1 schedule depicts the money demand schedule derived from equation (5.1) of the model, it also has a negative slope because a rise in the domestic price level increases the demand for money requiring a fall in real income to maintain money demand equilibrium.[2] The slope of the Y^d schedule may be flatter or steeper than the M^d schedule. The condition for the M^d schedule to be flatter than the Y^d schedule is that $\eta(\Theta + \beta) < \alpha$. For our analysis we shall assume that this condition is satisfied.

---

[1] The absolute slope of the Y^d schedule is given by the reciprocal of the summation of the elasticities of aggregate demand with respect to the real exchange rate and real interest rate, i.e. $1/(\Theta + \beta)$.

[2] The absolute slope of the M^d schedule is given by the income elasticity of money demand divided by the share of the domestic good in the aggregate price index i.e. η/α.

Price level

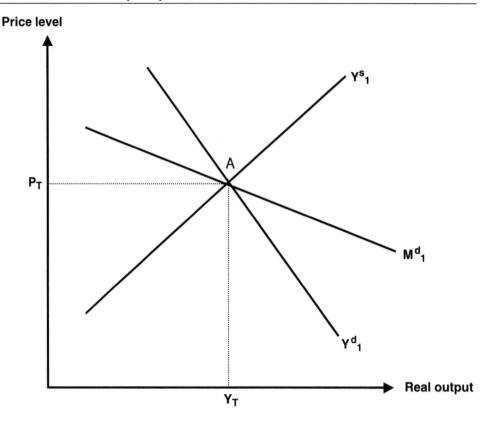

Figure 5.1   Equilibrium of the model

The aggregate supply curve has a positive slope since a rise in the domestic price level for a fixed nominal wage reduces the real wage facing producers encouraging them to take on more workers which results in increased output. It has a positive slope given by $1/\sigma$.

Equilibrium of the system is determined by the simultaneous interaction of all three schedules through a common point. In the absence of unanticipated disturbances to the economy, output is at its target level Y_T and the price level at its target level P_T. In the analysis we shall also assume that these are the optimal target values of the authorities and that the economy is initially in full equilibrium. If the system is initially in full equilibrium only unanticipated disturbances will cause the schedules to shift from their equilibrium levels, inducing corresponding adjustments in price and output. Under NPTR the exchange rate, price level, real output and interest rate all adjust to equilibrate the system causing shifts in both the M^d and Y^d schedules. For example, an appreciation of the exchange rate shifts the Y^d schedule to the left due to a loss of competitiveness with a resulting fall in exports as well as the fact that an appreciation leads to an expected future depreciation as the shocks impinging upon the economy are known to be self-reversing. As a result, the domestic interest rate is forced up further shifting the Y^d schedule to the left. The rise in the domestic interest rate lowers the demand for money which for a given money stock requires a shift to the right of the M^d schedule. By contrast, under a PTR the money supply and domestic interest rate are adjusted by the central bank to stabilise

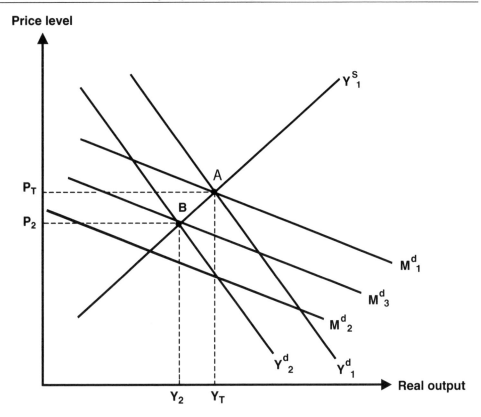

Price level

Figure 5.2   Money demand shock

the domestic price level. We now examine the impact of NPTR compared to a PTR in the face of three economic shocks.

5.6   A MONEY DEMAND SHOCK

Suppose that there is an unanticipated rise in money demand, this has the effect of shifting the M^d schedule to the left.

An increase in money demand causes a shift to the left of the money demand schedule from M^d_1 to M^d_2. Under NPTR an appreciation of the exchange rate shifts Y^d_1 to the left to Y^d_2 due to the fall off in export demand and rise in the domestic interest rate as there is an expected future depreciation of the currency. The rise in the interest rate leads to a fall off in money demand shifting M^d_2 to M^d_3. Temporary equilibrium is attained where all three schedules intersect at point B with price level P_2 and output level Y_2. Thus, it can be seen that under a NPTR a rise in the demand to hold money leads to a fall in both the domestic price and output level.

If a PTR is pursued the authorities will need to expand the money supply which will shift the money market schedule to the right from M^d_2 back to M^d_1, they have to raise the money supply to match the increased demand for money. The result will be that both the domestic

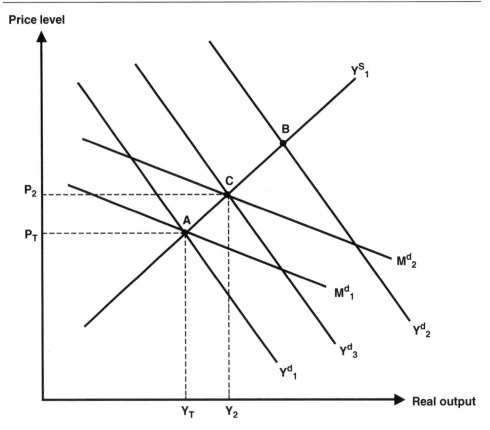

Figure 5.3   An aggregate demand shock

price level and output level are unchanged, indeed so too will be the domestic interest rate and exchange rate. Hence the increase in money demand is met by an equivalent increase in the money supply so that the domestic price level and output level are unchanged. Clearly in the face of a money demand shock a PTR makes good sense compared to a NPTR since it stabilizes not only the domestic price level but also the real output level.

5.7   AGGREGATE DEMAND SHOCK

Assume that there is an unanticipated increase in aggregate demand, this has the effect of shifting the Y^d schedule to the right from Y^d_1 to Y^d_2.

This means that there is an excess demand for money due to the rise in price and output which will cause the exchange rate to appreciate. Under a NPTR the appreciation of the domestic currency which will have two effects; the aggregate demand schedule will shift to the left from Y^d_2 to Y^d_3 due to the fall off in exports and the money demand schedule will shift to the right from M^d_1 to M^d_2 due to the rise in the domestic interest rate. Equilibrium of the system is obtained at point C with price P_2 and output Y_2.

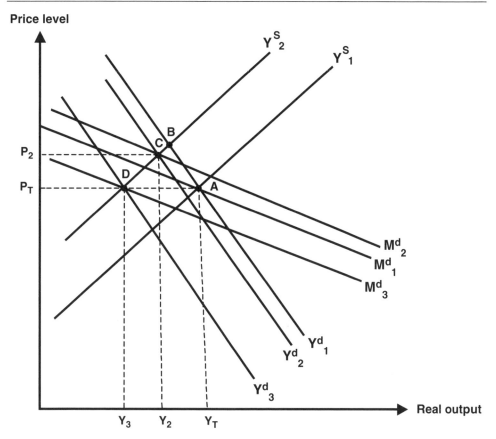

Figure 5.4   An aggregate supply shock

If there is a PTR then the authorities can by decreasing the money supply and raising the domestic interest rate shift the money demand and aggregate demand curves to the left back to M^d_1 and Y^d_1 which means a higher interest rate and an appreciation of the domestic currency but once again they are able to stabilise the domestic price and output level perfectly. The rise in the domestic interest rate and appreciation of the currency can in principle offset the aggregate demand shock effect on the price and output level. Once again the central bank would be correct in its presumption that stabilising the price level is also a means to stabilise the real output level. The higher interest rate is required since the appreciation leads to an expected depreciation.

5.8   AN AGGREGATE SUPPLY SHOCK

Assume that there is an unanticipated fall in aggregate supply, this has the effect of shifting the aggregate supply schedule to the left from Y^s_1 to Y^s_2 as depicted in Figure 5.4.

An aggregate supply shock causes there to be an excess demand for money at point B since Y^S_2 and Y^d_1 intersect to the right of the money demand schedule. Under a NPTR the excess demand for money resulting from the shock leads to a appreciation of the exchange rate. This has the effect of shifting the aggregate demand schedule to the left from Y^d_1 to Y^d_2. In addition, the appreciation leads to the expectation of a future depreciation, which via the uncovered interest rate parity condition raises the domestic interest rate constituting an additional reason for the leftward shift of the Y^d schedule. The rise in the domestic interest rate by reducing the demand for money shifts the M^d schedule to the right from M^d_1 to M^d_2. The result is that short run equilibrium under NPTR is obtained at point C with a rise in the domestic price level to P_2 and fall in domestic output to Y_2.

If the authorities pursue a PTR then they will reduce the money supply to offset the effects of the aggregate supply shock on the domestic price level which shifts the M^d schedule to the left from M^d_2 to M^d_3 and which raises the domestic interest and appreciates the domestic currency even more than in a NPTR resulting in a further fall in aggregate demand from Y^d_2 to Y^d_3. The result is that in a PTR there is a fall in output to Y_3 which is larger than in the case of a NPTR. This case is very important because it shows that in the face of an aggregate supply shock a PTR leads to a larger change in real output than would under a NPTR. Of course, while output is more variable in a PTR, the price level is more stable but the price level stability is brought about at the expense of increased output instability. The precise costs of a PTR regime pursued by an independent central bank in terms of output instability is essentially an empirical matter, evidence by Alesina and Summers (1993) suggest the trade-off may not be that costly but as we have shown, in the presence of aggregate supply shocks the effects can be quite adverse.

In sum, we have seen that while a PTR is a good idea in the face of transitory money demand and aggregate demand shocks it is not such a good idea in the face of an aggregate supply shock. In fact, a PTR exacerbates the effects of the aggregate supply shock on the level of real output compared to a NPTR. As such, it may be important for central banks to allow a higher degree of price flexibility if they can identify the shock as an aggregate supply shock, we now briefly turn our attention to consider if it is possible to identify the shock impinging upon the economy.

5.9   THE SEARCH FOR AN INDICATOR

From our analysis, it follows that the central bank requires, if possible, a means of identifying the source of the shock impinging upon the economy since in the face of an aggregate demand shock a PTR is best while in the face of an aggregate supply shock a NPTR performs best in terms of output stability. Since asset markets respond very speedily to news and shocks, there has been an increasing interest in the economics profession in searching to extract information from contemporaneously observable financial data information about the likely source of the shock impinging upon the economy, see for example, Lahiri (1992). If the authorities could extract such information they would be able to adopt more appropriate policy responses. We shall not go too deeply into this matter but rather illustrate that things are not at all easy, consider the case where the aggregate demand schedule is steeper than the Md schedule as depicted in Figure 5.5.

If there was an aggregate demand disturbance this would shift Y^d_1 to Y^d_2 and M^d_1 to M^d_2 under NPTR as we saw earlier equilibrium would be at point B with a rise in price and output to P_2 and Y_2 respectively. Under a NPTR excess demand for the currency results in an appreciation of the exchange rate and rise in the domestic interest rate. If there is instead an inflationary supply side shock that shifts the aggregate supply curve up to the left from Y^s_1 to Y^s_2, then under a NPTR equilibrium is given by point C with a rise in price and a fall in output to P_2

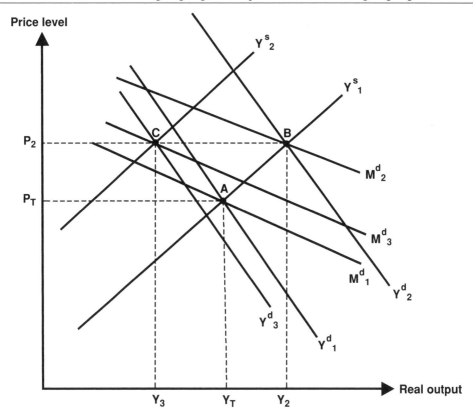

Figure 5.5   Distinguishing between shocks

and Y_3 respectively. Under a NPTR excess demand for the currency results in an appreciation of the exchange rate and rise in the domestic interest rate. In this case for simplicity, the price level effect is assumed of the two shocks is assumed to be identical with a price rise from P_T to P_2. The key difference is that an inflationary aggregate demand shock we know that a PTR is best for output stability, while in the case of an aggregate supply shock a NPTR is best for output stability. However, in both cases, there is an appreciation of the exchange rate and a rise in the domestic interest rate. Thus, the two financial variables do not permit us to distinguish between the two types of shock. In this case the failure to distinguish between the two types of shock is of importance because following an aggregate demand shock a PTR is superior to a NPTR. Whereas in the case of an aggregate supply shock a NPTR is superior to a PTR.

From the above example, it is quite clear that extracting information from contemporaneously observable financial data and using this to determine the appropriate policy response is not an easy task. Even in the simple case of trying to distinguish between an aggregate demand and an aggregate supply shock things may not be at all clear from financial data. Clearly, two financial variables such as the interest rate and the exchange rate alone are insufficient indicators. It might be useful, for instance, to add stockmarket data to the range of central bank indicators, since a rise in aggregate demand would likely lead to a rise in the stockmarket while an adverse aggregate supply shock would likely lead to a fall in the stockmarket.

Before finishing this section, it is worth reminding ourselves that things become a lot more complicated if one includes the possibility of two or more shocks impinging upon the economy at the same time and so forth. Also it is not only the source of the shock that is important but also the nature, the economy is subjected to both transitory and permanent disturbances and therefore a means of distinguishing between these two types of shock compounds the problems of using contemporaneous financial data as a guide to the appropriate policy response. All in all the use of financial variables to identify the source of shock to the economy is an under-developed research area and could prove to be an exciting area for future research.

5.10   CONCLUSIONS

We have seen that a price targeting regime (PTR) is a good idea in the face of money demand and aggregate demand shocks but it will lead to an undesirable outcome for the stability of real output in the face of an aggregate supply side shocks to the economy. This is not a trivial issue because these days central banks have in general moved to some sort of PTR system and this may lead to real economic problems in the face of aggregate supply disturbances. The effects are likely to be exacerbated once interdependence of the afflicted economies is considered. If all the central banks were to continue with PTR in the face of a common adverse aggregate supply shock then the falls in real output will be even greater once interdependence of output is considered. This is a worrying feature of the present consensus that central banks should focus primarily on price stability – given that we are talking about the Eurozone area, the United States and Japan.

The authorities would be able to achieve superior output stabilisation policies if they can identify the source and nature of the shock impinging upon the economy. In this context, while the use of information contained in contemporaneously observable financial data may prove useful, it might not prove conclusive as a guide to the appropriate policy response. We have argued that the authorities are well advised to derive their information from as many different sources as possible including using stockmarket data in addition to interest rate and exchange rate data. One should be careful, however, with interpretation particularly if the economy is subjected simultaneously to two or more shocks as the number of indicators remains the same while the number of possible combinations rises. In addition, there is the problem of distinguishing between permanent and transitory shocks.

The current popularity of price targeting/inflation control as a means of achieving a superior medium to long term economic performance critically depends upon the relative frequency of shocks originating on demand side of the economy be it shifts in money demand or aggregate demand compared to those on the aggregate supply side of the economy. In the case of an aggregate supply side shock the present arrangements may lead to larger fluctuations in real economic activity than is desirable and require more flexibility on the part of central banks to their price targets.

REFERENCES

Alesina, A. and Summers, L. (1993) Central Bank independence and macroeconomic performance: Some comparative evidence, *Journal of Money, Credit, and Banking*, **25(2)**, 151–161.
Coenen, G. and Wieland (2005) A small estimated euro area model with rational expectations and nominal rigidities, *European Economic Review*, **49(5)**, 1081–1104.

Lawler, P. (2005) Central bank inflation contracts and strategic wage setting in a multi-union economy, *Economic Letters*, **86(3)**, 323–329.

Lahari, K. (1992) Leading economic indicators: A leading indicator of inflation based on interest rates, *International Journal of Forecasting*, **8(4)**, 649–50.

Svensson, L. (1999) Inflation targeting as a monetary policy rule, *Journal of Monetary Economics*, **43**, 607–654.

6

Optimal Monetary Policy with Endogenous Contracts: Is there a Case for Price-Level Targeting and Money Supply Control?

Patrick Minford

6.1 INTRODUCTION

There have been many strands in economists' thinking about the best way to use monetary policy. Monetary policy is the tool which aims to set the money supply and so the price level, in so doing also affecting interest rates; alternatively it can be put that it aims to set interest rates, so setting prices, and in so doing also affects the money supply. These are equivalent descriptions; here I will talk about policy setting the money supply. But later on I will ask whether in setting the money supply central banks should aim to keep interest rates steady for a period (so-called 'interest rate control') or should instead keep the money supply steady for a period (money supply control).[1] But let us begin by discussing the main questions raised by monetary policy: what inflation rate should it aim for and what should it do in response to the business cycle ('stabilisation policy')?

6.2 CONSIDERATIONS IN DESIGNING MONETARY POLICY ARRANGEMENTS

To start with, money is a transactions technology medium and, because it is fiat or paper money, it is also costless to create; so its marginal use cost (the rate of interest) should be equated with its zero creation cost. The marginal cost is usually called 'shoeleather' cost because in models of demand for cash the alternative to holding cash is to put it in the bank to earn interest on deposit, at the cost of more trips to the bank wearing out one's shoes. This argument led Friedman (1969) to argue for a zero nominal interest rate, implying a rate of deflation equal to the real rate of interest (since the real rate of interest is defined as the ordinary or nominal interest rate minus the expected rate of inflation). If applied strictly this would imply a moving deflation target equal to the moving real rate of interest; however in practice one would get most of the benefits if the price level target were fixed to move steadily downwards at a fixed rate of deflation rather than of inflation. Plainly the Friedman argument ignores the issue of the 'zero bound' on short-run nominal interest rates; this problem arises if there is a need to

---

[1] By money supply here I mean M0, the monetary base, whose demand is reasonably stable. Should its velocity be disturbed by factors such as new technology on the shadow economy, then I assume allowance can be made for these disturbances.

Issues in Monetary Policy. Edited by K. Matthews and P. Booth.
© 2006 John Wiley & Sons, Ltd.

cut interest rates in order to prevent or end a recession. If interest rates are zero it would be impossible to cut interest rates below zero (since money in circulation pays a zero interest rate all short-run deposits, Treasury Bills and other short-run debt would be switched into money, thus eliminating the assets paying negative interest and so effectively getting rid of negative interest rates.) Hence there has been a general reluctance to set the inflation target below 2–3%, let alone at a negative rate; central banks have greatly feared the implied impotence of interest rates getting as low as zero – a situation well illustrated by the difficulties in deflationary Japan. Here I assume that the Friedman argument cannot be used because of the zero bound. However the further away from the Friedman optimum interest rates are the greater the 'shoeleather' costs. So one desiderandum of monetary policy would be that inflation can be set as low as possible without hitting the zero bound; this means that our policy should have to vary interest rates less rather than more if at all possible.

A second strand has emphasised that money supply growth generates inflation which provides an implied 'inflation tax' as a source of government revenue. In public finance, different taxes create different distortions (i.e. disincentives to efficiency); it is optimal, on its own, that the marginal distortion per unit of revenue be equated across taxes. Otherwise a tax, which if expanded would create a smaller extra distortion than other taxes, should be increased, and the others reduced until this inequality of marginal (i.e. extra) distortions is eliminated. Thus the inflation tax should be raised on this view until the marginal distortion on a unit of revenue be equal to that from general income tax – this would qualify Friedman's argument above in principle since it could be assumed that the distortion on money holdings in raising a unit of inflation tax revenue be equated to the distortion created by a unit of general tax revenue. This argument might point to a positive rate of inflation; however in practice the size of money holdings (M0) are so small in most developed countries that the yield of the inflation tax (which is the rate at which holdings of notes and coins in circulation are devalued, i.e. the rate of inflation times the stock of M0) is trivial as a percent of GDP.[2] It is normal therefore to assume for this reason that there is no case on these grounds for an inflation tax; I make this assumption here too.

A third aspect is there are other distortions in the economy due to market imperfections. Money growth and consequent inflation may help to alleviate these; for example in a sticky-price world higher inflation may reduce excess price margins. However this argument relies on the use of price shocks to affect real variables systematically; price setters would come to anticipate such policy behaviour. This would imply that people would come to expect inflation for this reason and this expectation in turn would raise inflation, while at the same time nullifying the effect on price margins. I therefore assume that one would not wish to make use of monetary policy to try and affect equilibrium relative prices and sales volumes.

These three aspects all involve the issue of what the inflation target should be. One can summarise these by saying that the zero bound issue indicates setting inflation high enough so that normal interest rates will just avoid the zero bound in virtually any conditions – but setting it no higher than this because of the costs of inflation identified by Friedman.

Finally, and this is the main focus of this chapter, money is of course the major instrument for stabilising the economy – that is for controlling the extent of boom and slump while also keeping inflation or prices at their target rate of inflation. Inflation targeting for example is a part of a 'feedback policy' used in stabilisation; in other words, monetary policy responds to inflation by loosening or tightening to bring the economy back to a track where it will generate the target rate of inflation. In the rest of this chapter I discuss different ways in which monetary

---

[2] M0 is about 3% of GDP in the UK.

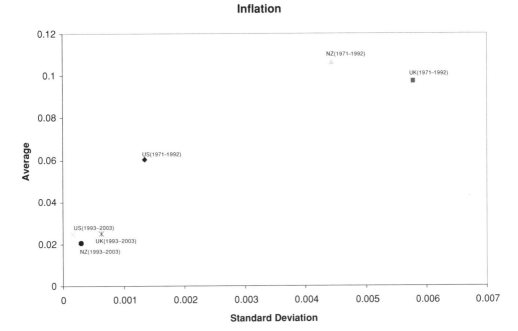

Figure 6.1   Inflation and inflation volatility in the US, the UK and New Zealand

policy should or should not respond to the state of the economy. The way I proceed is to set up a model of the economy that I believe to be a good one both theoretically and empirically and to examine within it the results of different possible types of response.

There has been a considerable success in the UK and many other countries with using inflation targeting – see Figures 6.1 and 6.2 which show how (in the UK, US and New Zealand, in all of which rather similar policies have been followed) not only has inflation come down since the advent of the new inflation-targeting policies but also the variability of both inflation and GDP has fallen massively. Here I ask whether this success of monetary policy can be built on by going further and targeting the price level (or the money supply level). By 'targeting' we mean here strictly that the money supply for the next quarter is chosen so that in the absence of further shocks the target variable is exactly on its target – this is no doubt too strict in practice but such strictness helps to bring out the differences of the various regimes with a useful clarity.

What do we mean by targeting the price level? The idea is illustrated by Figure 6.3. Under inflation targeting if there is a period of high inflation (prices rising faster than the target), the policy in the following period is to bring inflation down again to the target; notice that this means that the price level is permanently higher. Now compare price level targeting: if the same shock occurs to prices policy now brings the price level back to the previous target track for prices. This implies that in the next period prices must not return to the same inflation target rate but must actually go below it so that prices get back on track. With money-level targeting the idea is analogous: if the money supply growth overshoots then in the next period it must be brought down so that the money supply returns to the original target track. We will show later that money-level targeting is quite like price-level targeting but not quite so severe. We will also show that when either of these two policies is being followed there is also a good case for money supply control rather than interest rate control.

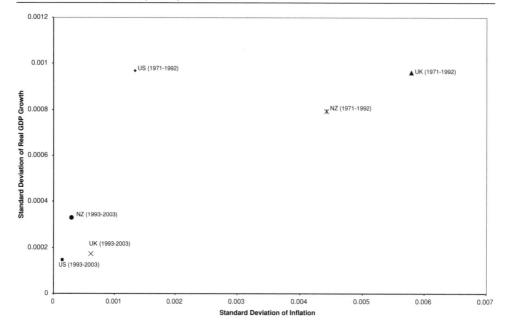

Figure 6.2   Volatility of inflation and real GDP growth in the US, the UK and New Zealand

To anticipate I will argue that price- or money-level targeting combined with money supply control are the best policies we can identify here, provided one is comfortable with a target track for inflation of 2–3% as is now normal in developed countries. If it seems that this imposes excessive costs of the Friedman sort, then this target track can be reduced by moving to interest-rate-setting without much loss of stability.

6.3   MONETARY POLICY: IS INFLATION TARGETING THE BEST WE CAN DO?

The model we use is 'classical' in nature: that is to say that it assumes markets are flexible and people act with full rationality, including in forming their expectations. However risk-averse households are also assumed to face excessive costs in arranging continuous borrowing to smooth their consumption in the short term (which of course they want to do in order to max-imise their utility); so they attempt to smooth their consumption through wage arrangements (i.e. 'contracts'). These may make wages to be fixed nominally in advance, or indexed to prices, or indexed to auction wages; a contract specifies that wages react in some proportion to each of these elements (proportions add to unity). Indexation is imperfect in two senses: the index used is biased in the short term because of fixed weights and it is paid retrospectively. These two features imply that 100% indexation is not automatic. What then happens is that households choose a degree of indexation that gives them the maximum consumption smoothing. This contract set-up imparts a varying element of nominal wage rigidity to the otherwise conven-tional classical model. Apart from these features of consumption and the wage contract, the model includes firms which invest and hire workers to maximise profits, given productivity,

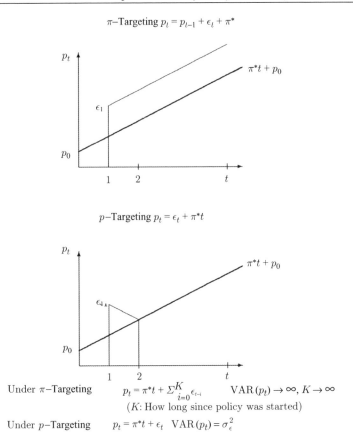

Figure 6.3 Comparison of Inflation(π)- and Price(p)-targeting (VAR=variance; t=time period)

and a government which carries out necessary spending, raising taxes and borrowing to finance it.[3]

In this model, if productivity and money supply shocks were temporary in nature ('stationary' – that is returning to their original value after a time), indexation would be minimal with only a slight tendency to rise as the variance of money shocks rose dramatically. However when shocks to either become permanent (as is clearly the case with productivity changes) indexation to prices becomes large, becoming largest when both shocks are persistent. The reason is that these shocks disturb prices and so the real worth of nominal wage contracts; indexation is of little use in remedying this disturbance if it is temporary because by the time the indexation element had been received the shock would have disappeared, but with permanent disturbances indexation can help offset it with a lag. This higher indexation also helps to alleviate the instability in unemployment which accompanies the greater shock persistence of

---

[3] There is no space to discuss the merits of this model. Suffice to say that it is well documented that consumption is not highly smoothed by household borrowing but varies with income and hence wages; that indexation varies; and that there is a degree of nominal wage rigidity (though not of the excessive variety assumed in certain recent models). Our model otherwise has the basic features of the 'real business cycle' set-up due to Kydland and Prescott, the 2005 Nobel prize winners for that work.

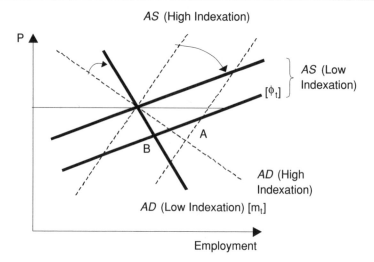

Figure 6.4 The effect of reduced indexation on slopes of AS and AD curves [ϕ_t = productivity shock; ϕ_t = monetary shock]

money – the point being that this persistence induces persistence in the economy's departure from its baseline and so disturbs unemployment too for longer.

In the OECD in the 1970s it is well-known that de facto indexation[4] was substantial; the calibrated model, when estimated variances and persistence of money and productivity shocks are fed into it, predicts high indexation in all countries covered, apparently in line with the facts. Also, contrary to much casual comment, there was little evidence of any diminution of indexation in the 1990s; the model also predicts as much, for even though the variance of money supply shocks fell in the 1990s, their persistence remained essentially unchanged. Since it is persistence in both shocks (monetary and real) that is inducing both the greater instability of real wages and the increasing indexation this produces, price level targeting is a natural avenue in which to investigate improvement in monetary policy. (Price level targeting can be considered as 'cumulative inflation targeting' where any past deviation from the inflation target is offset with an opposite deviation the following period). The reason is that such a policy will eliminate the effect of persistence in shocks from the price level and so from the real value of a nominal wage contract. It should therefore get us back towards the 'stationary world' in which the model finds that welfare is higher than in the 'non-stationary world' of high all-round persistence and high indexation.

From society's viewpoint reducing indexation improves the economy's stability in the face of supply shocks because it both flattens the Aggregate Supply (or 'Phillips Curve') and steepens the Aggregate Demand curve, as illustrated in Figure 6.4.

The resulting intersections for a supply shock as shown at A (high indexation) and B (low indexation). Thus the drop in indexation is stabilising to both employment and prices in the face of a supply shock. Of course for a money (demand) shock the result is greater employment

---

[4] Whether explicit or implicit; we also allow for wages to react in an 'auction' manner, which has an effect similar to indexation and is an element we find to be rather constant.

instability, though probably less price instability; however, demand shocks can, in principle, be controlled and offset by monetary policy and so are avoidable.

In order to assess the welfare of society from different monetary policy rules we measure the average household's utility, which is assumed to depend on its consumption and its leisure, each of them as well as the two combined have diminishing marginal utility. The workings of the model in detail need not detain us here.[5] In summary we may note that the model can be thought of in terms of the figure above; with an Aggregate Demand curve whose position is shifted by money and other demand shocks and a Phillips Curve or Supply Curve whose position is shifted by productivity (supply) shocks. We can think of the role of monetary policy as reacting to the supply shocks with appropriate choices of money supply – while also attempting to minimise pure money or demand shocks. I will show some of the results of investigations with the model below.

6.4   INTEREST RATE CONTROL – WHAT DOES IT DO?

Up to this point we have been considering rules for controlling the money supply for the current period. In practice most central banks control interest rates for the current period, letting the money supply therefore be whatever is necessary to meet precisely that interest-rate target. In effect what this rule does is to force money to respond to other shocks – i.e. here the supply shock – so as to fix interest rates, instead of being an autonomous random variable as we have assumed hitherto.

The problem we are dealing with here is a well-worn issue of monetary policy – whether monetary policy should set interest rates in the very short run, operating, period (of say a month ahead) or should fix the money supply. The seminal work of Poole (1970) noted that, if one wished to stabilise output, the answer depended on the relative variability of shocks to demand from, on the one hand, non-monetary sources such as investment or government spending and, on the other hand, from monetary sources. If money is the source of the variability then holding interest rates fixed will stop this variability spilling over into demand; on the other hand if non-monetary sources are the cause of the variability in demand, holding interest rates constant will not dampen them whereas fixing the money supply will cause interest rates to lean against these sources and dampen them.

Within this model, an important feature is a high responsiveness of investment to real interest rates and also to productivity shocks (which change the return on capital). Hence aggregate demand is heavily affected by non-monetary shocks. In Poole's terms this implies that it is better for money supply rather than interest rates to be controlled if one wishes to stabilise output. We consider the results from the model below; and also there discuss whether output stability is the only issue.

6.5   MONEY SUPPLY TARGETING AND FEEDBACK RULES – A STOCHASTIC SIMULATION ANALYSIS

We now proceed to consider some specific targeting rules, along the lines of our opening discussion. Our method is that of 'stochastic simulation'. In stochastic simulations we shock the model repeatedly to create 'scenarios' of what would happen to the economy. Each scenario

---

[5] A full account can be found in Minford, Nowell and Webb, 2003, and of the workings for this chapter in Minford and Nowell, 2003).

Table 6.1   Price- and inflation-targeting in the full model

	Inflation target contract structure optimal for inflation target	Price level target	Price level target with contracts Optimized
variance of real consumed wage	100	99	96
variance of unemployment	100	119**	69**
Household welfare[†]	100	96	113**
wage contract shares (%)			
nominal share	22	22	92
indexed share	71	71	0
auction share	7	7	8

[†]The weighted sum of the variances of real consumed wage and of unemployment.
**Statistically significant at 1% level.

is a 'run' of the model over a number of quarters, where the shocks for each quarter are drawn randomly from its measured distribution. Our stochastic simulations here are done for 50 runs of 40 quarters; thus if we treat each quarterly outcome in all 50 runs as a separate observation, we have a sample of 2000 observations from which to derive the variances and utility that interest us. We assumed that the standard deviation of demand and supply shocks are equal, which seems to tally with reality (Minford *et al.*, 2004).

Comparing price- and inflation-targeting in the full model (Table 6.1) we find that for *given* contract structure the variance of real wage goes down while that of unemployment goes up as one moves to price-level away from inflation targeting. As contract structure is optimised (with the consequent near-elimination of indexation) real wage variance drops further while unemployment variance drops below its original level under inflation targeting. Again the substantial gains come with the shift in contract structure.

The message of Table 6.1 is that price level targeting is worse for economic stability than inflation-targeting if you assume indexation remaining constant – very much in line with the standard macroeconomists' view that having to push prices back down after an inflation (like Mr Churchill going back onto gold in 1925 at the pre-war parity to restore prices to their pre-war levels) is deflationary and destabilising to the economy. Though consumption alone is slightly more stable because prices and so real wages are more stable, naturally enough, when prices are targeted; but unemployment is a lot more unstable.

All this however changes in the last column once indexation adjusts to the new environment (by in fact disappearing). There is now a general and marked reduction in instability, for the reason given earlier that the behaviour of supply and demand is different with low indexation.

6.5.1   Comparing money- and price-level targeting

We now ask whether targeting the level of the money supply instead of the price level could give us any improvement. The answer shown in Table 6.2 is: it depends whom in that average we call the representative household one wishes to please most – those in regular employment or those regularly unemployed. Moving to targeting the money supply means that prices are plainly less stable and hence real wages and the consumption of the employed is also less

Table 6.2   Stochastic simulation results for the two nominal level targets

	Pure money rule	Price level rule
variance of real consumed wage	100	96
variance of unemployment	56**	69**
household welfare[†]	113**	113**
wage contract shares (%)		
nominal share	59	92
indexed share	37	0
auction share	4	8

[†]The weighted sum of the two variances.
**Statistically significant at 1% level.

stable. For them money-targeting is less good than price-targeting, even though they protect themselves against this to an extent by choosing more indexation.

However for the unemployed matters are different. For them under price-level targeting with maximum nominal rigidity money shocks (i.e. shocks to monetary demand) have a bigger effect on employment (see Figure 6.6) than under money-level targeting; furthermore with money-targeting money shocks become random again, whereas under price-targeting they have to accommodate last quarter's productivity shocks which makes them persistent. Hence under money-targeting employment is both less vulnerable to money shocks and also these shocks, being less persistent, have a lower cumulative variability; thus employment is more stable than under price-targeting.

Depending on just how these two elements in average welfare are weighted together one can say that welfare is either the same or slightly higher on average under money – than under price-targeting. There is not much in it. The key point is that money-targeting is something of a compromise between rigorous price-targeting and inflation targeting; as such, particularly because it is better for employment stability, it could be attractive.

One could go further along this route and investigate variations on these two basic feedback rules, to see if we could do better still. But we leave such finer issues here and proceed instead to discuss the question of money supply or interest rate control.

6.5.2   Should we use interest rates rather than the money supply as the short-term instrument of control?

To this point we have identified two feedback rules for monetary policy that are superior to inflation targeting in terms of delivering macro stability. We now come to the vexed question of choosing the instrument of short run control. We pointed out above that, in line with Poole's analysis, stabilising output (and so employment) would be best done by controlling the money supply in this model because the main shocks to demand in it come from the non-monetary sources of productivity and thus investment. Table 6.3 below confirms this: whether there is a money-level or price-level feedback rule in place, interest-rate control always raises the variability of unemployment.

Table 6.3   Stochastic simulation results, money supply control vs. interest rate setting

	A) Price level rule with money supply control =100	B) Price level rule with interest rate setting; contracts optimised
variance of real consumed wage	100	98
variance of unemployment	100	107
Household welfare -weighted sum of variances	100	97
wage contract shares (%)		
nominal share	92	92
indexed share	0	0
auction share	8	8

	A) Money level rule with money supply control = 100	B) Money level rule with interest rate setting; contracts optimised
variance of real consumed wage	100	95
variance of unemployment	100	171
household welfare -weighted sum of variances	100	72**
wage contract shares (%)		
nominal share	59	14
indexed share	37	78
auction share	4	8

**Statistically significant at 1% level.

What is less clear on the face of it is why it also invariably lowers the variability of real wages (and so of consumption). We can understand it as follows. The variability of real wages is greatly affected by the variability of prices, especially when wage contracts are heavily fixed in nominal terms.

Take first the price-level feedback rule. Here wage contracts are heavily nominal. Now what interest rate control does is to force nominal interest rates to be constant; nominal interest rates are defined as equal to real interest rates plus the percentage difference of expected future prices and current prices. In this model real interest rates move very little because of their very large effect on investment demand; and expected future prices do not move at all under price level targeting. Hence for nominal interest rates to be constant prices too must move very little. Thus real wages are less disturbed by price movements than with money supply control when prices move normally with money and productivity shocks.

Now consider the other money-level feedback rule, where there is more indexation. Interest rate control now under the same argument as above forces expected inflation to offset real interest rate movements. As these latter are very small, this means expected inflation movements must also be very small; or in other words expected future prices must be equal to current prices. The last can only happen if the money supply shock is made very small – the reason is that the productivity shock is permanent and has the same effect on both current and expected future prices while any money supply shock, being temporary, only affects current prices.

With money supply variability suppressed, price variability falls; but at the same time price persistence rises and drives up indexation, dampening real wage responsiveness to price shocks as well and boosting unemployment responsiveness to productivity shocks.

Summarising we could say that interest rate control also controls prices more. This is good for consumers and workers, smoothing their real wages, but destabilises employment and output, which is bad for those on the margins of the labour market.

6.5.3   How important is the zero bound in setting the inflation target rate?

We saw earlier that there was a conflict, in choosing the target inflation path, between, on the one hand, setting the lowest possible rate, even negative and equal to the real rate of interest if possible, as recommended in Friedman's optimal inflation analysis, and, on the other hand, setting a high enough rate to enable 'head room' for interest rates to fall in recessions in the presence of the zero interest rate bound. Since the latter has generally appeared to be of dominant importance, in practice the target inflation path has been set at a sufficient rate to allow interest rates to drop by their normal range, as, for example, measured by their standard deviation. One might wish to allow a normal nominal interest rate to equal three standard deviations from zero, say; this would imply an inflation rate target equal to three standard deviations minus the normal real interest rate (say 3%). An interest rate three standard deviations from zero will hit zero only 0.1% of the time under the normal distribution of shocks, which prevails in this model.

Within this model we find that inflation targeting (with or without interest rate control) yields a standard deviation for the short-run nominal interest rate of 0.81%. Price-level targeting generates more interest rate variability under money supply control: roughly double, with a standard deviation of 1.54%. This comes about because, as just discussed, the nominal interest rate is made up in this case of the real interest rate plus the expected percentage rise in prices, since the expected future price level is being held constant via price-targeting; also the real interest rate itself is inversely correlated with the price level – a productivity shock raises the real interest rate and lowers prices; a money supply shock raises prices and lowers real interest rates. Under inflation targeting the nominal and real interest rate are the same because expected future inflation is being fixed by inflation-targeting. Thus price-level targeting raises the variance of nominal interest rates by both the variance of prices and twice the covariance of prices with real interest rates.[6]

Money-level targeting with money supply control generates just a slightly smaller standard deviation for nominal interest rates (at 1.51%) as price-level targeting with money supply control. The slight reduction comes about because expected future prices are correlated directly with current prices via productivity shocks; when productivity rises, the rise is permanent and

---

[6] Notice that we have been assuming throughout this chapter that the zero bound is not binding by virtue of setting the target for price rises high enough. If however the zero bound had been binding, we should find that price-level targeting would have been more stabilising than inflation targeting because it generates real interest rate changes independently of changes in nominal interest rates, purely through prices moving relative to a fixed expected future price level. We have not investigated this point here, since it impossible to do so in this model – there is no elasticity of demand for money to the nominal interest rate and hence if we imposed the zero bound so that the real interest rate was constrained to be minus the expected inflation rate, the model would be over-determined, with one real interest rate needed to achieve market-clearing and another imposed by the zero bound. Thus we have assumed that the zero bound is avoided. However, we are thereby potentially understating the benefits of price-level targeting in a model where the zero bound could occur as a natural solution. For example, suppose that price-level targeting achieved as good stabilisation with or without the zero bound; then we could set target inflation at its optimal rate as given by the Friedman optimum quality of money rule and not concern ourselves about the zero bound issue. This is something we are considering within a different model context in further work.

so raises prices now and in the future equally, thus partially offsetting the inverse correlation of prices with real interest rates. However, money supply shocks now have no effect on expected future prices because they will be eliminated by next period.

If we turn to regimes with interest-rate control we obtain, not surprisingly, lower nominal interest rate variability. Under inflation targeting interest-rate-setting makes no effective difference since the only variation in interest rates comes from real interest rates and this is negligible (a standard deviation of 0.26% which is well within the range of variation under interest-rate-setting). Under price-level targeting interest rate control brings the standard deviation of nominal interest rates down to 0.87%; while under money-supply targeting it brings it down to 0.6%. The difference between these two is bigger than under money supply control because under interest-rate control the money supply must react positively to productivity and so the correlation of expected future prices with current prices is larger.

What does this mean for the target inflation rate – if we set that to keep nominal interest rates three standard deviations from zero in a shock-free environment? If the normal real interest rate is 3%, then under inflation-targeting the target inflation rate could be as low as −0.6%. Under price-level and money-level targeting with money supply control it could be 1.6 and 1.5% respectively. With interest-rate control it could come down to −0.3% under price-level targeting and −1.2% under money-level targeting. Thus depending on how big shoeleather costs of money demand are, there is a wide range of choice for the target inflation rate; the bigger they are, the more one would be driven towards money-level targeting with interest-rate control, the policy that allows the lowest target inflation rate – though still short of the rate of deflation that would set nominal interest rates normally at zero.

Within the model here, there are no costs from holding less money as inflation and interest rates rise (this is because in the model money has to be held in a fixed quantity equal to spending) and we do find that the optimal policy otherwise is money- or price-level targeting with money supply control. Under this policy the avoidance of the zero bound suggests an inflation target of around 1.5%, much in line with current central bank practice. If one believed the costs associated with money-holding were higher, this would indicate moving to interest-rate control with these same targeting policies.

6.6   CONCLUSIONS

In this chapter we have investigated the nature of optimal monetary policy, within a classical model of flexible wages and prices and rational households and firms; the only special feature is a wage contract optimally chosen to smooth real wages and consumption. We found that monetary rules targeting the level of a nominal variable, whether money or prices, can do so without increasing macro instability, compared with monetary rules that target rates of change of the nominal variables; indeed they somewhat decrease macro instability (somewhat increase the welfare of the representative agent). The reason is the strong shift in contract structure away from indexation to nominal. This shift is strongest when a price-level rather than money-level target is in place – but in welfare terms it is hard to choose between the two, as there is a trade-off between the interests of the employed (who prefer the price rule) and the unemployed (who prefer the money rule).

We also considered within this model the familiar issue, originally addressed by Poole, of whether money supply or interest rates should be controlled for the current period, as the 'instrument' of monetary policy. We find in our model here that controlling the money supply raises welfare somewhat compared with controlling interest rates. On the other hand, control of interest rates reduces interest rate variability obviously and so makes it possible to set the inflation target lower while still avoiding the zero interest rate bound – in a model with significant shoeleather costs of money demand this could swing the argument in favour of interest rate control.

Thus the conclusions of this chapter are mildly encouraging to two ideas of interest to monetary authorities. First, that they can afford to aim for stability in the price level (or, less radically, in the money supply). Second, that the money supply may well be the best operating instrument.

ANNEX

6.6.1   The representative agent model (RAM)

The model used in the paper (Minford *et al.*, 2003) has two exogenous shocks driving it, a monetary (demand) shock, m_t, to the money supply presumed to originate from monetary policy, and a supply (productivity) shock, f_t. The productivity shock is (rather naturally) modelled as a random walk throughout. Of course whether the money supply shock is transitory or permanent depends on the monetary rule; if it targets, for example, the level of money it will be transitory, if it targets the money supply growth rate, it will be turned into a random walk.

The representative household is assumed to be entirely liquidity-constrained; this assumption emphasises the importance of the contract choice, since a choice that minimises the variance of the spendable real wage is therefore identical with one minimising the variance of the employed agent's consumption. In a more realistic model with consumption smoothing this motive would have been implemented by including some transactions cost on smoothing, thus providing a motive for smoothing the real wage itself; however, this involves greater complexity than the stark assumption made that the transactions costs are in effect insuperable.

The household is embedded in an environment of profit-maximising competitive firms which on a large proportion of their capital stock face a long lag before installation (a simple time-to-build set-up) and a government that levies taxes and pays unemployment benefits (which distort households' leisure decisions and introduce a 'social welfare' element into monetary policy). Firms and governments use the financial markets costlessly and settle mutual cash demands through index-linked loans; since there is no binding cash constraint on these agents, these loans are assumed to be unaffected by the imperfections of the price index which are short term in nature. This model is too simplified in many ways to match the data of a modern economy whether in trend or dynamics; however its focus is purely on the wage contract decision and its simplicity is justified in terms of its ability to match the OECD facts about wage contracts.

In calibrating the model the authors chose parameters perceived as plausible for modern OECD economies. The contract length is set at 4 quarters; the elasticity of leisure supply (s) at 3; the share of stocks and other 'short-term' capital (k) at 0.3; the average life of other capital at 20 quarters; the share of labour income in value-added ($\square$) at 0.7 (the production function is Cobb-Douglas); the elasticity of the official price index to unanticipated inflation (c) at 0.2 (implying that a 1% unexpected rise in inflation would result in a 0.2% temporary overstatement of the price level faced by the representative consumer). The initial values assume 10% unemployment; a capital-output ratio of 6; an average (= marginal) tax rate of 0.10; a real interest rate of 5%.

The government is assumed to smooth both the tax rate and the growth rate of the money supply by borrowing (from firms). Nevertheless it cannot avoid noise in its money supply setting – the source of this could be its inability to monitor the money supply quickly or even at all (for example in the USA the use of dollars by foreigners around the world makes it impossible to know what the domestic issue of dollars is).

Money supply raises prices in the long run, and in the short run also raises output, with persistence extending up to 15 quarters but with most effect over after 10. In the high-indexed case there is less real effect and less persistence than in the high-nominal case.

These fairly standard properties stem from the model's deliberate drawing on elements that have been shown by past work to be useful in explaining the business cycle and also natural rates as discussed for example by Parkin (1998), though he notes we are still some way from building dynamic stochastic general equilibrium models that can fully explain the business cycle. The elements here include: time-to-build investment, cash-in-advance, nominal contracting (as noted above), household liquidity constraints, and (on the natural rate side) the influence of unemployment benefits on labour supply. With suitable country-by-country calibration one would expect to be able to model OECD countries' business cycle and natural rate experience with at least some modest success.

Minford et al., (2003) found that in the face of stationary productivity and money supply shocks indexation would be minimal with only a slight tendency to rise as the variance of money shocks rose dramatically. However when shocks to either became highly persistent indexation to prices or to their close competitor, auction wages, (which together we term 'real wage protection') become large, becoming largest when both shocks are persistent. The reason was that productivity shocks would disturb prices and so the real worth of nominal wage contracts; indexation was of little use in remedying this disturbance if it was temporary because by the time the indexation element had been spent the shock would have disappeared, but with a permanent disturbance indexation can help offset it with a lag. If into this already-indexed world of persistent productivity shocks, monetary persistence is also injected, indexation rises further, to help alleviate the increased disturbance to real wages. This higher indexation also helps to alleviate the instability in unemployment which accompanies the greater shock persistence of money – the point being that this persistence induces persistence in the economy's departure from its baseline and so disturbs unemployment too for longer.

The authors looked at experience in the OECD in the 1970s where it is well-known that real wage protection was substantial; their calibrated model, when estimated variances and persistence of money and productivity shocks were fed into it, predicted high protection in all countries they could cover, apparently in line with the facts. They also found, contrary to much casual comment, that there was little evidence of any diminution of real wage protection in the 1990s; the model also predicted as much, for even though the variance of money supply shocks fell by then, their persistence remained essentially unchanged.

A1   Supply of work
$$a_t = a_c \times (W_t/(B_t \times P_{t-4}))^{-s} \times e_t$$

A2   Demand for capital goods
$$K_t = (1-k) \times (1-m) \times E_{t-20}\,[d_t \times (1/R_t) \times (1-T_t)] + k \times (1-m)$$
$$\times d_t \times (1-T_t) \times (1/r_t)$$

A3		Output function
d_t	$=$	$f_t \times K_t^{(1-m)} \times \{(1 - a_t) \times N\}^m$

A4		Wage rate, solved for W_t
$\bar{W}_t$	$=$	$(1 - v - w) \times W_t + v \times E_{t-4}[W_t/P_t] \times P_t + w \times E_{t-4}[W_t]$

A5		Official price index
$\ln(P_t)$	$=$	$ln(p_t) + c \times (\ln(p_t) - \ln(E_{t-1}[p_t]))$

A6		Goods market clearing, solved for r_t after substituting for K_t from Eqn.2
d_t	$=$	$M_{t-1}/p_t + K_t - K_{t-1}$

A7		Labour market clearing, solved for p_t
$N \times (1 - a_t)$	$=$	$(m \times d_t \times (1 - T_t) \times p_t)/\bar{W}_t$

A8		Money market clearing, solved for $\bar{W}_t$
M_t	$=$	$N\{\bar{W}_t \times (1 - a_t) + B_t \times P_{t-4} \times a_t\}$

A9		Efficiency
R_t	$=$	$E_t[f(r)]\frac{1}{20} - 1 \quad ; f(r) = \text{Product}_{i=1}^{20}\left(1 + \frac{r_{t+i}}{4}\right)$

A10		Money supply
M_t	$=$	$\bar{M}_t + m_t$

A11		Government budget constraint
b_t^g	$=$	$(M_{t-1} - M_t + N \times B_t \times P_{t-4} \times a_t - d_t \times p_t \times p_t \times T_t)/p_t$ $+ \left(1 + \frac{r_{t-1}}{4}\right) \times b_{t-1}^g$

A12		Firm's budget constraint
$d_t \times (1 - T_t)$	$=$	$K_t - K_{t-1} + \left(\bar{W}_t \times (1 - a_t) \times N\right)/p_t + b_{t-1}^p \times \left(1 + \frac{r_{t-1}}{4}\right) - b_t^p$

NOTES

1. By Walras's Law the bond market clearing equation, $b_t^p + b_t^g = 0$, is redundant.
2. To normalise the variables d_t, K_t, r_t, p_t and $\bar{W}_t$ to their base run values constant factors were applied to the right-hand sides of the following equations in their solved form: A2 1.11 (multiplicative); A3 0.629 (multiplicative); A6 + 0.0135 (additive); A7 0.7 (multiplicative); A8 0.9574 (multiplicative).

Variables and coefficients for RAM

Endogenous variables : base run values

a_t	Supply of work	0.10
K_t	Demand for capital goods	6.00
d_t	Output function	1.00

W_t	Wage rate	1.00
P_t	Official price index	1.00
r_t	Real interest rate (fraction per annum)	0.05
p_t	Price level	1.00
$\bar{W}_t$	Average wage	1.00
R_t	Long term real interest rate (fraction per annum)	0.05
M_t	Money supply	1.00
b_t^g	Government bonds outstanding	0.00
b_t^p	Firms' bonds outstanding	0.00

Exogenous variables : base run values

B_t	Benefits	0.60
e_t	$N(1.0,0.01)$	1.00
f_t	$N(1.0,0.01)$	1.00
M_t	Money supply target	1.00
m_t	Money shock	0.00
T_t	Tax rate	0.10

Coefficients

a_c	=	0.46
s	=	3.00
k	=	0.30
m	=	0.70
N	=	1.00
c	=	0.20

REFERENCES

Andrews, M.J., Minford, P. and Riley, J. (1996) On comparing macroeconomic models using forecast encompassing tests, *Oxford Bulletin of Economics and Statistics*, **58(2)**, 279–305.

Ascari, G. (2000) Optimising agents, staggered wages and persistence in the real effects of money shocks, *Economic Journal*, **110** (July), 664–686.

Attanasio, Orazio, and Guiso, Luigi (1998) The Demand for Money, Financial Innovation, and the Welfare Cost of Inflation: An Analysis with Household Data, NBER Working Paper No. W6593, June, 1998.

Bank of Canada (1994) *Economic behaviour and Policy Choice under Price stability*, Ottawa.

Berg, C. and Jonung, L. (1999) Pioneering price level targeting: the Swedish experience 1931–37, *Journal of Monetary Economics*, **43(3)**, June, 525–551.

Barro, R.J., and Gordon, D. (1983) Rules, discretion and reputation in model of monetary policy, *Journal of Monetary Economics*, **12**, 101–22.

Casares, M. (2002) Price setting and the steady-state effects of inflation, European Central Bank working paper No. 140, May, ECB, Frankfurt.

Christiano, L., Eichenbaum, M. and Evans, C. (2002) Nominal rigidities and the dynamic effects of a shock to monetary policy, Mimeo, Northwestern University.

Clarida, R., Gali, J. and Gertler, M. (1999) The science of monetary policy: a New Keynesian perspective, *Journal of Economic Literature*, **37(4)**, 1661–1707.

Collard, F., and Dellas, H. (2003) Inflation targeting, mimeo, University of Bern.

Duguay, Pierre (1994) Some thoughts on price stability versus zero inflation, working paper, Bank of Canada – presented at the conference on Central Bank Independence and Accountability, Universita Bocconi, Milan, March.

Erceg, C.J., Henderson, D.W., and Levin, A.T. (2000) Optimal monetary policy with staggered wage and price contracts, *Journal of Monetary Economics*, **46**, October, 281–313.

Fischer, S. (1994) Modern central banking, in Capie, F. *et al. The Future of Central Banking*.

Friedman, M. (1969) The Optimum Quantity of Money in *The Optimum Quantity of Money and other essays*, Chicago: Alldine.

Fuhrer, J. and Moore, G. (1995) Inflation persistence, *Quarterly Journal of Economics*, **110(1)**, 127–159.

Gali, J., and Monacelli, T. (2002) Monetary policy and exchange rate volatility in a small open economy, Mimeo, Universitat Pompeii Fabra.

Goodfriend, M. and King, R. (2001) The case for price stability, NBER working paper 8423.

Hall, Robert E. (1984) Monetary strategy with an elastic price standard, in *Price Stability and Public Policy*, Federal Reserve Bank of Kansas City, Kansas City, 137–159.

Henderson, D.W., and McKibbin, W.J. (1993) An assessment of some basic monetary-policy regime pairs: analytical and simulation results from simple multi-region macroeconomic models, in R.C. Bryant, P. Hooper and C.L. Mann (eds), *Evaluating policy regimes – new research in empirical macroeconomics*, Washington DC: Brookings Institution.

Khan, A., King, R., and Wolman A.L. (2002) Optimal monetary policy, Federal Reserve Bank of Philadelphia working paper No. 02–19.

Kiley, M.T. (1998) Monetary policy under neoclassical and new-Keynesian Phillips Curves, with an application to price level and inflation targeting, *Finance and Economics Discussion Series* 1998–27, Federal reserve Board, Washington, DC.

McCallum, Bennett T. and Nelson, Edward (1999a) Nominal income targeting in an open economy optimising model, *Journal of Monetary Economics*, **43(3)**, June, 553–578.

McCallum, Bennett T. and Nelson, Edward (1999b) An optimising IS-LM specification for monetary policy and business cycle analysis, *Journal of Money, Credit and Banking*, **31(3)**, August, Part 1, 296–316.

McCallum, Bennett T. (2003) Comment on 'Implementing Optimal Policy Through Inflation-Forecast Targeting' forthcoming in edited proceedings of the NBER Conference on Inflation Targeting, January 23–25, in Bal Harbour, Florida.

Minford, A.P.L. (1980) A rational expectations model of the United Kingdom under fixed and floating exchange rates, in K. Brunner and A.H. Meltzer (eds) *On the State of Macroeconomics*, Carnegie Rochester Conference Series on Public Policy, **12**, Supplement to the Journal of Monetary Economics.

Minford, A.P.L. (1995) Time-inconsistency, democracy and optimal contingent rules, *Oxford Economic Papers*, **47**, 195–210.

Minford, A.P.L. and Peel, D.A. (2002) Exploitability as a specification test of the Phillips Curve mimeo, Cardiff University, downloadable from Minford's Cardiff web page, http://www.cf.ac.uk/carbs/econ/webbbd/pm.html.

Minford, A.P.L. and Peel, D.A. (2003) Calvo contracts- a critique mimeo, Cardiff University, downloadable at http://www.cf.ac.uk/carbs/econ/webbbd/pm.html.

Minford, A.P.L., Nowell, E. and Webb, B. (2003) Nominal contracting and monetary targets – drifting into indexation *Economic Journal*, January, **113**, 65–100, downloadable at http://www.cf.ac.uk/carbs/econ/webbbd/pm.html.

Minford, A.P.L. and Nowell, E. (2003) Optimal monetary policy with endogenous contracts: is there a case for price-level targeting? mimeo, Cardiff University, downloadable at http://www.cf.ac.uk/carbs/econ/webbbd/pm.html.

Nessen, M. and Vestin, D. (2000) Average inflation targeting, mimeo, December 2000, Sveriges Riksbank, Stockholm.

Parkin, J.M. (1998) Unemployment, inflation and monetary policy, *Canadian Journal of Economics*, **31(5)**, 1003–32.

Poole, W. (1970) The optimal choice of monetary instrument in a simple stochastic macro model, *Quarterly Journal of Economics*, **84**, 197–221.

Rotemberg, J.J. and Woodford, M. (1997) An optimization-based econometric framework for the evaluation of monetary policy, in B.S. Bernanke and J.J. Rotemberg, (eds)., *NBER Macroeconomics Annual* 1997, 297–346.

Smets, F. (2000) What horizon for price stability? *European Central Bank working paper* No. 24, July 2000, ECB, Frankfurt.

Svensson, L.E.O. (1997) Optimal inflation targets, 'conservative' central banks, and linear inflation contracts, *American Economic Review*, **87**, 98–114.

Svensson, L.E.O. (1999a) Price level targeting versus inflation targeting: a free lunch? *Journal of Money Credit and Banking*, **31(3)**, 277–295, August.

Svensson, L.E.O. (1999b) Price stability as a target for monetary stability: defining and maintaining price stability, discussion paper No. 2196, August 1999, Centre for Economic Policy Research, London.

Svensson, Lars E.O., and Woodford, Michael (2003) Implementing optimal policy through inflation-forecast targeting Working Paper, Princeton University.

Taylor, J.B. (1993) Discretion versus policy rules in practice, *Carnegie-Rochester Series on Public Policy* **39**, 195–214.

Vestin, David (2000) Price-level targeting versus inflation targeting in a forward-looking model, mimeo, IIES, Stockholm University.

Wallis, K.F. (1995) Large-scale macroeconometric modelling in H. Pesaran and M. Wickens (eds) *Handbook of Applied Econometrics*, Blackwell.

Williams, J.C. (1999) Simple rules for monetary policy, mimeo, Federal Reserve Board, February 1999, Washington DC.

Woodford, M. (2005) *Interest and Prices*, Princeton University Press.

7
Forecasting Inflation: The Inflation 'Fan Charts'

Kevin Dowd[1]

7.1 INFLATION FORECASTING

Since 1992, the principal objective of UK monetary policy has been to target inflation, and the Bank of England has achieved this target with great success. Successful inflation-targeting requires that the Bank take a forward-looking view of inflationary pressures in the economy, and this presumably relies on the Bank being reasonably competent at forecasting inflation and other relevant macroeconomic variables. At the same time, it was also felt that it would be helpful for the Bank to publish its key forecasts: publication of the Bank's forecasts would help to communicate the Bank's 'view' to the market, and (assuming that they were reasonably accurate) strengthen the Bank's credibility. Publication would also expose the Bank to outside scrutiny, and therefore further its public accountability.

Accordingly, in February 1993, the Bank started publishing a quarterly chart showing a path for the 'central projection' of inflation up to two years ahead. However, forecasting is a notoriously inexact science, and even with the best forecasting model, realised outcomes are almost always different from those projected. Forecasts are therefore uncertain. To accommodate this uncertainty, the chart also included an 'uncertainty band', or shaded area around the central projection. The edges of the band were equal to the central projection plus or minus an estimated forecast error, and gave a rough idea of the uncertainty attached to the forecast inflation rate.

In February 1996, the band was replaced by a more explicit representation of inflation uncertainty. This is the famous 'fan chart', which represents a forecast of the inflation probability density function for the current quarter and the next eight quarters ahead.[2] The parameter values underlying the fan charts were made available from the third quarter of 1997 (1997Q3) onwards, and from that point on it became possible (in principle[3]) for outsiders to replicate the inflation fan charts and then subject the Bank's inflation density forecasts to independent

[1] The author thanks Philip Booth for his helpful comments. This work was carried out under an ESRC grant (RES-000-27-0014) and the author thanks the ESRC for their financial support.

[2] A probability density function gives the probability that a random variable – in this case, the inflation rate – will take a particular specified value, and can be used to determine the probability that inflation will fall within a particular range. It can also be regarded as providing a description of the randomness of the random variable concerned. The term 'probability density function' is often abbreviated to 'pdf' or 'density function'.

[3] In fact, the parameterisation of the Bank's inflation 2PN model has been the source of some confusion over the years. The original definitive reference, Britton *et al.* (1997), mistakenly reported that σ was the standard deviation, and their density formula also had an error in the sign of γ. The latter error was quickly corrected by Wallis (1999), but the former error was only corrected when the Bank revised its internet guidance notes on the 2PN in 2003. A correct restatement of the Bank's 2PN inflation density function and its parameterisation is provided by Wallis (2004).

assessment once enough observations had been accumulated to carry out an evaluation. In the space of a few years, the Bank's inflation forecasting had gone from a simple forecast of the likely central projection – which we can consider to be a forecast of the mode (or most likely value) from an unspecified inflation density function – to a forecast of the complete inflation density function itself. Furthermore, the key information – the type of density function used, and the values of the parameters fed into it – was now made public. Thus, the inflation fan charts represent a major innovation (and, indeed, a world first) in central bank forecasting and accountability: never before had a central bank made such an explicit, statistically complete and scientifically refutable inflation forecast.[4]

This chapter examines these forecasts and evaluates how well they have performed. The answer provided here will come as a surprise to many: despite the Bank's undoubted success in achieving its inflation target, and despite the fact that the Bank's 'central projection' forecasts are also quite good, the Bank's density forecasts as such are demonstrably inadequate. Although the Bank is pretty good at forecasting likely or expected inflation, it tends to overestimate inflation uncertainty (measured in terms of the dispersion of possible outcomes) for medium (i.e. 1-year) and longer-term (i.e. 2-year) horizons. The problem is that the Bank keeps forecasting a range of probable inflation outcomes that is much wider than the range of recent historical outcomes – in other words, bizarre as this might sound, the Bank as an inflation density forecaster does not seem to learn from its own success in keeping actual inflation low and stable. In fact, the Bank's performance is so poor at inflation density forecasting that one can easily construct naïve competitors that generate superior forecasts – a depressing conclusion when one considers the huge amount of time and effort that go into producing the forecasts on which the fan charts are based.

Section 2 now explains the fan charts in more detail, and section 3 looks at how they are constructed. Section 4 then looks at how well the Bank's density forecasts have performed, and section 5 offers some conclusions.

7.2   THE INFLATION FAN CHARTS

Each fan chart shows the inflation central projection surrounded by a series of prediction intervals at various levels of probability.[5] These intervals cover 10%, 20%, ..., 90%, of the forecast probability. Thus, the 10% prediction interval covers the central 10% of the pdf-mass centred around the forecasted mode or most likely value; the central 20% covers the central 20% of probability mass centred around the mode; and so on. Each of these intervals is shaded, with the 10%-interval darkest and the shading becoming lighter as we move to broader intervals. Interval forecasts are given for horizons up to eight quarters ahead, and typically 'fan out' and become more dispersed as the horizon increases.[6]

---

[4] The Swedish central bank, the Sveriges Riksbank, was also developing similar inflation density forecasting models at much the same time. The first Swedish inflation fan chart was published in the Riksbank's *Inflation Report* for 97Q4, but no 'hard' quantitative information was provided about the Swedish forecast density functions until the 98Q2 Swedish *Inflation Report*.

[5] A prediction interval is a range within which a random variable is supposed to occur with a specified probability. For example, if there is a 10% probability that inflation will fall in the range between 2.4 and 2.6, then we can say that this range is a 10% prediction interval. We can have prediction intervals for any probability between 0 and 100%.

[6] The Bank actually published two different types of RPIX inflation fan chart. The first, which was first published in February 1996, and first published with its parameters in August 1997, is based on the assumption that short-term market interest rates would remain constant over the horizon period. In February 1998, a second type of RPIX fan chart was introduced, the market-rate model, based on the assumption that short-term interest rates would follow market expectations over the horizon period. The two differed only in their mode parameters, and yield similar results. The last RPIX fan chart forecasts were published in February 2004, following the switch-over from an RPIX to a CPI target in late 2003, and the only inflation fan charts currently published by the Bank are CPI ones.

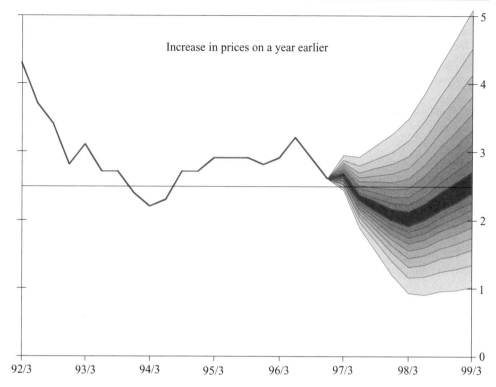

Figure 7.1   The August 1997 Inflation Fan Chart
Notes: The Figure shows previous realised values and predicted intervals for RPIX inflation, measured as the percentage increase in prices over the previous 12 months (measured against the *y*-axis), for the market rate model. The Figure is reproduced with permission from the Bank of England.

A typical example is the fan chart that appeared in the *Inflation Report* for August 1997, reproduced here as Figure 7.1. This chart gives prediction intervals for inflation for each of the nine quarters from 97Q3 to 99Q3, and these intervals – the so-called 'rivers of blood' – tend to fan out as the horizon increases. For example, the broadest interval, the 90% interval, fans out to the range [1.01%, 5.08%] for the end of the horizon period, indicating that the MPC was 90% confident that inflation for 99Q3 would be in this range. The fan chart also provides prediction intervals at probabilities of 80%, 70%, and so on. Observe too that the fan chart is asymmetric, indicating that the forecast inflation density function is skewed – typically, as in this case, skewed upwards towards higher values of inflation.

7.3   THE BANK'S FORECAST INFLATION DENSITY FUNCTION

The inflation fan charts are based on the assumption that the probability density function governing the RPIX inflation rate takes a particular form known as a two-piece normal (2PN), which we can think of as a normal density function – the classic bell curve – with an ad hoc adjustment for skewness.[7] This density function has three parameters. The first is the mode,

---

[7] These density functions are described in more detail in the Annex.

usually represented by μ (the Greek letter mu). This is the most likely value of the random variable being forecast. So, for example, if $\mu = 2.5$, then the most likely inflation value over the forecast horizon concerned is 2.5. The second parameter is a measure of the skew or asymmetry. The third parameter, usually represented by σ (the Greek letter sigma), describes the uncertainty or dispersion of the random variable. This parameter is closely related to the standard deviation, which is a more familiar measure of dispersion. However, σ is not the same as the standard deviation, except in the special case where the skew is zero.

When it publishes a fan chart, the Bank also reports on its website the parameter values on which the fan chart is based.[8] These values are published for each of three parameters (i.e. μ, a skew parameter, and σ), and each forecast horizon (ranging from the current-quarter to nine quarters ahead).

The parameter values themselves are determined judgementally by the Bank. Prior to May 1997, the judgement concerned was that of the Governor and Directors of the Bank, acting on the basis of advice from Bank staff. Since then, these parameter forecasts have been based on the judgements of the Monetary Policy Committee (MPC) also acting on the basis of internal advice. The advice given is partly based on the results of the quantitative forecasting models used within the Bank, but is also based on the extensive economic intelligence gathered by the Bank, much of which is collected by its network of regional agents. In fact, a very considerable amount of time and effort goes into the preparation of the forecasts on which the fan charts are based.

Once the MPC specifies the parameter values for each horizon period, then the inflation forecasting model is complete and any density forecasts or associated prediction intervals can be ascertained from it.[9]

7.4   EVALUATING THE BANK'S INFLATION FORECASTS

At the most basic level, evaluating the inflation density forecasts is straightforward. A simple glance at any fan chart shows the problem: from 1993 onwards, the inflation rate has been very stable and fairly close to its target value of 2.5%, and yet any fan chart also shows major inflation uncertainty, especially as one looks further out into the future. So, although realised inflation has been stable, the forecasts suggest significant probabilities that inflation could fall well outside its recent historical range.

7.4.1   Backtesting of the fan charts

To examine this issue in more depth, I carried out some backtesting of the Bank's inflation forecasts over three different horizons – a short horizon of one-quarter-ahead, a medium horizon of four-quarters-ahead, and a long horizon of eight-quarters ahead. Backtesting involves the comparison of density forecasts against the realised values of the variable being forecasted,

---

[8] The website address is: http://www.bankofengland.co.uk/inflationreport/rpixinternet.xls.

[9] To complicate matters a little, the prediction intervals represented in the fan charts themselves are not based on the more familiar symmetric prediction intervals that one usually finds in the literature. Instead they are based on prediction intervals centred around the mode μ. This means, for example, that if the distribution is asymmetric, then the lower and upper tails of the 50% prediction interval do not necessarily have probability masses of 25% each. The Bank's corporate view is that these non-central prediction intervals make it easier for an audience to understand the Bank's forecasts. However, Wallis (1999) argues that the Bank would do better to report symmetric prediction intervals, because they are more 'natural' from the perspective of the forecasting literature. I agree with Wallis, but the issue is one of communicative style rather than substance, and what really matters is how well the Bank's density forecasts actually perform, not the precise way in which those density forecasts are represented.

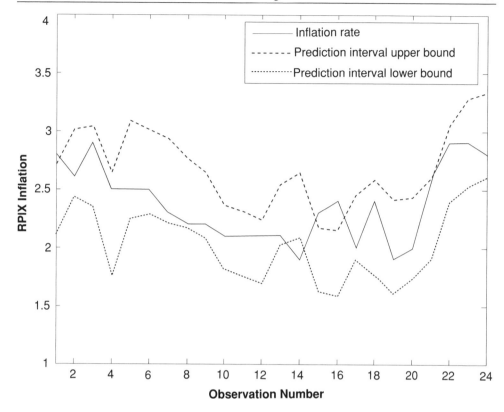

Figure 7.2 Backtesting chart for inflation density forecasts at horizon 1 quarter ahead
Notes: Obtained using data from 97Q3 to 03Q3. The actual (expected) numbers of non-exceedances, lower exceedances and upper exceedances are 19 (16), 1 (4) and 4 (4).

in order to come to a view about the adequacy of the model's forecasts.[10] Backtesting of risk models is standard practice in financial institutions with financial risk forecasting models, and the same methods can be applied to the Bank of England's inflation density forecasts as well.

To illustrate, Figure 7.2 shows a backtest chart of the short horizon forecasts. This chart consists of a plot of the realised inflation rate compared against the bounds of the 66.7% prediction interval.[11] The fact that the prediction interval covers 66.7% of predicted outcomes implies that if the model forecasts well, we would expect two out of three outcomes to be within the prediction interval, and one out of three to be outside it. Furthermore, as this prediction interval is symmetric, we would expect equal numbers of outcomes on equal sides of it. Hence, with 24 observations considered in the Figure, we would expect 2/3 of the observations (i.e. 16 observations) to fall within the prediction interval, 1/6 of the observations (i.e. four outcomes)

---

[10] Backtesting seeks to ensure that a risk forecasting model generates risk forecasts that are compatible with the actual behaviour of the random variable being forecast. In the case of a regular financial institution, this random variable would typically be the profit or loss generated by a portfolio over some horizon period. Backtesting is important because financial institutions' risk forecasting models are used to make 'real' risky decisions: not unnaturally, institutions want to reassure themselves that their models are sound before they bet real money on them.

[11] All results reported in this chapter are based on the constant-rate fan inflation fan chart model, which assumes that short-term interest rates are constant over the forecast horizon. However, results for the market-rate model are much the same.

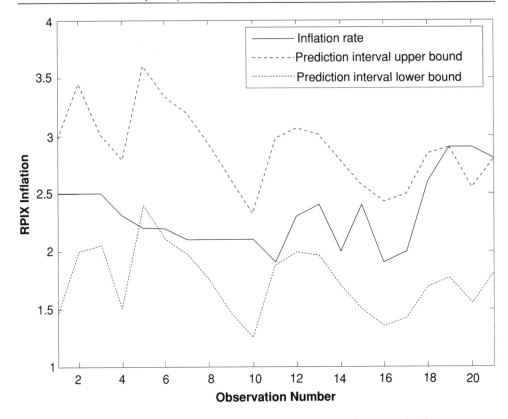

Figure 7.3   Backtesting chart for inflation density forecasts at horizon 4 quarters ahead
Notes: Obtained using data from 97Q3 to 03Q3. The actual (expected) numbers of non-exceedances, lower exceedances and upper exceedances are 19 (14), 1 (3.5) and 1 (3.5).

to fall below it, and the same number to fall above it. Given these predictions, the outcomes shown in Figure 7.2 are pretty good: we get 19 observations within the prediction interval, one observation below it and four above it. Thus, the actual numbers of observations outside and within the prediction interval are close to their expected values. The conclusion that the Bank's forecasting model performs well over a one-quarter ahead horizon is also confirmed by more formal statistical tests (see Dowd (2004)).

Figure 7.3 shows the corresponding backtest chart for a forecast horizon of four quarters ahead. Over this horizon, we get 21 observations in total, and would expect 14 of these to fall within prediction interval and 3.5 to fall on either side of it. However, in this case we actually get 19 observations falling within the interval, and only one on each side of it. The interval forecasts thus appear to be rather wide, which suggests that the model is over-predicting inflation risk over this horizon. Again, this impression is confirmed by the results of more formal statistical tests, which indicate that the model's forecasting performance is questionable (*loc. cit.*).[12]

---

[12] It is also confirmed by the results first reported by Wallis (2003) and reinforced by Clements (2003) and Wallis (2004). They too find that the performance of the Bank's model over the four-quarter ahead horizon is questionable, whilst also finding, as I did, that the performance of the Bank's model over very short horizons is quite acceptable. However, they did not examine forecast horizons longer than a year ahead.

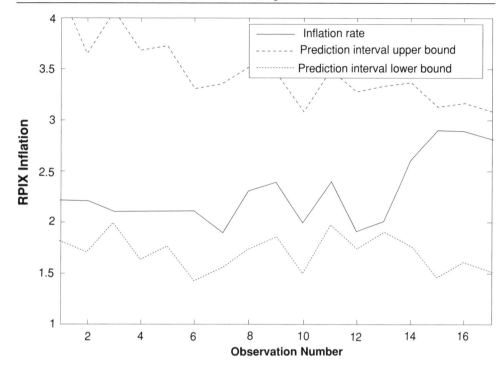

Figure 7.4   Backtesting chart for inflation density forecasts at horizon 8 quarters ahead
Notes: Obtained using data from 97Q3 to 03Q3. The actual (expected) numbers of non-exceedances, lower exceedances and upper exceedances are 17 (11.34), 0 (2.83) and 0 (2.83).

Finally, Figure 7.4 shows the corresponding backtest chart for the long forecast horizon of eight quarters ahead. We get 17 observations over this horizon, all of which fall well within the prediction interval. As we would have expected only 11.34 observations to fall within this interval, it is obviously too wide, and this leads to the conclusion that the model is clearly over-estimating inflation risk. This conclusion is also supported by the results of more formal statistical tests, which tell us the model's forecasts over this horizon are decisively rejected (*loc. cit.*).

In short, backtesting results indicate that the Bank's forecasts are adequate over short forecasts horizons, questionable over medium horizons, and decisively rejected over long horizons. Although the fan chart forecasts are fine for short horizons, they clearly deteriorate and eventually become unacceptable as the forecast horizon gets longer.

7.4.2   The credibility of the fan charts vs. the stability of the inflation rate

As noted earlier, what is most striking about the fan chart forecasts is the way in which their width rises as the forecast horizon lengthens. For example, if one looks again at the August 1997 inflation fan chart given in Figure 7.1, we see that the MPC thought that there was a very significant probability that inflation would *not* remain within plus/minus one percentage point of its 2.5 percent target rate over the horizon to 99Q3. Yet inflation remained within this range in every quarter over that horizon period, and on every subsequent quarter, despite the fact that later fan charts also suggested significant probabilities that that range would be missed.

There is an uneasy tension between the inflation forecasting model, which seems to suggest a significant risk of inflation breaching this range, and the subsequent behaviour of inflation, which looks *ex post* as though there was never any serious danger of a breach occurring.

This raises an obvious question: how likely is it that the MPC's forecasts were right and inflation just happened to remain in this range? To address this question, I estimated the probability that no breach of this range would have occurred by end of the RPIX fan chart period if we take the Bank's model to be correct and we feed into it the MPC's forecasts of the parameters involved. There are various ways to carry out the calculations and details of the methodology are given elsewhere (Dowd, 2005), but my sense of the 'best' estimate was a little under 2%. Such an estimate would suggest that the Bank was fortunate, though by no means incredibly so, to have avoided missing this target range and suffering the resultant indignity of having to send an open letter explaining its failure to the Government.

Yet this test is not nearly stringent enough, because the realised inflation rate has never even come close to breaching the [1.5%, 3.5%] range over the period considered. Instead, inflation always fell within the considerably narrower range of [1.89%, 3.00 %]. Hence, if the probability of the inflation rate breaching the first range was small, the probability of it remaining within this narrower band was much smaller still. What might this latter probability actually be? To answer this question, I carried out some further calculations and estimated the probability of this tighter target range remaining unbreached at about 0.006%, or 6 in 100,000. This estimate suggests that although it is statistically *possible* that the Bank's forecasts have been good ones, it is highly *unlikely* that they were: the odds strongly suggest (i.e., suggest beyond a reasonable doubt) that the Bank has been over-predicting inflation risk.

7.4.3   The Bank's forecasts vs. those of a naïve alternative

We can also examine the adequacy of the Bank's forecasts by comparing them with those of an alternative forecasting model. To make it easy for the Bank, let's see how the Bank's model performs against a manifestly poor competitor. For the sake of argument, suppose we have a competitor model that forecasts a simplistic normal density function around the Bank's mode forecasts. To be precise, this competitor forecasts a normal density function with a mean equal to the Bank's μ forecast and a standard deviation equal to 0.33 over all horizons. I chose this value because it ensures a high probability that inflation would remain within the [1.5%, 3.5%] range, in line with the empirical evidence just discussed, but the reader can regard this value as little more than pulled out of thin air. This competitor is clearly very naïve,[13] and the Bank's model ought to be able to thrash it decisively.

We now set up a three-match competition between the two models. The results of this competition are shown in Table 7.1, and make interesting reading. Over the short (one-quarter-ahead) horizon, both models perform well, and there is little to choose between them. We would expect 16 observations within the prediction intervals, and the naïve model generates 18 such observations whilst the Bank model generates 19. So the naïve model performs a little better, but let's call this a draw as they are so close. Over the medium term (four-quarter-ahead) horizon, the naïve model clearly does better. Over this horizon, there are 14 expected within-interval observations; the naïve model generates 12 and the Bank model generates 19. This result is a clear win for the naïve model. And over the long horizon, there is little to choose

---

[13] This model is the simplest model I could think of, and to call it naïve is a gross understatement. It totally ignores the extensive information on which the Bank's forecasts are based, its calibration is highly arbitrary, and it makes no allowance for any skewness.

Table 7.1 A forecasting competition: the bank model vs. a naïve competitor

Parameter	Horizon ahead (quarters)	Expected number	Observed Bank model	Numbers Naïve model
Number of observations below interval	1	4	1	1
Number of observations within interval	1	16	19	18
Number of observations above interval	1	4	4	5
Number of observations below interval	4	3.5	1	4
Number of observations within interval	4	14	19	12
Number of observations above interval	4	3.5	1	5
Number of observations below interval	8	2.83	0	7
Number of observations within interval	8	11.34	17	7
Number of observations above interval	8	2.83	0	3

between the two models. The results are: the expected number of observations is 11.34, the naïve model produces 7, and the Bank's model produces 17. Hence, the naïve model has a forecast error of 4.34, and the Bank model a forecast error of 5.64: so let's be generous and call this a draw because it is relatively close. If we follow standard football practice and award three points for a win, one point for a draw and zero points for a loss, then the naïve model overall wins by five points to two.[14] Given the relative sophistication of the two models, this result represents a very poor performance by the Bank's model – a bit like Manchester United losing to a team of rank amateurs.

7.4.4 The MPC's density forecasts vs. the empirical inflation rate

The root of the problem with the inflation fan charts is that the type of inflation process assumed by the MPC does not match the way inflation actually behaves. As noted already, in a typical fan chart, the forecasted risk bounds tend to move further apart, the further ahead one forecasts into the future. The MPC is saying, in effect, that it is (typically) more uncertain about future inflation, the further ahead if looks. In making such forecasts, the MPC is (implicitly or explicitly) assuming that the inflation rate is a diffusion process. Diffusion processes are widely used in finance to model the prices of assets such as stocks, and they have a certain plausibility in that context because one can reasonably assume that stock prices follow random walks, and an implication of a random walk is that the relevant stock price becomes more uncertain, the further ahead one looks into the future – in other words, a random walk is a plausible model for a stock price, and a random walk leads to a diffusion process. However, the same argument does not apply to inflation under a successful inflation targeting regime. If inflation is successfully targeted, then it will have a tendency to revert to a mean value that is close to the target value: if inflation is higher than this level, it tends to fall; and if it is lower than this level, it tends to rise. Indeed, this is exactly what we would expect of a successfully targeted inflation rate: the tendency of inflation to revert to a mean close to the target rate of

---

[14] I am ignoring complaints from supporters of the naïve model that they were robbed because the referee was biased, and that the true score should have been 9–0. They are right, of course, but the referee was going out of his way to avoid accusations of bias *against* the Bank.

2.5% is, in fact, the key evidence that the Bank has been successful in achieving its inflation target.

Thus, there is an incompatibility between the diffusion process assumed by the Bank when forecasting inflation risk, and the mean-reverting process actually delivered by the Bank's own monetary policy. This distinction between diffusion and mean-reverting processes matters because the two processes generate quite different empirical behaviours. Perhaps the most important difference is that the diffusion process gives significant probabilities for very low or very high inflation rates (e.g. rates less than 1% or over 5%), whereas the mean-reverting process gives such outcomes negligible probabilities. Using a diffusion process to forecast a mean-reverting random inflation rate will therefore lead to major over-estimates of medium and longer-term inflation risk – and this is exactly what we find. In a nutshell, perhaps the main problem with the fan charts is, in fact, that they are fan charts, i.e., and fan out.

7.5 CONCLUSIONS

The evidence presented here points to a clear conclusion: the density forecasts reflected in the Bank's inflation fan charts are manifestly inadequate. One suspects that this conclusion will come as a surprise to many readers, including some in the Bank itself. After all, the Bank periodically reviews the forecasting performance of its fan chart models and publishes occasional assessments in its *Inflation Report*. Furthermore, it recently commissioned the distinguished Australian econometrician Adrian Pagan to independently examine its modelling and forecasting practices, and Pagan's report was largely complimentary (Pagan, 2003). So neither Bank insiders, nor Pagan, came to any damning conclusions about the adequacy of the Bank inflation forecasts.

But how can those forecasts be so poor without anyone inside the Bank apparently noticing? Part of the answer is that the Bank's (published) forecast evaluations have largely focused on forecasts of *expected* inflation – focusing on bias, *ex post* forecast errors, etc. – and the Bank's forecasts of expected inflation have been pretty good. Indeed, any forecast evaluation exercise that focuses on a comparison of expected and realised outcomes is likely to come to a positive conclusion about the adequacy of the Bank's forecasting model. But there is much more to density forecasts than forecasts of mere expected values, and (evaluations of the latter aside) the Bank seems to have conducted relatively little, if any, evaluation of the density forecasts as such. Although the Bank's inflation forecasting models have evolved from models that forecast (only) expected inflation into models that forecasts inflation density functions, the forecast evaluation practices used by the Bank seem to have remained stuck in a time warp as new developments in risk model evaluation passed them by. The only problems they could have detected with the 'traditional' (i.e., expected-value) forecast evaluation methods that they were using were biases or patterns in forecast errors, and there were no such problems to find. On the other hand, the problems that *do* exist with the Bank's forecasts – which are mainly problems related to inadequate volatility or σ forecasts – were missed by Bank staff because they were (one presumes) not using evaluation methods that could have detected them.[15]

---

[15] Pagan also focuses on expected-value forecasting rather than density forecasting as such, and concludes, 'The Bank has been quite sensitive to the need to perform ex-post forecast evaluation. ...I feel that the work in this area has been of high quality and certainly of adequate quantity' (Pagan, 2003, p. 2). In private correspondence Professor Pagan also informs me that he had doubts on the extent to which evaluation of the fan charts fell under his terms of reference. In retrospect, it is a shame that the Bank didn't give Professor Pagan a clearer mandate to evaluate the fan charts.

All of which points to a curious paradox at the heart of the MPC regime that currently determines UK monetary policy. The paradox is that the MPC has produced good monetary policy decisions using demonstrably poor inflation forecasts – forecasts that are poor in so far as they tend to give an exaggerated sense of medium to longer term inflation risk. This said, the Bank's forecasts of expected or likely inflation are good, so maybe these are the only forecasts that the MPC really needs to make successful monetary policy decisions. But then why bother with all the song and dance of density forecasting, when all the Bank really needs are old fashioned forecasts of likely values?

ANNEX – THE TWO-PIECE NORMAL DENSITY FUNCTION

The 2PN density function is usually represented as a density function that takes the lower half of a normal density function with mean μ and standard deviation σ_1, and the upper half of a normal with mean μ and standard deviation σ_2, where the lower half and upper half probabilities are scaled to give a common value where they meet. More formally, the 2PN pdf is defined as:

$$f(x; \mu, \sigma_1, \sigma_2) = \begin{cases} C \exp\left\{-\dfrac{1}{2\sigma_1^2}(x - \mu)^2\right\}, x \leq \mu \\[2mm] C \exp\left\{-\dfrac{1}{2\sigma_2^2}(x - \mu)^2\right\}, x \geq \mu \end{cases} \tag{A1}$$

where

$$C = \sqrt{\frac{2}{\pi}} \frac{1}{(\sigma_1 + \sigma_2)}$$

and μ is the mode (see, e.g., John (1982)). The value of this function gives us the probability that inflation will take a particular value x, given values of the parameters μ, σ_1 and σ_2. The distribution is negatively skewed if $\sigma_1 > \sigma_2$ and positively skewed if $\sigma_1 < \sigma_2$. In the special case where $\sigma_1 = \sigma_2$ the distribution has a zero skew and a standard deviation equal to σ_1 (and σ_2).

However, the Bank uses a 2PN based on an alternative set of parameters. The alternative parameterisation is:

$$f(x; \mu, \gamma, \sigma) = \begin{cases} C \exp\left\{-\dfrac{1}{2\sigma^2}(1 + \gamma)(x - \mu)^2\right\}, x \leq \mu \\[2mm] C \exp\left\{-\dfrac{1}{2\sigma^2}(1 - \gamma)(x - \mu)^2\right\}, x \geq \mu \end{cases} \tag{A2}$$

where $-1 < \gamma < 1$, and γ and σ are related to σ_1 and σ_2 via:

$$(1 + \gamma)\sigma_1^2 = \sigma^2 \text{ and } (1 - \gamma)\sigma_2^2 = \sigma^2$$

For each forecast horizon the Bank's spreadsheets report values for the mode μ, the skew (equal to the difference between the mean and the mode), and the uncertainty σ.

A typical 2PN density function is shown in Figure 7.5. This Figure gives the eight-quarter ahead density function associated with the parameter values of the August 1997 *Inflation Report*. As we can see, this density function has a mode of 2.50 and a positive skew (or skew to the right). In this particular case, the skew value is 0.53, so the 2PN has a mean value of

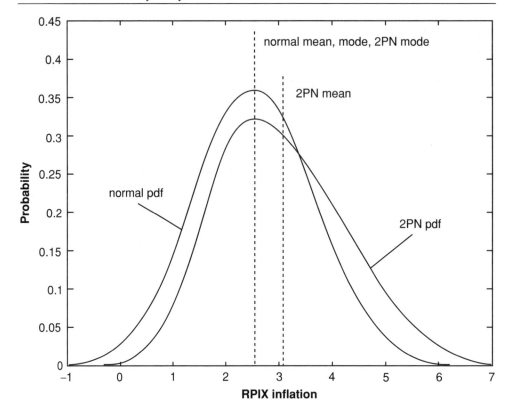

Figure 7.5 Normal and 2PN inflation density functions
Notes: The 2PN is calibrated using the eight-quarter ahead parameter values associated with the August 1997 inflation fan chart: $\mu = 2.50$, $\sigma = 1.11$, $\gamma = 0.53$. The normal is calibrated using $\mu = 2.50$ and $\sigma = 1.11$.

2.50+0.53=3.03 percent: the mean exceeds the mode. The density function also has a (quite high) σ value of 1.11. For comparison, the Figure also shows the corresponding normal density with the same μ and σ parameters. The normal density function is symmetric, and has a mean equal to the μ value of 2.50.

REFERENCES

Britton, E., Fisher, P. and Whitley, J. (1997) The Inflation Report projections: understanding the fan chart, *Bank of England Quarterly Bulletin* **38**, 30–37.
Clements, M.P. (2004) Evaluating the Bank of England density forecasts of inflation, *Economic Journal*. **114**, 855–877.
Dowd, K. (2004) The inflation 'fan charts': An evaluation, *Greek Economic Review*, **23**, 99–111.
Dowd, K. (2005) Too good to be true? The (in)credibility of the UK inflation fan charts, Forthcoming, *Journal of Macroeconomics*.
John, S. (1982) The three-parameter two-piece normal family of distributions and its fitting, *Communications in Statistics – Theory and Methods*, **11**, 879–885.
Pagan, A. (2003) *Report on Modelling and Forecasting at the Bank of England*, London: Bank of England.

Wallis, K.F. (1999) Asymmetric density forecasts of inflation and the Bank of England's fan chart, *National Institute Economic Review* (January), 106–112.

Wallis, K.F. (2003) Chi-squared tests of interval and density forecasts, and the Bank of England's fan charts, *International Journal of Forecasting*, **19**, 165–175.

Wallis, K.F. (2004) An assessment of Bank of England and National Institute inflation forecast uncertainties, *National Institute Economic Review* No. 189, July.

8
Asset Prices, Financial Stability, and the Role of the Central Bank

Forrest Capie and Geoffrey Wood

8.1 INTRODUCTION

It has become more and more common for central banks to be made 'independent' of government. This 'independence' has taken two main forms. One, rather unusual, is that accorded to
the European Central Bank. That bank has been given the task of maintaining price stability
in the Euro area, but left to decide for itself what price stability means in practical terms. The
other form is that given to the Reserve Bank of New Zealand, and, in almost identical terms,
to the Bank of England. Both these institutions were given a target for the rate of inflation,
which they were required to hit.

They were also given another responsibility, however – that of maintaining what is termed
in the Bank of England Act of 1998 financial stability. It is sometimes claimed that price
stability is easy to define while financial stability is somewhat amorphous. We first argue that
distinction is not as clear as many claim; the meaning of price stability is not self evident. After
that, we consider what financial stability can mean, and how it can be made an operational
concept. We also discuss why both goals are important; and then turn briefly to the separation
of roles between the Bank of England and the Financial Services Authority, a discussion useful
both for making clear the UK institutional setting and illuminating the meaning of financial
stability. We conclude by considering the relevance of asset prices and the general price level
for financial stability.

8.2 WHAT IS PRICE STABILITY?

Price stability has nowhere been defined as constancy of a particular index of prices. Rather,
where a precise definition has been given, or, in the case of the ECB, chosen, it is for a low
(by recent standards) rate of inflation, measured in terms of a particular price index. Both the
chosen rate and the chosen index can be contentious.

First consider the rate of inflation. The ECB is sometimes accused of choosing a rate that is
too low. Now, how can a rate above zero be too low? There are two possible answers. The first
of these rests on the now widely, but regrettably not universally, acknowledged fallacy that a
little inflation is good for growth. The second of these is rather better founded in principle;
we have no views on its practical significance in this case. The difficulty is that goods change.
Quality changes, in many cases it improves, and how can this be allowed for if, for example,
the price of the goods does not change? The answer is obvious in principle; we should assume

Issues in Monetary Policy. Edited by K. Matthews and P. Booth.

that the price has fallen, but it is not easy to decide by how much the price should be assumed to have fallen. On these grounds it can legitimately be argued that a small annual rate of price level increase of a bundle of goods of improving quality corresponds to constant purchasing power over an unchanging bundle of goods of unchanging quality.

The choice of index is also not clear cut. This was illustrated in the UK recently, when the Chancellor of the Exchequer announced (in 2003) that the inflation target to be aimed for by the Bank of England would cease to be the well-known and thoroughly familiar retail prices index (RPI), and become the narrower, and unfamiliar, harmonised index of consumer prices (HICP). Substantial criticism greeted the change, commenting on both the difficulty of explaining policy henceforward, and the difficulty of hitting a relatively novel index with only a short run of data available.

The Chairman of the Federal Reserve remarked some years ago that price stability was when no-one worried about changes in the value of money in their decisions; that is exactly what is intended, but the above brief discussion illustrates how difficult it is to formalise that idea.

8.3   FINANCIAL STABILITY

One might say exactly the same of financial stability. One can see when a country has a stable financial system, but it is not so easy to make clear exactly what that means. A helpful way of thinking about a part of the problem is to define stability as the absence of crisis. That of course needs a definition of crisis. Happily, one is to hand. One which has become classic was provided by Anna Schwartz in 1986.

> A financial crisis is fuelled by fears that means of payment will be unobtainable at any price and, in a fractional reserve banking system, leads to a scramble for high-powered money ... In a futile attempt to restore reserves, the banks may call in loans, refuse to roll over existing loans, or resort to selling assets. No financial crisis has occurred in the United States since 1933, and none has occurred in the United Kingdom since 1866. (Schwartz, 1986, p. 11)

But there is more to financial stability than the absence of crisis. Suppose one has been able to balance a pencil on its point. It might not be falling over, but it is hardly stable, for the slightest push would topple it. In other words, before a system can be described as stable it must not just be free of current crises, but must have stabilising mechanisms such that when it is hit by some shock, the shock is dampened, and dies out rather than spreading through the system. Only then can the system be described as genuinely stable.

What can the central bank do to provide such a mechanism? Do its responsibilities extend to that? The answer is that they certainly do, and the mechanism was invented some two hundred years ago. The mechanism is the Lender of Last Resort (LOLR). What is that, and why was it invented, when, and by whom?

8.4   THE LENDER OF LAST RESORT

The classic role of lender of last resort can best be illustrated by reference to a financial crisis. Schwartz's definition of a financial crisis, given above, is in a line which runs back to Henry Thornton and to his Paper Credit of 1802. It focuses on the banking system, and is concerned with the possibility that a bank failure would lead to a scramble for cash, which in turn can cause more bank failures, lead to a sharp contraction in the money stock, and then in turn to recession, perhaps even to depression. That chain of events is certainly not unknown; it is a brief sketch of what happened in the Great Depression in the United States. The chain can be broken by the central bank acting as lender of last resort – that is, providing cash to the system so as to match the sudden, panic-driven, demand for it. Indeed, were it believed that the central bank would act in that way, there might be no panic driven surges in the demand for cash. When urging the Bank of England to commit itself always to supply cash in the event of a banking panic, Walter Bagehot argued along just those lines:

> What is wanted and what is necessary to stop a panic is to diffuse the impression that though money may be dear, still money is to be had. If people could really be convinced that they would have money ... most likely they would cease to run in such a herd-like way for money. (Bagehot, 1873, pp. 64–65).

The Bank of England learned to behave in that fashion and there were no crises after 1866. The Federal Reserve learned the lesson in the Great Depression and there were no crises after that. Yet the importance of that role has in recent years been downplayed. We maintain that there is still possible need for classic lender of last resort action, and that it is other actions that require justification.

Capital markets today are said to be so much more widely developed than they were in the nineteenth century that any solvent firm can get liquidity if needed, and significant flights to cash are no longer likely. That is not true. For example, if a computer failure meant that the entire liquidity of the system was stuck in one place, there would be a sudden shortage of liquidity, just as in a classic banking panic. Classic lender of last resort action – the injection of liquidity to meet a sudden temporary increase in demand for it – would still be necessary.

But should that 'classic' role be extended? Some have argued that being a 'crisis manager' is part of that role. Should central banks try to forestall events which could otherwise very well require them to act as a classic lender of last resort, or might be imperfectly resolvable even with such action?

This is clearly the way that the Federal Reserve viewed its recent role in engineering the rescue of Long-Term Capital Management (LCTM). By preventing the collapse of LTCM, the Federal Reserve saw itself forestalling problems, possibly substantial, at several large banks. But there is actually a much more persuasive justification than that for the Federal Reserve action (Edwards, 1999). In the LTCM episode the institutional mechanism for resolving LTCM in an orderly liquidation did not exist. Usually bankruptcy law provides for an automatic stay of the firm's assets. This prevents individual creditors from disposing of assets under their control and thus gaining an advantage over other creditors. LTCM's situation was different, and very special, because of its huge derivatives position. Derivatives contracts have statutory exception to the automatic stay provisions of the US bankruptcy code. Derivatives contracts have clauses that give the counterparties the right to terminate the contract in the event of a default *of any kind* by a counterparty. Further, in the event of such default and termination, counterparties have the right to liquidate any of the defaulting counterparties' assets that they have in their control, *even if the assets are not directly related to the derivatives contracts in question*. Thus, default by LTCM on any of its obligations would surely have triggered a 'run' by its derivatives counterparties. The Federal Reserve in effect inserted itself as a 'trustee-in-bankruptcy' where the law did not provide for one, and thus prevented the financial market turmoil that could have emerged from a legal lacuna.

There may, therefore, be a role for central banks in acting as crisis managers when the institutional mechanism or legal procedures are not in place for there to be an orderly liquidation of an institution. Such circumstances may not be as unusual as one might on the basis of past experience expect, in view of the rapid liberalisation of financial markets around the world and the growing internationalisation of financial transactions. There are bound to be situations where the laws in one country conflict with those in another, and where the legal ambiguities are such that the liquidation of a financial transaction or institution may prove to be more difficult and time consuming than expected, rather than as quick and orderly as is desirable.

But note that such expansion of the role is intended to promote stability of monetary conditions. It is a new way, necessary because laws have not been adapted adequately to changes in financial markets, to achieve a long-established goal.

8.5   DO ASSET PRICES MATTER?

Some scholars and practitioners argue that not only is lender of last resort still important, but it is so important that it should encompass not only banking system stability, but also the stabilisation of asset markets. Should central banks concern themselves with stabilising them?

It would surely not be thought prudent if central banks started to use monetary policy to control house prices. More generally, if there were a boom in asset prices based on a rational assessment of improved future prospects, we would not want it stopped. And if it really were irrational, could monetary policy stop it?

This is not to suggest central banks should not monitor asset prices for any information they may give about the future behaviour of the economy. And of course it would be legitimate to intervene if the problem were a sudden shortage of liquidity. Indeed, that is a traditional central banking role. It was carried out well by, for example, the US Federal Reserve in 1987, when it injected liquidity when trading was drying up for lack of it; and then withdrew it before it had any undesired inflationary consequences.

That recommendation may suggest an asymmetric response to asset price fluctuations – ignore booms, but provide liquidity if trading dries up for lack of it during a price slump. This is how the US Federal Reserve has behaved in some episodes (October 1987, as noted above, and also October 1988, and 2001); and it has been criticised for doing so. There have been two criticisms. First is the claim that it has led to the 'Greenspan Put' – the claim that in effect the Fed is underpinning the market. This would seem a little unfair, for the aim of the policy is to facilitate trading rather than stabilise prices. (The first may of course contribute to the second – or not.) Discussing that criticism would be a diversion from the subject of this chapter, but discussing the other criticism is not.

Some maintain that when asset price rises become 'unsustainable' they generate a probability of a sharp reversal. Central banks should worry about 'bubbles' because of the risk of subsequent 'bursts'. There must surely be doubts about that advice. First, the evidence that asset price crashes cause, precipitate, or predict recessions is not compelling (Wood, 2000). Second, any harmful consequences for the banking system that might occur following the collapse are prevented by liquidity injection if needed. Third, the record of central banks when tightening money because they are worried about a 'bubble' is not encouraging; on more than one occasion their doing so has produced a sharp downturn in the real economy. All in all, the conclusion on balance seems to be that the preferable policy – perhaps only because it is the lesser of two evils – is to let asset price booms run their course but ensure that there is sufficient liquidity in any ensuing price crash.[1]

---

[1] This conclusion is forcefully and elegantly argued in Trichet (2003).

8.6 SHOULD INSTITUTIONS BE PROPPED UP?

Some writers have broadened the definition of financial stability well beyond that implied by the absence of a crisis, to that of maintaining institutions in operation (see, for example, Crockett, 2003). The argument for the importance of institutions can in part be traced to Bernanke's work on the Great Depression in the USA, and in part to the 'too big to fail' doctrine. Bernanke argued that the depth and length of the Great Depression could not be explained by the monetary contraction alone. It was, he suggested, also due in part to the number of banks which failed leading to the absence of 'channels of transmission' of credit from lenders to borrowers. This reduced investment and hence prolonged the recession. A puzzle with this is why the failed banks were not taken over, and run by new management with new shareholders; that, after all, is what often has happened in more recent years when a bank has failed. The explanation may well be that so many banks were failing, and so deep was the recession, that there was too much uncertainty for such take-over activity. It is therefore not clear that the results Bernanke found can support concern with institutions in times less extreme than the Great Depression.

Can any bank be too big or too important to fail? Certainly in the nineteenth century, the answer would have been no, as is well illustrated by the failure of Overend and Gurney. The consequences of that firm's failure were contained by classic LOLR action. In this context it is necessary only to note the vast (relative) size of that financial institution – by balance sheet ten times bigger than the next biggest. That historical episode does not help the 'too big to fail' doctrine.

Be that as it may, it is useful to consider what can be meant by 'fail'. Two aspects of the word must be clarified. The first is to note that in general large, well diversified, banks do not just collapse suddenly. Rather they decline, losing market share and perhaps shrinking absolutely as well as relatively. Thus so long as banks are allowed to grow and diversify, the problem we are discussing is unlikely to be common.

But although difficult, it is possible for a large bank, or group of banks which comprises a substantial part of a country's banking system, to get into difficulties quickly. Where there are such failures there can be a role for the central bank, a role properly described as crisis manager rather than as lender of the last resort.

The central bank could act as an honest broker, finding a firm in the private sector willing to take over and run the failed institution, buying it for a token sum, injecting new capital, and supplying competent management: that was exactly how the Bank of England behaved when Barings failed in 1995. If such a buyer cannot be found sufficiently promptly to keep the institution running, and if it is important that it be kept running without even a brief pause, then the central bank can organise public sector purchase and capital provision, and run the organisation until a private sector buyer can be found or a gradual run-down can take place.

The troubled institution (or set of institutions) is allowed to 'fail', in the sense that shareholders lose wealth and the management jobs; but the business is kept running rather than immediately liquidated. This leaves unsettled what should happen to depositors. Should they lose also? The answer surely must be that they should be protected to the extent of whatever deposit protection was in place before the failure, and no further; otherwise, what was the point of the deposit protection scheme?

Now, it is necessary to pause at this point and look back at the nineteenth century. After all, as observed above, when Overend and Gurney failed in 1866, it was huge relative to the rest of the system – bigger by that comparison than any bank today. No problems occurred as a consequence of not keeping it running; what short-lived problems there were resulted from the Bank of England being tardy in acting as lender of last resort. Why did no problems result from the bank's closure? One can conjecture that this was a result of the network of bank interdependencies being less extensive than now; but that is only conjecture, for no work has been done to test that conjecture. Indeed, and casting doubt on that conjecture, Overend's was extensively connected with other banks through its very large bill book. Accordingly, therefore, while the case for keeping an institution running (as described above) seems persuasive, it lacks the strong empirical backing that would be provided by demonstration of what has changed between 1866 and now to make such action necessary.

Another argument advanced for bailing out insolvent banks is that in a time of crisis it is difficult to tell an illiquid from an insolvent bank. Accordingly, a central bank should simply decide whether or not it wishes to lend to a bank, and not concern itself with the bank's solvency. Bagehot's advice was to the contrary; in a crisis, 'advances should be made on all good banking securities and as largely as the public ask for them' (p. 70). This advice, Goodhart (1999) observed, was '... to distinguish, in part, between those loans on which the central bank might expect, with some considerable probability to make a loss (bad bills and collateral) and those on which little, or no, loss should eventuate' (1999, p. 351). That is surely right. But Bagehot's advice was also intended to serve another purpose. Showing that there is nothing new in the insolvency/illiquidity argument, one finds it tackled with his characteristic lucidity by Hawtrey (1932):

> In the evolution of the Bank of England as the lender of last resort, we have seen how at the beginning it was inclined to ration credit by refusing all applications in excess of a quota, but later on its restriction took the form of limiting the kind of security it would take. It is not ordinarily possible to examine in detail the entire assets of an applicant for a loan. Demonstration of solvency therefore cannot be made an express condition of the loan, at any rate at a time when the need for cash has become urgent. But the furnishing of security makes scrutiny of the general solvency of the borrower unnecessary. The secured debt being covered by assets more than equivalent to it, there is less need to enquire whether the remainder of the borrower's assets will be sufficient to cover the remainder of his debts (pp. 126–127).

Nevertheless, one can perhaps imagine circumstances where a well-run bank is hit by a shock, one no fault of its own and which it could with sufficient liquidity survive, but for which it has insufficient collateral for the amount of liquidity required. It has obtained all it can from the market, but needs more. What should the central bank do then? Manifestly, it could first lower the standard of collateral it will accept. If that should not prove sufficient, one might start to have doubts about the troubled bank being well run; but be that as it may, there might just conceivably, if these doubts are stilled, be a case for very short term unsecured lending. It cannot be emphasised enough, however, that this case depends on a sequence of events, every one of them in itself unusual, occurring one after another; and even then the case is far from overwhelming.

8.7   FINANCIAL BENEFITS OF MONETARY STABILITY

Central banks usually have two responsibilities nowadays: financial stability and monetary stability. What is the connection between them? How should we expect long-term price predictability to affect financial stability? We should not perhaps expect price stability to deliver perfect financial stability as a by-product, but it should certainly make it easier to attain. For it both reduces rate volatility at every point in the yield curve,[2] and facilitates assessment of credit and interest rate risk. Does the evidence support this conjecture? We can look at evidence from the years of the gold standard to see.

It is a little difficult to make direct and straightforward comparisons between the gold standard era and the present day, for the behaviour of prices then was somewhat different from now. The trend was flatter. Indeed, in Britain (and in most of the world) prices drifted down from 1870 to the mid 1890s, and drifted up thereafter until 1914. On average, over the period, the price level ended up essentially steady; this is quite different from now, when the price level rises steadily, albeit more slowly than it has done in the recent past. The short term, too, is different, for prices sometimes rose and fell quite sharply year by year during the period of the Gold Standard.

Britain and the USA had very similar price experience, but very different financial stability experience. In the gold standard period the British banking system was very stable, while that of the USA experienced a stream of failures. Why? Two factors were crucial – the lender of last resort and the difference between good and bad regulation. Britain had in the Bank of England an effective lender of last resort from 1866. This provided stability in the banking system; hence the absence of crises thereafter. The USA, in contrast, did not have a central bank until 1914, and even then it did not act consistently in that role until after the Great Depression. That is well known. What is also well known, but perhaps less often noted in this context, is the effect regulation has on banking structure. In Britain banks were allowed to merge, and to diversify both geographically and by activity. In the USA, in contrast, geographical diversification was restricted, and unit banking close to being the norm. The system was thus failure prone, and failures were common. Two points follow. First, while financial stability benefits from price stability, other factors matter. Second, we have a clear demonstration that regulation can impede financial stability. Regulation needs to be designed carefully. A more recent example of the same point is provided by Japan. In the aftermath of the collapse of asset prices there, the Japanese banking system was very weak and so in turn was the Japanese economy. This resulted because the banks had been allowed to count the appreciated assets in their capital – so when asset prices collapsed, so did their capital. Bad banking practice to do it, and bad regulation to allow it to happen.

8.8   CONCLUSIONS

In twenty-first century economies, just as in eighteenth, nineteenth and twentieth century economies, where there is a monopoly supplier of liquidity that body should supply liquidity to the banking system when the system is hit by shocks such that the demand for liquidity surges. That lender of last resort should not attempt to stabilise asset prices; but if fluctuations in them cause the demand for liquidity to surge, lender of last resort response is then appropriate. Although market discipline should be relied on as much responsible, some regulation is also necessary in such a system – both to prevent moral hazard resulting from the existence of a lender of last resort, and to ensure that an inadequately capitalised bank does not threaten the whole banking system.

---

[2] It has this effect all along the yield curve because policy rates are stable at the short end, and long-term rates are not pushed around by changing inflation expectations.

There is also a role for a body – and that which acts as lender of last resort is the obvious one – which can intervene when legal lacunae threaten the stability of the system. But there can be no justification for any further extension of the classic LOLR role.

REFERENCES

Bagehot, W. (1873) *Lombard Street*, London: John Murray.

Bernanke, B. (1983) Non monetary effects of the financial crises in the propagation of the Great Depression, *American Economic Review*, **73(3)**, (June), 257–276.

Crockett, A. (2003) Strengthening Financial Stability in *The Regulation of Financial Markets* ed. Booth, P.M. and Currie, D.A., Institute of Economic Affairs, London.

Edwards, F. (1999) Hedge funds and the collapse of long term capital management, *Journal of Economic Perspectives*, **13**, Spring, 189–210.

Goodhart, C.A.E. (1999) Some myths about the lender of last resort, *International Finance*, **2(3)**, (November), 339–360.

Hawtrey, R. (1932) *The Art of Central Banking*, London: Longman, Green and Co.

Seabourne, T. (1986) The summer of 1914 in *Financial Crises and the World Banking System* ed. Capie, F.H. and Wood, G.E., London: Macmillan.

Schwartz, A.J. (1986) Real and pseudo financial crises in *Financial crises and the World Banking System* ed. Capie, F.H. and Wood, G.E., London: Macmillan.

Trichet, J.-C. (2003), Asset Price Bubbles and their implications for Monetary Policy and Financial Stability in *Asset Price Bubbles : The Implications for Monetary, Regulatory, and International Policies* ed. Hunter, W.C., Kaufman, G.G. and Pomerleano, M., Chicago: MIT Press.

Wood, G.E. (2000) The lender of last resort reconsidered, *Journal of Financial Services Research*, **18(2/3)**, (December), 203–228.

Money, Asset Prices and the Boom-Bust Cycles in the UK: An Analysis of the Transmission Mechanism from Money to Macro-Economic Outcomes

Tim Congdon[1]

9.1 INTRODUCTION

How does money influence the economy? More exactly, how do changes in the level (or the rate of growth) of the quantity of money affect the values of key macro-economic variables such as aggregate demand and the price level? As these are straightforward questions which have been asked for over 400 years, economic theory ought by now to have given some reasonably definitive answers. But that is far from the case.

Most economists agree with the proposition that in the long run inflation is 'a monetary phenomenon', in the sense that it is associated with faster increases in the quantity of money than in the quantity of goods and services. But they disagree about almost everything else in monetary economics, with particular uncertainty about the so-called 'transmission mechanism'. The purpose of this chapter is to describe key aspects of the transmission mechanism between money and the UK economy in the business cycles between the late 1950s and today, and in particular in the two pronounced boom-bust cycles in the early 1970s and the late 1980s. Heavy emphasis will be placed on the importance of the quantity of money, broadly-defined to include most bank deposits, in asset price determination. However, in order better to locate the analysis in the wider debates, a discussion of the origins of certain key motivating ideas is necessary.

9.2 TRADITIONAL ACCOUNTS OF THE TRANSMISSION MECHANISM

Irving Fisher of the University of Yale was the first economist to set out, with rigorous statistical techniques, the facts of the relationship between money and the price level in his 1911 study of *The Purchasing Power of Money*. Fisher's aim was to revive and defend the quantity theory of money. In his review of Fisher's book for *The Economic Journal*, John Maynard Keynes

---

[1] The author is most grateful to Walter Eltis, Milton Friedman, Charles Goodhart, David Laidler, Allan Meltzer and Gordon Pepper for comments on earlier drafts of this chapter, but all remaining mistakes and infelicities are very much his responsibility. He is also most grateful to Dr Peter Warburton for the econometric appendix, which analyses one type of 'real balance effect', and to Mr Richard Wild of National Statistics for help in the preparation of an index of asset prices.

Issues in Monetary Policy. Edited by K. Matthews and P. Booth.

was mostly friendly, but expressed some reservations. In his words, 'The most serious defect in Professor Fisher's doctrine is to be found in his account of the mode by which through transitional stages an influx of new money affects prices.'[2] In the preface to the second edition Fisher summarised Keynes' criticism as being the claim that, although his 'book shows *that* changes in the quantity of money do affect the price level', it 'does not show *how* they do so'.[3] In other words, Keynes felt that Fisher had not provided a satisfactory version of the transmission mechanism.

Fisher quickly responded to Keynes. In fact, he used the opportunity of the preface to the second edition of *The Purchasing Power of Money* to direct Keynes to pages 242–247 of another of his works, *Elementary Principles of Economics*, which had been published in 1912 between the first and second editions. In those pages, entitled 'An increase in money does not decrease its velocity', Fisher noted that economic agents have a desired ratio of money to expenditure determined by 'habit' and 'convenience'. If 'some mysterious Santa Claus suddenly doubles the amount [of money] in the possession of each individual', economic agents have excess money balances. They try to get rid of their excess money by increasing their purchases in the shops, leading to 'a sudden briskness in trade', rising prices and depleting stocks. It might appear that only a few days of high spending should enable people to reduce their money balances to the desired level, but 'we must not forget that the only way in which the individual can get rid of his money is by handing it over to somebody else. Society is not rid of it'. To put it another way, the payments are being made within a closed circuit. It follows that, under Fisher's 'Santa Claus hypothesis', the shopkeepers who receive the surplus cash 'will, in their turn, endeavour to get rid of it by purchasing goods for their business'. Therefore, 'the effort to get rid of it and the consequent effect on prices will continue until prices have reached a sufficiently high level'. The 'sufficiently high level' is attained when prices and expenditure have risen so much that the original desired ratio of money to expenditure has been restored. Prices, as well as the quantity of money, will have doubled.[4]

Three features of Fisher's statement of the transmission mechanism in his *Elementary Principles of Economics* are,

(1) the emphasis on the stability of the desired ratio of money to expenditure,
(2) the distinction between 'the individual experiment' (in which every money-holder tries to restore his own desired money/expenditure ratio, given the price level, by changing his money balances) and 'the market experiment' (in which, with the quantity of money held by all individuals being given and hence invariant to the efforts of the individuals to change it, the price level must adjust to take them back to their desired money/expenditure ratios), and
(3) the lack of references to 'the interest rate' in agents' adjustments of their expenditure to their money holdings.[5]

These are also the hallmarks of several subsequent descriptions of the transmission mechanism. In 1959 Milton Friedman – who became the leading exponent of the quantity theory in the 1960s

---

[2] Johnson and Moggridge (eds) (1983), Vol. XI, p. 376.
[3] Barber (ed.) (1997a), p. 27.
[4] Barber (ed.) (1997b), pp. 242–244.
[5] The analysis on pp. 242–7 of *Elementary Principles* is different from that in chapter four of *Purchasing Power*, even though chapter four had purportedly been on the same subject of 'the transition period' (i.e., the passage of events in the transmission mechanism). Chapter four of *Purchasing Power* is highly Wicksellian, with much discussion of the relationship between interest rates and the rate of price change, and then between real interest rates and credit demands. This Wicksellian strand was dropped in pp. 242–247 of *Elementary Principles*.

and 1970s – made a statement to the US Congress about the relationship between money and the economy. He recalled Fisher's themes. After emphasising the stability of agents' preferences for money, he noted that, 'if individuals as a whole were to try to reduce the number of dollars they held, they could not all do so, they would simply be playing a game of musical chairs'. In response to a sudden increase in the quantity of money, expenditure decisions would keep on being revised until the right balance between money and incomes had returned. While individuals may be 'frustrated in their attempt to reduce the number of dollars they hold, they succeed in achieving an equivalent change in their position, for the rise in money income and in prices reduces the ratio of these balances to their income and also the real value of these balances'.[6] Friedman has also emphasised throughout his career the superiority of monetary aggregates over interest rates as measures of monetary policy.

The claim that, in a long-run equilibrium, the real value of agents' money balances would not be altered by changes in the nominal quantity of money was also a central contention of Patinkin's *Money, Interest and Prices*, the first edition of which was published in 1955. *Money, Interest and Prices* exploited the distinction between the individual and market experiments in a detailed theoretical elaboration of what Patinkin termed 'the real-balance effect'. In his view 'a real-balance effect in the commodity markets is the *sine qua non* of monetary theory'.[7]

9.3 ASSET PRICES IN THE TRADITIONAL ACCOUNTS

Despite the lucidity of their descriptions of the transmission mechanism, the impact of Fisher, Friedman and Patinkin on the discussion of macro-economic policy in the final 40 years of the twentieth century was mixed. In the 1970s Friedman had great success in persuading governments and central banks that curbing the growth of the money supply was vital if they wanted to reduce inflation. However, his theoretical work on money was contested by other leading economists and did not command universal acceptance. By the 1990s the preponderance of academic work on monetary policy focused on interest rates, with the relationship between interest rates and the components of demand in a Keynesian income-expenditure model attracting most attention.[8]

The relatively simple accounts of the transmission mechanism in Fisher's *Purchasing Power of Money* and some of Friedman's popular work were particularly vulnerable on one score. They concentrated on the relationship between money and expenditure on the goods and services that constitute national income, but neglected the role of financial assets and capital goods in the economy; they analysed the work that money performs in the *flow* of income and expenditure, but did not say how it fits into the numerous individual portfolios which represent a society's *stock* of capital assets. As Keynes had highlighted in his *Treatise on Money* (published in 1931), money is used in two classes of transaction – those in goods, services and tangible capital assets (or 'the industrial circulation', as he called it), and those in financial assets ('the financial circulation').[9] The need was therefore to refurbish monetary theory, so that money was located in an economy with capital assets and could affect asset prices as well as the price

---

[6] See Friedman 'Statement on monetary theory and policy', given in Congressional hearings in 1959, reprinted on pp. 136–145 of Ball and Boyle (eds) (1969). The quotations are from p. 141.

[7] Patinkin (1965), p. 21.

[8] See, for example, the Monetary Policy Committee of the Bank of England paper on *The transmission mechanism of monetary policy* in response to suggestions by the Treasury Committee of the House of Commons, 1999, particularly p. 10.

[9] Johnson and Moggridge (eds) (1971) Vol. V, ch. 15, pp. 217–230.

level of goods and services. Much of Friedman's theoretical work for a professional audience was a response to this requirement.

The purpose of this chapter is to show that in the four closing decades of the twentieth century money was crucial to asset price fluctuations in the UK. It will appeal, in particular, to the first two of the three distinctive features of the naïve transmission mechanism discussed by Fisher in 1912 and Friedman in his 1959 Congressional testimony, namely the stability of the relevant agents' demand for money and the need to differentiate between the individual and market experiments. It will argue that these ideas are useful in the context of the financial markets where asset prices are set, just as they are in the markets for the goods and services which enter consumer price indices.

9.4   THE OWNERSHIP OF CAPITAL ASSETS IN THE UK

Before relating money to asset prices some remarks on ownership patterns are necessary. Ample official data on the UK's wealth are available. Partly to achieve diversity in their asset portfolios and partly to enjoy the advantages of specialised investment management, many households build up their assets through long-term savings products marketed by financial institutions. The twentieth century also saw a rise in the proportion of corporate equity quoted on the stock exchange in tandem with the institutionalisation of saving. As a result, financial institutions became the principal holders of UK quoted equities in the closing decades of the century (see Table 9.1).[10] They also held substantial portfolios of commercial property and other assets, such as government and corporate bonds. Indeed, over most of the 40 years to the end of the century the institutions were so large that their activities were crucial in the determination of asset prices and particularly of share prices. A key question arises from the institutions' heavyweight role in asset markets. Is it sensible to view their attitudes towards their holdings of equities, and other assets, as being powerfully influenced by their money balances or not?

Table 9.1   Beneficial ownership of UK shares, 1963–89

Table shows % of total equity owned

	1963	1975	1989
Insurance companies	10	15.9	18.6
Pension funds	6.4	16.8	30.6
Unit trusts	1.3	4.1	5.9
Investment trusts and other OFIs	11.3	10.5	2.7
Total institutional	29	47.3	57.8

Source: Economic Trends, January 1991.

9.4.1   The monetary behaviour of the different sectors of the UK economy

Fortunately, abundant information has been published on the money supply holdings of the different sectors of the UK economy. Following the Radcliffe Committee's recommendation that more money supply statistics be compiled, the Bank of England and National Statistics

[10] Ted Doggett, 'The 1989 Share Register Survey', pp. 116–21, *Economic Trends* (London: HMSO for the Central Statistical Office), January 1991 issue.

Table 9.2   Key facts about different sectors' money holdings in the UK
economy, 1964–2003

*Table relates to annual changes, quarterly data, with the first rate of change
calculated in Q2 1964.*

*Note that differences in the 'level' series are often very different from the
'changes' series published by National Statistics, because of changes in
population and definition.*

	Mean increase, %	Standard deviation of growth rates
Personal sector	10.9	4.1
Corporate sector (or 'ICCs')	11	10.6
Financial sector (or 'OFIs')	18.3	15.7

Source: National Statistics website, updated to 22 February 2004, data series VQTP,
VQTN, VSNQ, VQSJ, VQSH and VQCL.

(formerly the Central Statistical Office) have since 1963 collected figures on the bank deposits held by various categories of UK agent. The three types of private sector agent tracked in the data are the personal (or 'household') sector, the corporate sector (known more technically as 'industrial and commercial companies' or 'non-financial companies') and the financial sector (also called 'non-bank [or other] financial institutions').

Some noteworthy facts about the monetary behaviour of the three components of the private sector are presented in Table 9.2. It demonstrates, in a particularly striking way, some important differences between the sectors in the 40-year period. The growth rate of financial sector money was almost double that of the personal and corporate sectors, and was also characterised by more pronounced volatility than that of the other sectors' money. The standard deviation of the annual growth rates of financial sector money was four times that of personal sector money and markedly higher than that of corporate sector money. The contrast between the different sectors' monetary behaviour is vital in understanding the transmission mechanism from money to the economy. Econometric work on the personal sector's demand-for-money functions in the UK during this period routinely found it to be stable, in the sense that standard tests on the significance of the relationship between personal sector money and a small number of other variables (including nominal incomes) were successful.[11] Similar work on the demand to hold money balances by companies and financial institutions had less satisfactory results.[12] However, it would be a serious mistake to believe that companies' and financial institutions' monetary behaviour was erratic and unpredictable.

In fact, the ratio of 'liquid' assets to total assets of life insurance companies and pension funds combined was much the same at the start of the twenty-first century as it had been in the mid-1970s, even though their assets had climbed more than 50 times.[13] (See Figure 9.1: life insurance companies and pension funds were the two principal types of long-term savings institution in the UK in this period. Assets are 'liquid' if they can be quickly and cheaply

---

[11] Thomas (1997a) and Chrystal and Drake (1997).

[12] Thomas (1997b) and Chrystal (1994).

[13] See the author's 'Money and asset prices in the UK's boom-bust cycles', research papers in the May 2000 and June 2000 issues of Lombard Street Research's *Monthly Economic Review* for more detail (the papers are available on request from the author at tim.congdon@lombardstreetresearch.com).

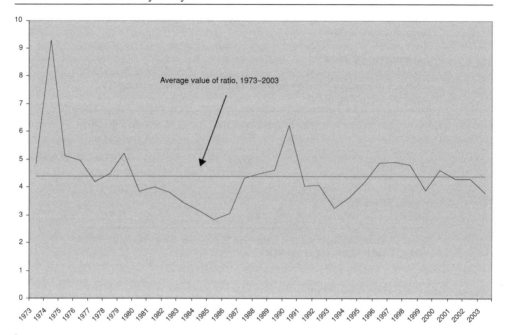

Figure 9.1   The institution liquidity ratio in the UK, 1973–2003. *Chart shows ratio of liquid assets to total assets at life assurance companies and pension funds combined.*

converted into other assets. Bank deposits are an example of a liquid asset, but the institutions might from time to time also hold liquidity in assets such as short-dated Treasury or commercial bills which are not money.) Indeed, the long-run stability of the ratios of money and liquidity to the total assets held by the UK institutions in the final three decades of the twentieth century is remarkable, given the wider economic turmoil and institutional upheaval of these years. It is reasonable to propose that the stability of the institutions' desired ratio of money to assets may serve the same purpose in a discussion of asset markets as Fisher's stability of persons' desired ratio of money to expenditure in a discussion of goods markets.

9.4.2   The monetary behaviour of financial institutions and asset prices: analytical sketch

Given the stability of the money/asset ratios in the leading financial institutions, it is easy to sketch – in a simplified way – a link between financial sector money and asset prices. As already noted, a crucial feature of Fisher's and Friedman's descriptions of the transmission mechanism was that payments were being made within a closed circuit. As a result, if agents had excess money, individuals' attempts to unload their excess balances by increased expenditure would not change the quantity of money. Spending and national income adjusted to the quantity of money, not the quantity of money to spending and national income. An analogous argument is readily presented in the case of financial institutions in asset markets.

   To help in understanding the processes at work, a highly stylised 'asset market' may be assumed. It could be regarded as a naive characterisation of Keynes' 'financial circulation'.

Suppose that the UK's financial institutions are the only holders of and traders in UK equities (i.e. they operate within a closed circuit), that equities constitute all of their assets and that the stock of equities (i.e. the number of shares in issue) never changes. Suppose that – for whatever reason – financial institutions' money balances jump sharply and that they have excess money. Whereas in the long run they try to keep their ratio of money to total assets at, say, 4%, their money/assets ratio (or 'cash ratio') now stand at 6%. In terms of figures, they might have £60bn of money and £1000bn of equities, whereas recently they had £40bn of money and £1000bn of equities. Each individual institution tries to get rid of its excess money by buying equities. *But the purchase of equities by one institution is the sale by another. For all the institutions taken together, the assumptions ensure that the flow of purchases and sales cannot change the £60bn of money in the system.* No matter how frenetic the trading activity and no matter the keenness of particular fund managers to run down their cash, the aggregate £60bn cannot rise or fall. The value of trading in equities in a year may be an enormous multiple of this £60bn, but still the £60bn cannot change.

How, then, is the 4% cash ratio restored? In one round of transactions the excess supply of money causes buyers to be more eager than the sellers and the price of equities edges up, perhaps by 10%, so that the value of the stock of equities is £1100bn The cash ratio falls to just under 5 1/2%(£60bn divided by £1100bn multiplied by 100). This is a movement towards the equilibrium 4% ratio, but it is not enough. The institutions still hold 'too much money'. In the next round of transactions the excess supply of money again causes buyers to be more eager than sellers and the price of equities moves forward again, perhaps by 15%. The value of equities rises to £1 265bn and the cash ratio drops to about 4 3/4 % (£60b. divided by £1 265 b. multiplied by 100) – and so on. In every round the value of the money balances stays at £60bn. *It does not change because – within the closed circuit assumed in the exercise – it cannot change.* The return of the institutions' cash ratio to the equilibrium 4% is achieved, after so many rounds of transactions, by a rise in the value of equities to £1 500bn. The institutions' asset values have adjusted to the amount of money they hold. It is a striking, but entirely realistic, feature of the example discussed that a rise in their money balances from £40bn to £60bn (i.e. of only £20bn) is associated with (or 'causes') a rise in equity prices of £500bn. The argument can be generalised freely. In the advanced economies of today specialised financial institutions are the characteristic holders of assets. It follows that, when they hold excess money, there is likely to be upward pressure on asset prices; conversely, when they have deficient money balances, asset prices tend to fall.

9.5   ASSET PRICES AND ECONOMIC ACTIVITY

The realism of the analytical sketch above is open to question and will be illustrated in the later narrative account of two boom-bust cycles. By contrast, the claim that asset prices are relevant to spending behaviour should not need extensive discussion. It should be sufficient to emphasise the ubiquity of arbitrage in asset markets and to note two kinds of linkage between asset markets and the rest of the economy. These linkages ensure that asset prices affect spending.

Arbitrage is important, because it links the price of equities with the price of the tangible assets and goodwill to which they relate and, at a further remove, to the price of all financial securities and all tangible assets. An excess supply of money may in the first instance boost the price of existing equities traded on the stock exchange, including – for example – the equities issued by property companies in the past. But that induces new issuance by property companies and the formation of new companies with a view to seeking a quotation. So owners of commercial property package their buildings in a corporate vehicle and try to sell these vehicles to financial institutions. The market price of all property is therefore boosted by ambitious stock market valuations. In a modern economy similar processes are at work for all assets. Further, arbitrage operates between different assets as well as between different forms of the same asset. If equities rise sharply in price, they may appear over-valued relative to commercial or residential property. The wide variety of wealth-holders found in a modern economy – including rich individuals and companies, as well as the large financial institutions – may then sell equities and use the proceeds to buy property. The excess supply of money – the condition of 'too much money chasing too few assets' – has pervasive effects.

Of course the power of arbitrage to remove asset price anomalies relies on the ability to switch payments between different types of asset market. A key assumption in the analysis – that of a specialised asset market, which constitutes a closed circuit where certain asset prices are set – has to be relaxed. Instead agents compare prices in all asset markets, and sell over-valued assets in one market and buy under-valued assets in another. Not only do they sell over-valued stocks to buy under-valued stocks and sell small-capitalisation stocks to buy big-capitalisation stocks and so on, but they also sell houses to buy shares and sell shares to buy houses.

Does that destroy the concept of a closed circuit of payments in which the ability of excess or deficient money to alter asset prices depends on the quantity of money being a given? The short answer, in an economy without international transactions, is 'not at all'. It is true, for example, that, if quoted equities become expensive relative to unquoted companies of the same type, the owners of unquoted companies will float them, which withdraws money from the pool of institutional funds. Conversely, when quoted companies become cheap relative to 'asset value', entrepreneurs organise takeovers, which inject money back into the institutional pool. To the extent that one type of participant has been a net buyer and it has satisfied its purchases by drawing on its bank balances, its bank deposits (i.e. its money holdings) must fall. But the money balances of another type of agent must rise. As in the analytical sketch, vast numbers of transactions may take place, but the quantity of money does not change.

In fact, it is possible to identify particular types of participant in asset markets, and to collect data on their purchases and sales. For the purpose of illustration Table 9.3 gives data on the markets in UK quoted ordinary shares in 1994. The net value of purchases and sales in a particular market, and indeed of all asset purchases and sales in the economy as a whole is zero. But the logically necessary equivalence of the value of purchases and sales does not mean that the prices of the assets bought and sold cannot change. In particular, prices change when all the agents participating in the numerous asset markets have excess or deficient money holdings. The arena of payments – the closed circuit within which the transactions take place – becomes all the markets, including the asset markets, that constitute the entire economy.[14]

What about the two kinds of influence of asset prices on spending on goods and services? First, investment in new capital items occurs when the market value of assets is above their replacement cost. Assets will continue to be bought and sold, and investments will be undertaken or suspended, until the market value of assets is brought into equivalence with their

---

[14] Of course, every economy has international transactions. Such transactions represent another escape-valve for an excess supply or demand for money balances, in accordance with the monetary approach to the balance of payments. But to discuss the possibilities would take this Chapter too far. In any case, the incorporation of 'an overseas sector' in data sets on transactions in particular assets is conceptually straightforward (see Table 9.3). The overseas sector's transactions become entries in the capital account of the balance of payments. Again, it is conceptually straightforward – although empirically very demanding – to expand the arena of payments, the closed circuit for transactions, so that it becomes the world economy.

Table 9.3   An asset market in the UK in 1994
The market in quoted ordinary shares (equities)

Net sellers of equities	Amount sold, £m.	Net buyers of equities	Amount bought, £m.
Banks	393	Life assurance and	8,531
Personal sector	679	pension funds	
Industrial and		Remaining financial	1,097
commercial cos.	9,261	institutions	
Public sector	3,646	Overseas sector	4,351
Sum of sales	13,979	Sum of purchases	13,979
by net sellers		by net buyers	
The sum of net sales and purchases was zero.			

Note: Each of the identified types of equity market participant had substantial purchases *and* sales. The gross value of their transactions was a very high multiple of their net purchases and sales. Stock exchange turnover in UK and Irish listed equities was £577bn in 1994 (in 1994 the UK's gross domestic product at market prices was about £670bn).
Source: Financial Statistics(London: Office for National Statistics), June 1998 issue, Tables 8.2A and 6.3A.

replacement value.[15] Secondly, consumption is affected by changing levels of wealth. When asset price gains increase people's wealth, they are inclined to spend more out of income.[16]

Another way of stating the wider theme is to emphasise that, in the real world, markets in goods and services and markets in assets interact constantly. Keynes' two circulations – the 'industrial circulation' and the 'financial circulation' – are not separate.[17] If excess money in the financial sector causes asset price gains, agents of all kinds will be inclined to sell a portion of their assets and buy more goods and services (i.e. to spend a higher proportion of their incomes); if deficient money in the financial sector causes asset price falls, agents will spend a lower proportion of their incomes on goods and services. The adequacy of money balances relative to a desired level, the direction of pressures on asset prices and wealth-influenced changes in the propensity to spend out of income should be seen as an indissoluble whole.

Before reviewing the realism of our account of money's role in asset markets, a polemical note can be injected into the discussion. In none of the above has a reference been made to 'interest rates'. Agents have been adjusting their spending on goods and services, and their asset portfolios, in response to excess or deficient money, and the prices of goods, services and assets have been changing in order to bring agents back into 'monetary equilibrium'

---

[15] The idea that investment adjusts until the market value of a capital asset equals the replacement cost is associated with James Tobin and 'the Q ratio', i.e. the ratio of market value of a firm's capital to its replacement cost: see Tobin (1969). But similar remarks have been made by many economists, including Friedman: see Friedman (1969) pp. 237–260 (in particular pp. 255–256) reprinted from a paper in 1961 in *The Journal of Political Economy*. When an excess supply of money affects asset markets, the result is 'to raise the prices of houses relative to the rents of dwelling units, or the cost of purchasing a car relative to the cost of renting one' and so on. In Friedman's view, 'the process operates through the balance sheet, and it is plausible that balance-sheet adjustments are sluggish in the sense that individuals spread adjustments over a considerable period of time' (p. 256).

[16] Numerous studies identify a relationship between wealth and consumption. See, for example, Byrne and Davis (2001).

[17] An implication is that the circular flow of income and expenditure – such a familiar part of the undergraduate macroeconomic courses – is misleading and unrealistic when it is taken to imply that national income stays in line with national expenditure unless autonomous injections of demand come from the government or overseas. Any agent can sell any asset, obtain a money balance and use the proceeds to buy a good or service which constitutes part of national output, and the purchase leads to increased national income and expenditure. Similarly, any agent can run down a money balance and buy a good or service, with the same effects. Assets differ from money in that the nominal value of money is given, whereas the nominal value of assets can vary without limit. The transactions involved in 'mortgage equity withdrawal' from the housing market – at present the topic of much interest – illustrate the merging of asset markets and markets in current goods and services. Much research on this has been conducted at the Bank of England: see, for example, Davey (2001). The author introduced the concept of mortgage equity withdrawal to the analysis of personal sector spending in a paper written jointly with Paul Turnbull in 1982 (Tim Congdon and Paul Turnbull 'The coming boom in housing credit', L. Messel & Co. research paper, June 1982, reprinted in Congdon (1992), pp. 274–287).

(i.e. a condition where the demand to hold money balances equals the supply of such balances).

9.5.1 Financial sector money in the boom-bust cycles

The causal role of money growth fluctuations in asset price volatility may be better appreciated by recalling the experience of two particularly big cycles in the UK, that between late 1971 and 1974 ('the Heath-Barber boom', and the stock market and property crashes of 1974) and that between 1985 and 1992 ('the Lawson boom' and the ensuing recession). The economy's instability in the Heath-Barber and Lawson booms was notorious, and contrasts with relative stability in most of the other 40 years from 1963.

An overview of the main facts about money growth and the economy in this 40-year period may be a helpful preface to the detailed narrative. In the first 25 years after the Second World War, UK policy-makers had suppressed inflation by a variety of non-market methods, including direct controls on prices and wages. In the monetary sphere the favoured approach was to curb the growth of bank balance sheets, usually by a crude quantitative limit on bank advances. But in September 1971 the banking system was liberalised in a set of reforms known as 'Competition and Credit Control'. The banks were to be free to grow their businesses as they wished, while 'the authorities' (i.e. the government and the Bank of England) would raise interest rates to prevent excessive money supply expansion. In practice officialdom was often reluctant to administer the interest rate medicine and credit booms continued for far too long. The September 1971 reforms were followed by over 20 years of macroeconomic volatility, with large fluctuations in the growth of bank credit and money, even more dramatic swings in asset prices, and somewhat smaller fluctuations in the growth of nominal national income. Figure 9.2 portrays the growth rates of money and nominal gross domestic product

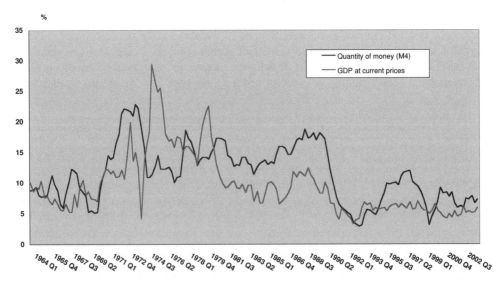

Figure 9.2 Money and national income, 1984–2003 *Annual % changes in M4 and GDP at current market prices, quarterly data seasonally adjusted*

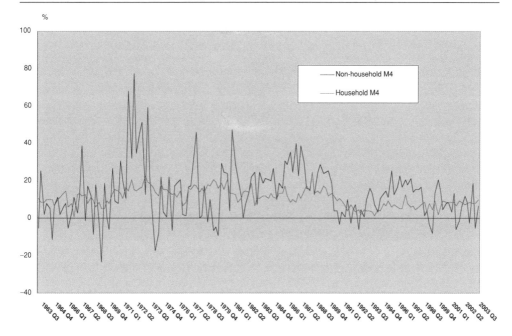

Figure 9.3   Household and non-household money in the UK 1983–2003 *Chart shows annualized growth rate in quarter, %.*

in the 40 years to 2003, with the turbulence of the middle two decades being evident in both series.

It was noted earlier that the different sectors of the economy – households, companies and financial institutions – had different monetary behaviours. More precisely, households' demand for money was markedly more stable than that of the other two sectors, with the standard deviation of the growth rates of financial sector money being four times that of household money and significantly higher than that of corporate sector money. Figure 9.3 illustrates this contrast, showing the growth rates of household and non-household money in the 40 years. A remarkable feature is that the annualised growth rate of non-household money exceeded 30% in no fewer than 12 quarters.[18] Monetary economics has many problematic aspects, but it should have been obvious to all policy-makers that something had gone wrong in an economy where the money balances of key groups of agents were exploding at this sort of rate. Figure 9.4 gives the growth rates of non-household money and an index of asset prices in the same period.[19] Asset prices were more volatile than either money or nominal GDP over the four decades, but the relationship between changes in non-household money and asset prices was not of markedly worse quality than that between changes in more familiar monetary variables and nominal GDP.

---

[18] The 12 quarters were Q3 1967, Q3 1972, Q4 1972, Q1 1973, Q3 1973, Q4 1977, Q1 1978, Q2 1981, Q1 1986, Q3 1986, Q1 1987 and Q3 1987. With two exceptions, all these quarters coincided with extreme asset price buoyancy. The two exceptions were Q3 1967, which was affected by the devaluation of the pound, and Q2 1981.

[19] An explanation of the method of compiling the asset price index is available from the author. The author is grateful to Mr Richard Wild of National Statistics for help in preparing the index.

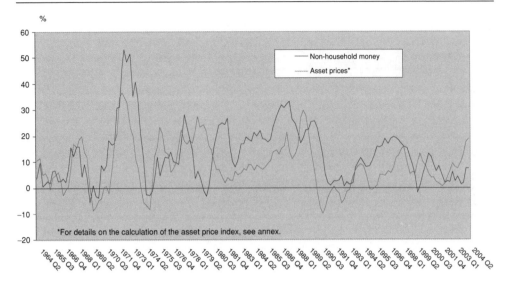

Figure 9.4   Non-household money and assest prices, 1964–2004 *Annual changes in M4 held by companies and financial institutions (i.e., non-households) and an asset price index, quarterly data.*

9.5.2   Financial sector money and asset prices in the Heath-Barber boom

The first of the boom-bust cycles is usually named after Edward Heath, who was Prime Minister at the time, and Anthony Barber, who was Chancellor of the Exchequer. As already noted, the Competition and Credit Control reforms of September 1971 were intended to end quantitative restrictions on bank credit, which had been in force for most of the preceding 30 years. Rapid growth in bank credit and, hence, in a broadly-defined measure of money followed in 1972 and 1973. In the year to the third quarter 1970 M4 increased by 10.7% and in the year to Q3 1971 it increased by 14.1%. In the following two years M4 advanced by 22.0% and 23.0% respectively.[20] The difference in the monetary behaviour of the economy's sectors was particularly clear in the cycle of the early 1970s. In the year to Q3 1970 personal sector money increased by 11.5% and in the year to Q3 1972 by 13.7%, both figures being roughly in line with total M4 growth. But in the next two years the underlying stability of personal sector money meant that it did not increase by as much as total M4, and it rose by 16.3% and 18.5% respectively.

To recall the earlier analysis, the households, companies and financial institutions comprising the UK private sector were the only holders of M4 money. For any given quantity of money, the less that was held by one sector, the more that had to be held by the other two sectors. Logically, the shortfall in personal sector money growth in 1972 and 1973 implied an extremely sharp acceleration in the growth rates of corporate and financial sector money. In the years to Q3 1970 and Q3 1971 corporate sector money grew by 2.7% and 22.2% respectively; in the year to Q3 1972 it soared by 48.2% and in the year to Q3 1973 by 39.2%. The violence of the change in corporate balance sheets between the two years before the boom and the two years of the boom itself is obvious. However, it was overshadowed by even more extreme movements in

---

[20] *Economic Trends: Annual Supplement*(London: National Statistics, 2002 edition), p. 245. The data on changes in the sectors' money balances in the following paragraphs come from the database in the National Statistics website, as it was in the spring of 2004.

financial sector money. In the year to Q3 1970 financial sector money increased by 22.8% and in the following year it fell slightly, by 1.3%. But in the year to Q3 1972 it jumped by 75.0% and in the year to Q3 1973 by 46.0%!

Further insights are gained by extending the analysis to particular types of institution and seeing how they responded to the money supply shock. Friedman's game of musical chairs – as agents interacted to bring money balances to a desired amount after an unexpected change to such balances – was played at the level of the thousands of organisations which belonged to the financial sector, as well as at the level of the three sectors which constituted the UK private sector. At the end of 1971 life insurance companies had short-term assets (mostly bank deposits) of £349m. In 1972 these short-term assets leapt by £202.3m (by 58.0%) and in 1973 by a further £201.1m (36.5%). At the end of 1971 private sector pension funds had short-term assets of £144m. In 1972 they increased by £74.0m (51.4%) and in 1973 by another £170.3m (almost 80%!).[21]

What happened to asset prices? At the time corporate bonds and government fixed-interest securities (or 'gilts') were a large part of life company and pension fund assets, but some observers were concerned that high money supply growth would lead to inflation and higher interest rates, and that higher interest rates would decimate the value of bonds and gilts. (These observers – such as Professor Alan Day of the London School of Economics, Peter Jay of *The Times* and Gordon Pepper of W. Greenwell & Co., the stockbrokers – were correct.) The institutions therefore wanted to increase their equity weightings (i.e. the proportion of their total assets in equities) while their money balances were exploding at annual rates of between 30% and 80%. As suggested in the analytical sketch above, the individual fund managers wanted to keep their cash ratios down, but – if they bought securities – they would be buying them mostly from other institutions. They would continue to have excess money holdings until share prices had increased. In practice stock exchange turnover soared and share prices rose dramatically. The *FT* Industrial Ordinary Share Index climbed from 322.8 (1st July 1935 = 100) in May 1971 to 533.7 a year later, an increase of 65.3%.[22]

Unfortunately, that was not the end of the story. The early 1970s were a period of considerable political and social uncertainty, and share prices were constrained by heavy selling by the personal sector. May 1972 was the stock market peak. Asset price buoyancy in the rest of 1972 and during 1973 was instead most marked in property. Both residential and commercial property registered enormous price increases, at a pace never before recorded in the UK's peacetime history. The economy as a whole was profoundly affected. The increase in real domestic demand in 1973 was 7.8%, almost the highest figure in the post-war period. The sequel to the cyclical excesses was a dramatic rise in inflation (to over 25% in early 1975) and the worst recession since the 1930s, as policy-makers struggled to bring inflation down to an internationally acceptable figure.

Once cause of the slide in activity was a severe squeeze on company liquidity in 1974, which was a by-product of a decline in aggregate money supply growth. In the year to the end of 1973, M4 rose by 22.1%, but in the year to end-1974 it increased much more slowly, by only 10.8%. The swing from monetary ease to restraint can be seen as more abrupt if one considers the inflation-adjusted rate of money growth, because inflation was higher in 1974 than in 1973. Corporate and financial sector money saw more extreme movements than aggregate money in the downturn, in line with the long-run behaviour patterns and just as they had in the upturn.

---

[21] *Financial Statistics* (London: Central Statistical Office), December 1974 issue, p. 89 and p. 93.
[22] The figures for the *FT* Industrial Ordinary Share Index are monthly averages.

In the year to Q4 1973 financial sector money advanced by 35.1%; in the first three quarters of 1974 it contracted. Share prices started to fall in late 1973 and plunged in 1974, with the *FT* Industrial Ordinary Index in November at little more than a third of its value in May 1972. Corporate sector money climbed by over a third in the year to Q4 1973, but declined by almost a tenth in the year to Q4 1974. Companies' attempts to protect their balance sheets were responsible for heavy rundowns in stocks and cutbacks in investment, while commercial property values slumped.

9.5.3 Financial sector money and asset prices in the Lawson boom

After the recession of 1980 and 1981, the early 1980s were a fairly quiet period in which output grew at a rate that was slightly above-trend trend, inflation was stable at about 5% a year, employment increased gradually and asset markets were steady. But in late 1985 a drastic change in monetary policy occurred, comparable in its cyclical consequences with Competition and Credit Control in 1971. The growth of the quantity of money had been held back in the early 1980s partly by a technique known as 'over- funding'. This involved sales of government debt to non-banks in excess of the budget deficit, and led to reductions in banks' assets and their deposit liabilities. For technical reasons apparently related to money market management, over-funding was stopped in the autumn of 1985. Broad money targets were suspended and, in due course, they were to be abandoned. An acceleration of money supply growth quickly became clear. Whereas M4 growth averaged 13.0% in the four years to end 1985, it averaged 16.9% in the following four years.[23]

The contrast in monetary conditions before and after autumn 1985 was in fact greater than implied by this 4%-a-year difference in the annual growth rates. A big fall in oil prices cut UK inflation in 1986 and dampened inflation expectations. The increase in personal incomes remained fairly steady in 1986 and 1987, and the rise in the personal sector's money holdings was more or less constant – at a little above $11^1/_2$% a year – from 1983 to 1987. The result – as in the Heath-Barber boom – was that the upturn in aggregate M4 growth led to an explosion in the money holdings of companies and financial institutions. In the four years to 1985 companies' M4 holdings grew on average by 11.6% per annum; in 1986 and 1987 they increased by 30.3% and 19.2% respectively. Financial institutions were in a somewhat different position, because a sequence of liberalisation measures had encouraged their rapid growth in the early 1980s, and much of this growth is best interpreted as a benign, once-for-all adjustment in their economic importance. The average growth rate of financial institutions' money holdings in the five years 1980 to 1984 inclusive was a very high 24.8%. Even so in the next five years – the years of the Lawson boom – the average growth rate was about 10% a year more, at 34.4%.

The upturn in the growth rate of non-personal money holdings was particularly marked in 1986 and 1987. Indeed, in 1987 financial institutions' money holdings jumped by 58.9%, a figure which was comparable with their experience in the Heath-Barber boom 15 years earlier. Again it is easy to trace a relationship between the money balances held by the financial sector as a whole and those held by particular types of institution. At the end of 1985 life insurance companies had £3262m held in 'cash and balances with the monetary sector' and £123m held in certificates of deposit (CDs); at the end of 1986 the corresponding figures

---

[23] *Economic Trends: Annual Supplement* (London: National Statistics, 2002 edition), p. 245.

were £4 062m and £173m; and at the end of 1987 they were £5 975m and £188m.[24] At the end of 1985 pension funds had £3 970m held in 'cash and balances with banks' and £156m in CDs; at the end of 1986 the corresponding figures were £5 697m and £229m; and at the end of 1987 they were £8 263m and £570m. [25] So the money balances of these two types of institution together advanced from £7 511m at the end of 1985 to £10 161m at the end of 1986 (or by 35.3%) and to £14 996m at the end of 1987 (representing 47.6% growth in 1987). In two years they almost exactly doubled, while financial sector money in aggregate increased by 104%.

And what happened to asset prices in this cycle? Table 9.1 showed that by the late 1980s insurance companies and pension funds owned about half of all UK equities, while other types of long-term savings institution (unit trust groups and investment trusts) held at least another 10%. It is therefore unsurprising that the surge in these institutions' money holdings should be associated with large stock market gains. In the two years to September 1987 – which, roughly speaking, were the first two years from the end of over-funding and the consequent acceleration in money supply growth – the *FT* all share index rose from 633.18 to 1, 174.38. In other words, share prices doubled. Share prices behaved much like financial sector money, and life company and pension fund money, in the same period. It is true that an abrupt fall in share prices in late October 1987 prompted comparisons with the Great Crash in the USA in the late 1920s, with several alarming forecasts being made of an impending slump in economic activity. However, an alternative view – that the stock market fall of October 1987 was due to market participants' anticipation of future inflation trouble – is also tenable. If so, the likely sequel would be attempts to move portfolios away from equities and into property. In fact, the late 1980s were a period of rapid property appreciation, with 1988 seeing the peak of the house price increases and a commercial property bubble.

The response of the economy to asset price gains had many similarities to the events of the Heath-Barber boom. The forecasts of a recession in 1988 were totally wrong. Domestic demand, measured in real terms, grew by 5.0% in 1986 and 5.3% in 1987; it then jumped by 7.9% in 1988, roughly matching the 1973 experience. In mid-1988 particularly large trade deficits were reported. Officialdom began to realise that the boom in spending was out of line with the economy's ability to produce. The boom caused a sharp fall in unemployment, and asset price inflation spread to markets in goods and services. Interest rates were raised sharply in late 1988 and 1989, with clearing bank base rates reaching 15% on 5 October 1989. Higher interest rates dampened the growth of bank credit and money.[26]

The monetary data give insights into the balance-sheet strains of the period. As in 1974, money supply growth in 1990 declined whilst inflation (again affected by international oil prices) was rising. The result was a squeeze on real money balances and a collapse in asset values. M4 growth fell from 18.1% in 1989 to 11.9% in 1990 and 6.0% in 1991. Company sector money – which had been soaring in 1986 and 1987 – contracted in the year to Q1 1991. The change of trend in financial sector money came later, but was more pronounced. Financial sector money dropped by 4.5% (i.e. at an annualised rate of almost 9%) in the first half of 1991 and showed little growth from mid-1991 to mid-1993. The imprint of these trends on pension

---

[24] *Financial Statistics* (London: Central Statistical Office), July 1987 and April 1989 issues, Table 7.13 in both issues.

[25] *Financial Statistics* (London: Central Statistical Office), July 1987 and April 1989 issues, Table 7.14 in both issues.

[26] Note that this is the first occasion that interest rates have been introduced into the narrative. The narrative would undoubtedly have been enriched and been brought closer to reality if they had been introduced earlier, but a perfectly sensible account of events has been given without them.

funds' cash holdings, in particular, was marked. The pension funds had 'cash and balances with banks' of £17 492m at end-1990, but only £9 834m at end-1992.[27]

The main asset classes did not respond in a neat and tidy way to the change in the monetary environment. Nevertheless, the impact of excess money until 1990 and deficient money thereafter is obvious in their price movements. The equity market had reasonable years in 1988 and 1989, but struggled in 1990 and share prices in January 1991 were lower than they had been in September 1987. But a big rally in early 1991 was the start of the long bull market. By contrast, the property market was badly hit by the monetary squeeze and asset price deflation continued until 1993. The fall in house prices in the four years to mid-1993 was the worst in the UK's post-war history and scarred the financial memories of the many millions of people who had been tempted to buy a home in the boom of the late 1980s. The UK's expulsion from the Exchange Rate Mechanism of the European Monetary System in September 1992 was so humiliating that it persuaded many key policy-makers that monetary policy should in future be based on domestic conditions, not the exchange rate.

9.6   CONCLUSION: MONEY AND ASSET PRICES IN THE TRANSMISSION MECHANISM

Nowadays most accounts of the transmission mechanism of monetary policy give pride of place to the level of interest rates or even to only one interest rate (i.e. the central bank rediscount rate) as the economy's *factotum*. An alternative approach, building on the work of Irving Fisher, Patinkin and Friedman, sees expenditure decisions as motivated by individuals' attempts to bring actual money balances into line with the demand to hold them. Many introductory statements in this tradition focus on the effect that these attempts have initially on expenditure on goods and services, and eventually on the price level. They rely for their conclusions on two features of the adjustment process, the stability of the desired ratio of money balances to expenditure, and the distinction between the 'individual experiment' and 'market experiment' in a closed circuit of payments where the quantity of money is kept constant. This chapter has shown that the same sort of story can be told about asset markets, relying on the stability of financial institutions' desired ratio of money balances to asset totals and the invariance of the pool of institutional money balances as asset prices are changing. It follows that, when the quantity of money held by key players in asset markets rises or falls abruptly by a large amount, powerful forces are at work to increase or lower asset prices.

Of course, the notion of a closed circuit of payments – for either goods and services or assets – is a simplification. In the real world, markets in goods and services are not separate from asset markets. If excess money leads to a rise in asset prices, almost certainly the rise in asset prices will influence expenditure on goods and services. In his 1959 statement to the US Congress, Friedman compared the rounds of payments as agents seek to restore monetary equilibrium (i.e. the equivalence of the demand for and supply of money balances) to a game of musical chairs. In this chapter the venue for the game of musical chairs was the UK economy, including its asset markets. Moreover, because of the availability of sectoral money supply data in the UK since 1963, it has become possible to say more about the identity and behaviour of the main players in the game. Three types of player in the UK in the 40-year period were individuals as such, companies and financial institutions. Companies and financial institutions

---

[27] *Financial Statistics* (London: Central Statistical Office), August 1992 issue, Table 7.22, p. 92, and December 1994 issue, Table 5.1B, p. 83.

were particularly active in asset price determination. It has been argued that corporate and financial sectors' money balances were consistently more volatile than personal sector money, and the volatility in their money holdings was reflected in asset prices. Very high growth rates of broad money were therefore responsible for the asset price follies in the upturn phase of both the Heath-Barber boom in the early 1970s and the Lawson boom in the late 1980s, and subsequent very sharp declines in broad money growth were responsible for the asset price busts which followed. It has been possible to give an account of events with only an occasional reference to interest rates. Changes to expenditure on goods and services, and decisions to buy and sell assets, could be interpreted – throughout the 40-year period – as responses to excess or deficient money holdings, not to the putative effect on an interest rate on investment or stock-building.

Admittedly, much of the account here has taken narrative form and suffers from the possible risk of being too selective with facts and figures. An econometric exercise by Dr. Peter Warburton has been undertaken to address this weakness and is reported in the Annex to this chapter. In the exercise changes in real private domestic demand are regressed on changes in real non-personal broad money. (Non-personal broad money is the money held by companies and financial institutions. Note that private domestic demand is the correct measure of demand for the purpose. Government spending must be excluded, because the government's spending is not sensitive to its money holdings, while exports must be excluded because they reflect demand conditions elsewhere in the world.) The results suggest that the highly volatile non-personal money holdings, often dismissed in Bank of England research as of no relevance to macroeconomic outcomes, did have a statistically significant effect on expenditure. In short, the boom-bust cycles in the closing four decades of the twentieth century reflected the UK economy's response to extreme fluctuations in money supply growth. Excess money was accompanied by asset price buoyancy, and provoked both above-trend growth in demand and exchange rate weakness. The eventual result was higher inflation. Similarly, deficient money growth was associated with asset price declines and slowdowns (or even contractions) in demand. The behaviour of the quantity of money, on the broad definitions, was fundamental to understanding the economy's changing cyclical fortunes over the 40-year period.

ANNEX
ECONOMETRIC ANALYSIS OF ONE TYPE OF REAL BALANCE EFFECT
by Peter Warburton

The purpose of this annex is to demonstrate that the relationship between the annual growth rate of real private domestic demand (RPDD) and that of real non-personal money balances (RMB) (defined as the annual growth rate of aggregated corporate and financial M4 balances, expressed in real terms), is statistically significant and robust over time.

In order to test for the presence of a lagged real balance effect, the start date of the regressions was advanced three years to 1967Q2. The results of the simple regression for this period are shown in equation (9.1) below, and contain a highly significant coefficient on the real money balances term, RMB.

A general dynamic functional form was adopted, using four lagged dependent variables, current and 12 quarterly lags of real money balances. Using the general to specific method, a parsimonious representation was derived, shown as equation (9.2). Noting the presence of some large outliers in data periods where important fiscal changes occurred (most notably, the introduction of Value Added Tax in 1973), a variant of this regression was developed using dummies, each expressed as four-quarter differences. This variant is equation (9.3). The implied steady states from both (9.2) and (9.3) are consistent with the parameters of the simple regression (9.1) with which we began.

Finally, the sample period was divided into two equal portions, 1967Q2 to 1984Q4 and 1985Q1 to 2002Q4 and the regressions were repeated. The results of the subdivided sample for equation (9.3) are shown as equations (9.4) and (9.5), respectively. For both halves of the sample, the RMB term achieves statistical significance, but the fit of the regression is much tighter for the second half than the first. The difference between the implied long-run coefficient on RMB between the two sub-periods is bordering on statistical significance at the 95% level, suggesting that the real balance effect was stronger post-1984. Overall, the relationship between changes in real demand and real money balances is robust across the two sub-periods.

What is striking about the results is the shortness of the lag structure for real money balances. With no significant lags in RMB beyond a single quarter, the regressions imply that the full impact of a disturbance to real money balances is absorbed quickly into real demand.

Viewed simply, these regressions imply that a 6% increase in the real money balances (of private non-financial corporations and financial corporations, combined) will lift real private domestic demand by 1%. The absence of a complex lag structure in the relationship implies that adjustment to the long-run elasticity would be completed within one year. With reference to the two sub-periods, a 7% increase in real money balances delivers the 1% rise in domestic demand pre-1985 while only a 5% increase is required to have this effect post-1984.

Simple regression, period 1967Q2 to 2002Q4

$$\%\Delta RPDD = 1.609 + 0.1785\%\Delta RMB \qquad (9.1)$$
$$(5.6) \qquad (8.5)$$
$$\text{Adjusted R-squared} = 0.34$$
$$SE = 2.98\%$$

Dynamic multiple regression, period 1967Q2 to 2002Q4

$$\%\Delta RPDD = 0.66 + 0.1057\%\Delta RMB - 0.0423\%\Delta RMB(-1)$$
$$(2.8) \quad (3.0) \qquad (1.1) \qquad\qquad (9.2)$$
$$+0.7611\%\Delta RPDD(-1) - 0.145\%\Delta RPDD(-4)$$
$$(12.6) \qquad (2.8)$$
$$\text{Adjusted Rsquared} = 0.69$$
$$SE = 2.03\%$$
$$\text{Long-run: } \%\Delta RPDD = 1.72 + 0.165\%\Delta RMB$$

Dynamic multiple regression, period 1967Q2 to 2002Q4

$$\%\Delta RPDD = 0.6254 + 0.0927\%\Delta RMB - 0.0335\%\Delta RMB(-1) \qquad (9.3)$$
$$(3.0) \qquad (3.0) \qquad (1.1)$$
$$+0.7242\%\Delta RPDD(-1) - 0.0849\%\Delta RPDD(-4)$$
$$(14.0) \qquad (2.0)$$

$$+8.451\Delta DUM73Q1 + 3.653\Delta DUM79Q4$$

$$(6.9)\qquad(3.0)$$

$$+3.739\Delta DUM88Q4$$

$$(3.1)$$

Adjusted Rsquared $= 0.79$

SE $= 1.67\%$

Long-run:$\%\Delta$ RPDD $= 1.734 + 0.164\,\%\Delta$ RMB

Analysis of parameter stability
Dynamic multiple regression, period 1967Q2 to 1984Q4

$$\%\Delta RPDD = 0.7264 + 0.0693\%\Delta RMB - 0.0054\%\Delta RMB(-1) \qquad (9.4)$$

$$(2.5)\quad(1.7)\qquad(0.1)$$

$$+0.6343\%\Delta RPDD(-1) - 0.108\%\Delta RPDD(-4)$$

$$(8.4)\qquad(1.7)$$

$$+8.386\Delta DUM73Q1 + 3.887\Delta DUM79Q4$$

$$(5.8)\qquad(2.7)$$

Adjusted Rsquared $= 0.76$

SE $= 1.96\%$

Long-run : $\%\Delta RPDD = 1.533 + 0.135\%\Delta RMB$

Dynamic multiple regression, period 1985Q1 to 2002Q4

$$\%\Delta RPDD = 0.478 + 0.1444\%\Delta RMB - 0.0832\%\Delta RMB(-1) \qquad (9.5)$$

$$(1.9)\quad(2.6)\qquad(1.5)$$

$$+0.8754\%\Delta RPDD(-1) - 0.1619\%\Delta RPDD(-4)$$

$$(11.8)\qquad(2.4)$$

$$+3.3845\Delta DUM88Q4$$

$$(3.4)$$

Adjusted Rsquared $= 0.83$

SE $= 1.30\%$

Long-run:$\%\Delta RPDD = 1.668 + 0.2136\%\Delta RMB$

REFERENCES

Ball, R.J. and Boyle, P. (eds) (1969) *Inflation*, Harmondsworth: Penguin Books.

Barber, W.J. (ed.) (1997a) *The Works of Irving Fisher* Vol. 4 *The Purchasing Power of Money*, London: Pickering & Chatto, 1997, originally published by Macmillan in New York in 1911.

Barber, W.J. (ed.) (1997b), *Works of Fisher* Vol. 5 *Elementary Principles of Economics*, London: Pickering & Chatto, 1997, originally published by Macmillan in New York in 1912.

Byrne, J. and Davis, E.P. (2001) Disaggregate wealth and aggregate consumption: an investigation of empirical relationships in the G7, *National Institute of Economic and Social Research Discussion Paper*, No. 180, London: National Institute.

Chrystal, K.A. (1994), Company sector money demand: new evidence on the existence of a stable long-run relationship for the UK, *Journal of Money, Credit and Banking*, **26**, 470–494.

Chrystal, K.A. and Drake, L. (1997), Personal sector money demand in the UK *Oxford Economic Papers* Oxford: Clarendon Press.

Congdon, T. (1992), *Reflections on Monetarism*, Aldershot: Edward Elgar.

Davey, M. (2001) Mortgage equity withdrawal and consumption, *Bank of England Quarterly Bulletin*, Vol. 41, Spring 2001, pp. 100–103, London: Bank of England.

Friedman, M. (1969) *The Optimum Quantity of Money*, London and Basingstoke: Macmillan.

Johnson, E. and Moggridge, D. (ed) (1983) *The Collected Writings of John Maynard Keynes* Vol. XI *Economic Articles and Correspondence*, London and Basingstoke: Macmillan Press for the Royal Economic Society.

Johnson, E. and Moggridge, D. (eds) (1971), *The Collected Writings of John Maynard Keynes* Vol. V *A Treatise on Money: the Pure Theory of Money*, London and Basingstoke: Macmillan Press for the Royal Economic Society.

Patinkin, D. (1965), *Money, Interest and Prices*, New York: Harper & Row, 2nd ed.).

Thomas, R. (1997a) The demand for M4: a sectoral analysis, Part I – The personal sector, *Bank of England Working Paper No. 61*, London: Bank of England.

Thomas, R. (1997b,) The demand for M4: a sectoral analysis, Part II – The company sector, *Bank of England Working Paper No. 62*, London: Bank of England.

Tobin, J. (1969) A general equilibrium approach to monetary theory, *Journal of Money, Credit and Banking* **1**, 15–29.

10

Money, Bubbles and Crashes: Should a Central Bank Target Asset Prices?

Gordon T. Pepper with Michael J. Oliver

For at least the last decade, there has been a growing sense of frustration among market professionals with the attempts by academics to account for the behaviour of financial markets. Practitioners
do not dispute the value of academic analysis, but assert that academic theories do not adequately
explain the behaviour of financial markets. The result is that many very experience practical people
have become highly critical of traditional teaching in universities.

The Stewart Ivory Foundation is a charity founded in 2001 to further the development of financial
education in Scotland. To cover omissions from conventional teaching the Trustees, who represent
the major investment management companies in Edinburgh, decided to sponsor the new course,
which is entitled, 'A Practical History of Financial Markets', as one unit of Edinburgh Business
School's MBA program.[1]

Russell Napier, Managing Director, The Stewart Ivory Foundation Education Company

10.1 INTRODUCTION

The Efficient Market Hypothesis (EMH) is the academic theory that dominates many financial
economists' thinking. In any sophisticated market there are many investment professionals who
scrutinise stock prices continuously to find stocks that are cheap and ones that are dear. They
assimilate all relevant available information, including everything that influences expectations
about the future. They buy stocks they think are cheap and sell ones they think are dear. The
prices of the former rise and those of the latter fall, until all stocks are correctly priced, when
prices are said to be 'efficient'. When unexpected new information becomes available the
market-makers adjust their prices and the other professionals act very quickly if they think that
the market-makers have adjusted them incorrectly. Prices respond almost instantaneously so
that no one else can make money and they are efficient once again.

Because prices become efficient again so quickly, the Efficient-Market Hypothesis states that
investors cannot *consistently* outperform a market making use of existing available information.
It should be appreciated that EMH does *not* state that the stock market is efficient in the
sense that prices correctly reflect the factors considered to be important by industrialists and

---

[1] Practitioners' criticism of academic work is reciprocated. Many academics do not respect analysis by practitioners and there is a
danger that they dismiss it without reading it properly. The Stewart Ivory Foundation/Edinburgh Business School's course consists of
five modules. Module 3, entitled 'The Monetary Theory of Asset Prices', is by Pepper. The first part of it is the basis of part A of the
present chapter. At the time of writing, the course has been given three times, twice in Edinburgh and once in London. The attendees
included many with lengthy practical experience, some of whom have economic degrees. Perhaps their assessments of the module -
'inspirational', 'cutting edge work', 'excellent', 'stimulating', 'steeped in the real world', 'insightful' – will encourage academics to
study the present chapter. Sceptical academics may also find it helpful to read the annex at the end of the chapter before starting on the
chapter itself. Pepper and Oliver (2006) is a revised and extended version of Module 3.

Issues in Monetary Policy. Edited by K. Matthews and P. Booth.
© 2006 John Wiley & Sons, Ltd.

fundamental analysts. This is a deduction from EMH that is wrong. The monetary theory of assets prices, discussed in this chapter, explains why.

In contrast to fundamental analysts who study the 'real' factors,[2] monetary analysts study the supply and demand for money and credit, and other flows of funds that influence the level of asset prices as a whole. More generally, if the existing amount of money in the economy as a whole is greater than the current demand for money some of the surplus is likely to be spent acquiring existing assets, the prices of which will tend to rise.[3] Conversely, if the existing amount of money is less that the demand for money, people will tend to sell assets to top up their bank balances and the prices of the assets will tend to fall.

The macroeconomic effects of booms and busts in asset prices have attracted a lot of attention since the break-up of the Bretton Woods regime in 1973. One area that has recently absorbed academic studies is how central banks should respond to movements in asset prices and in particular, the question of whether in fact a central bank should target asset prices (Bordo and Jeanne, 2002; Cecchetti et al., 2000; Vickers, 1999). This chapter examines money, bubbles and crashes from the perspective of a practioneer and is divided into two. The first part provides a monetary theory of bubbles and crashes. The second part turns to address the question of whether a central bank should target asset prices.

PART A: THE MONETARY THEORY OF BUBBLES AND CRASHES

As an appetiser to what is to be discussed in this part, consider an economy starting to slide down into a recession. As it does so, the stock market usually falls. At some stage the market stops falling and people start to 'see through' the recession and focus on the coming economic recovery. After its fall, some investors judge the market to be cheap and start to buy stocks.

In such circumstances a corporation is quite likely to make a cash bid for another corporation, Corporation A, and to finance the takeover by borrowing from a bank. The stock market rises when the bid is announced. When the bid goes through, the holders of stock in Corporation A receive bank deposits in exchange for their stock. They may well subsequently reinvest the proceeds in other stocks. It is important to realise that such a reinvestment does not destroy the bank deposit because the sellers of the stocks in which the reinvestment is made receive bank deposits in exchange for their stocks. For example, if one of the ex-stockholders in Corporation A switches out of a bank deposit into Corporation B, the person who sells the stock in Corporation B receives the deposit. If this person reinvests the money in Corporation C, the seller of Corporation C's stock receives the deposit. This third person may reinvest the money and so on. Each time the reinvestment takes place the market tends to rise. The initial credit transaction, that is, the corporation borrowing from a bank to finance the takeover, has a one-off effect whereas the consequential increase in the money supply has a continuing effect. The borrowing to finance the takeover produces a one-off rise in the market. The monetary consequence of the borrowing can be responsible for a rise in the market that continues for some time.

---

[2] The real factors include the extent of competition, share of market, export prospects, available new capacity, and the amount of research and development. The corporation's accounts are also scrutinised, including the dividend, earnings, profits, sales, costs and profit margins. The historical record is examined to find out how fast the corporation has grown in the past and whether the growth has been financed by retained earnings or new issues of stock. The quality of management is judged and expectations of the future are assessed, and so on.

[3] The supply and demand for money are usually out of equilibrium, see annex to this chapter.

If substantial borrowing to finance stock purchases persists for more than a year or so, the continuing monetary effects compound. After a year or so of this happening, the result can be the formation of a bubble in asset prices.

In due course the bubble will burst. If people start to sell assets to repay loans the previous upward spiral turns into a downward one. Worse still, the value of collateral in general can fall below that of the assets being secured. People can become forced sellers of assets. The laws of supply and demand are reversed. A fall in prices forces more people to sell instead of encouraging buyers. The result can be full-scale debt-deflation.

To understand how this process occurs, we first need to examine the types of traders who buy and sell securities.

10.2   TYPES OF TRADERS IN SECURITIES

There are two basic reasons why someone purchases or sells a security. The first type of transaction, a 'liquidity trade', occurs when someone needs either to raise cash or has surplus money to invest. The second type of transaction, a 'portfolio trade', occurs when someone switches from one stock into another, or into or out of cash, in the hope that the transaction will improve the return on a portfolio. Another distinction is between two types of portfolio trade. An 'information trade' occurs when there has been some unexpected new information that affects the value of a stock. A 'price trade' occurs when the price of a stock has altered in spite of there not being any new information justifying the alteration.

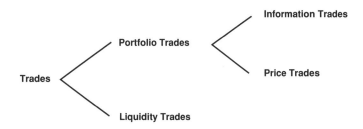

When new information becomes available, market-makers adjust their prices and information traders act very quickly if they think that they can make a profit, with prices responding until no one else can do so. Prices then become 'efficient' once again.

Information trades establish efficient prices but liquidity trades move prices away from the efficient level. A sale of a stock to raise money will initially depress the stock's price. If the price falls without there being any news justifying the fall, price traders will normally judge the stock to be cheap and will purchase it until the price reverts to the efficient level. In the opposite case of a liquidity purchase, the price of the stock will initially rise. If there is no news justifying the rise, price traders will normally judge the stock to be dear and will sell until the prices revert to the efficient level.

Summarising, liquidity trades move prices away from the efficient level and price trades normally push prices back again. There are an enormous number of potential price traders. Anyone can buy stock. Potential sellers include everyone who holds stock and anyone who is prepared to sell stock that they do not own. The potential number of price trades is accordingly very large compared with liquidity trades and they are usually sufficient to be able to correct any price discrepancies caused by liquidity trades.

There is a remaining possibility. It is that a rise in price of a stock can lead to expectations of a further rise in price and a fall in price can lead to expectations of a further fall; in other words, expectations can become extrapolative.[4] If this happens prices will depart further from the previous level.

It might be thought that there is a remote possibility of expectations becoming extrapolative. Indeed they are rarely so for an individual stock, but expectations can easily become extrapolative for a market as a whole. It will be argued that they do so when liquidity transactions persist in one direction, that is, when there are more liquidity purchases than sales, or vice versa, for any length of time. There are three stages to the argument. The first is that the balance of liquidity transactions can persist in one direction for many months. The second is how this leads to extrapolative expectations. The third explains why price traders who understand what is happening do not push prices back to the level justified by fundamentals. Each will be described in turn below.

10.2.1 Persistent Liquidity Trades

Any stockbroker will confirm from practical experience that a frequent reason for a stock exchange transaction is that the client either needs to raise cash or has cash to invest.[5] A private individual, for example, may need cash to finance a large item of expenditure; for instance, a new car; a large tax demand may have arrived; or an estate may be in the process of being wound up. Industrial and commercial corporations need funds to finance industrial investment and any rise in inventories. House building has to be financed. Life assurance corporations receive premiums, and pension funds receive contributions, which need investing. There is no doubt whatsoever that liquidity transactions are numerous. But the fact that they are numerous does not necessarily mean that liquidity purchases can exceed sales or vice versa for prolonged periods.

A liquidity transaction has been defined to be a transaction that takes place because someone either needs to raise cash or has surplus money to invest. In the former case the amount of money that the person had was less than he or she wanted. In the latter case the person had more money than desired. This suggests that the existing amount of money in the economy should be compared with people's current demand for money.

10.2.2 Demand for money

Money is held for two main purposes. First, to facilitate transactions, for example, expenditure on goods and services, increases as national income and expenditure rise, whether in real terms or because of inflation. Secondly, as a medium for savings. The main determinants of the demand for money for saving purposes are wealth and the merit of bank deposits as an investment relative to the alternatives available. The latter depends on how the rate of interest on bank deposits compares with the expected return on other assets, after taking risk of below average return or loss into account.

Interest rates have a direct and an indirect effect on the demand for money. The former is rather complicated. Money has various forms: notes and coin, demand deposits (current

---

[4] The expectations of monetary analysts are extrapolative, not adaptive or myopic, see the annex to this chapter.
[5] For elaboration on cash-flow accounting, see the annex to this chapter.

accounts), time deposits (deposit accounts), and so on. Notes, coin and demand deposits tend to be held for transactions purposes and are called 'narrow money'. Notes and coin do not earn any interest and demand deposits have a lower rate of interest than that on time deposits. When interest rates rise, people tend to run down their holdings of narrow money and switch into time deposits. Hence narrow money tends to fall when the *level* of interest rates rises and the opposite happens when interest rates fall.

Broad money is narrow money plus time deposits. The demand for broad money is not directly affected by changes in the *level* of interest rates because the switching only affects its composition and not its total. Changes in *relative* interest rates affect broad money because these affect the demand for money for savings purposes.

Interest rates have an indirect effect on the demand for money via their influence on national income and expenditure.

10.2.3 Supply of money

Money can be created in two ways. Governments can 'print money' and bankers can create 'fountain-pen money'.

Printing-press money

In a modern economy bank deposits are the most important form of money. A government 'prints money' when it borrows from the banking system. Banks' liabilities and assets have to balance. If their assets rise, their deposits, which are their main liabilities, do so too. The overall effect is that the money supply increases as banks' holdings of government debt rise.

Fountain-pen money

Banks create fountain-pen money when they make a loan. The simplest case is when two people use the same bank and one of them increases his overdraft when he makes a payment to the other. The latter's bank deposit rises. In the bank's books, loans rise on the asset-side of the balance sheet and deposits rise on the liability-side. The money supply increases as the entry is made in the bank's books. Until the late twentieth century the records were kept manually by clerks using fountain pens and the money was created at the stroke of a banker's pen. This is the explanation of the term 'fountain-pen money'.

Interest rates

Interest rates are almost invariably set by the central bank.[6] They are not determined by market forces and, as a result, they rarely bring the supply and demand for money into balance. Further, compared with other factors, they have a weak impact on the supply of both printing-press and fountain-pen money. A government does not, for example, alter its expenditure plans or tax rates because interest rates have changed. The supply of fountain-pen money depends on bank lending which is influenced by many factors other than interest rates. The result is that the supply of money is often either in excess of or less than people's demand for money. A crude way of illustrating this is to compare monetary growth with that of GDP. Figure 10.1 shows the percentage change in M4 in the UK less that of GDP. It will be seen that in some

---

[6] Switzerland is a possible exception.

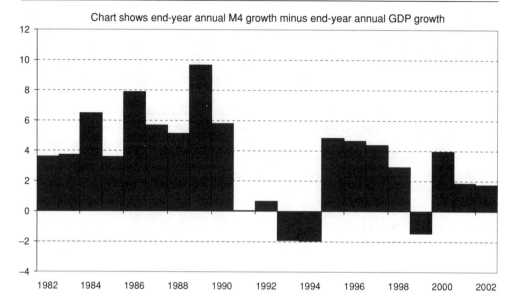

Figure 10.1 Excess monetary growth

years the growth of M4 has been substantially in excess of that of GDP, whereas in other years it has been lower.

If the amount of money in the economy is in excess of the demand for money the excess can be spent in three ways:

(1) On goods and services. Economic activity will rise as a result and this may lead in due course to an increase in the price of goods and services. This type of inflation may be called product-price inflation.
(2) On existing domestic assets. Equity, bond and property prices will tend to rise as a result. This is a type of inflation, which may be called asset-price inflation.
(3) On non-sterling assets, for example sterling deposits may be exchanged for dollar ones, in which case sterling will tend to fall.

The second is the subject of this chapter.

10.3   EXTRAPOLATIVE EXPECTATIONS

10.3.1   Sentiment

A market responds if liquidity transactions persist in one direction. Prices rise if the transactions are net purchases and fall if they are net sales. People then think up plausible explanations for why the market is behaving as it is. At its simplest there are always bullish and bearish factors present in a market. If the market rises the bullish ones are advanced as the explanation for the rise. If the market falls the bearish ones are advanced. The truth is that both factors have already been allowed for in prices and the explanations for the behaviour of the market are invalid. The erroneous explanations nevertheless receive publicity and affect sentiment. People tend to be bullish when prices are rising and bearish when they are falling. Few, if any, observers of a market dispute that the direction in which the market is moving can have an important influence on sentiment. It is not argued that this always happens but merely that it can happen. This is another way of stating that expectations can become extrapolative.

10.3.2   Intuition

Many speculators are influenced by intuition and this is often a reflection of the amount of money about. If people have money to invest not all the funds will be invested as they accrue; some will be allowed to accumulate. When unexpected good news occurs decision-taking inertia is broken and accumulated funds are invested. The greater the accumulation of liquidity, the larger will be the rise in the market and the market's response to good news will be clear. In the opposite case, people needing to raise cash are often prompted into action by unexpected bad news. The size of the fall in the market depends on how many people are waiting to raise cash. If many people are waiting the market's response to bad news will be clear. On the other hand, if institutions have funds awaiting investment, they are likely to bargain hunt on bad news when prices fall and the market may well bounce back.

Professionals who are close to a market observe how the market is reacting to news. A market tending to react to good news and to ignore bad gives the impression of wanting to go up; a market reacting to bad news and ignoring good gives the impression of wanting to go down. Speculators who rely on intuition are strongly influenced by the amount of money about although they may not realise it. Intuition is another reason why rising prices can lead to expectations of further rises, and vice versa for falling prices.

10.3.3   Decision-Taking Inertia

The importance of decision-taking inertia in a world of uncertainty needs stressing. Investment decisions often appear obvious with the benefit of hindsight and, therefore, to have been easy to take. At the time the decisions are taken, in contrast, the uncertainties nearly always appear to be great. The easiest option is to do nothing. Further, investment managers are only too well aware how difficult it is to outperform a market and that, in the event, successful transactions will most probably be almost exactly balanced by unsuccessful ones. Many investment managers take the view that their chance of overall success is increased if they confine their transactions to ones about which they are reasonably confident at the time they take the decision. If they are not reasonably confident, they are reluctant to act.

Funds for investment constantly arrive. Life assurance corporations receive premiums. Pension funds receive contributions. Mutual funds (unit trusts) receive money from new investors. Because of decision-taking inertia, this 'new money' is often not invested as soon as it arrives but tends to accumulate. The institutions' reaction to unexpected news depends not only on the amount of new money waiting investment – that is, on the *stock* of money – but also on the tendency for the funds to grow or diminish – that is, on the *flow* of new money. For example, if the stock of new money is both unusually high and growing, an institution is likely to become anxious not to miss buying opportunities; it will be keen to bargain-hunt on bad news or be willing to accept rising prices on good news.

10.3.4   Crowds

For the reasons given, price movements tend to persist when monetary forces are powerful and 'following the trend' (buying when the market is rising and selling when it is falling) becomes profitable. Speculators are remarkably good at detecting 'the game in town' making money. They join in. Prices rise or fall further. This encourages others. The herd instinct prevails. A crowd forms. People in a crowd act differently from the way they would act if they were alone. The behaviour of a crowd is different from the sum of the behaviour of individuals if they are acting in isolation. Patterns in the charts follow. Chartists react to these patterns and buy or sell as the case may be. This is another reason why rising prices can lead to expectations of further rises and, in the opposite case, falling prices lead to expectations of further falls.

Fundamental factors are, of course, very important. Major market movements occur when both fundamental factors and monetary forces are in the same direction.

10.3.5   Discounting Liquidity Transactions

An explanation is needed for why speculators, who understand what is happening, do not, in accordance with the Efficient-Market Hypothesis, discount liquidity transactions in the same way as they do news announcements and push prices back to the level justified by fundamentals.

One crucial reason why liquidity transactions are not discounted in the same way as news announcements is that whereas the latter occur at a *point* of time the former are spread over a *period* of time. If actual purchases and sales are to match, a continuous sequence of speculative transactions would be needed to offset the liquidity transactions as they occur. But speculators do not in practice act in this way.

The main reason for inaction by people who understand financial bubbles and who are quite sure that the market is much higher than can be justified by fundamentals is that they do not know when the bubble will burst. The danger is that stocks will be sold too soon; that the market will carry on rising for some time; and that the rise will be substantial. Indeed the final rise in a market just before a bubble bursts is frequently hectic. Departing from the herd can be very risky. An investment manager can lose his job. A fund management firm can lose clients. The firm may not even survive as an independent entity. The short-run risks can easily become unacceptably high.

10.3.6   Short-term risk versus profits in the longer-term

According to Modern Portfolio Theory, when people choose investments they select stocks that will maximise their expected yield, subject to minimising risk of below average return or loss. (Note that many believers in the EMH wrongly focus on volatility rather than risk of below average return.) There is a trade-off between maximising yield and minimising risk. When a financial bubble is building up an investor may confidently expect a sale of stocks to result in abnormally high profits *in the long term* but risk of loss *in the short term* can rise to such an extent that the opportunity has to be declined. In particular, there is great danger of a short-term loss if stocks are sold whilst the growth of the money supply is still excessive. In these circumstances many investors will have missed the market. Liquidity will have accumulated that should have been invested and will still be growing. When unexpected bad news occurs and prices fall, these investors are likely to hunt for bargains. If they do so, anyone who has sold stocks will make a loss as prices bounce back up.

An excellent example of what can happen occurred in the second half of the 1990s when Mr Tony Dye was Chief Investment Officer of P&D Fund Managers. At the time the firm was one of the four largest fund mangers in the UK. As a financial bubble built up in US and UK equity prices Mr Dye became convinced that prices had risen well above what could be justified by fundamentals. In the mid 1990s P&D started to switch out of common stocks. Unfortunately for them, prices continued to rise and the short-run performance of the funds concerned became worse than that of their competitors. Their clients became unhappy and some of them took their funds away. P&D received considerable adverse publicity. Mr Dye came under great pressure and eventually left the group, ironically a few days before markets reached their peak. P&D's parent corporation, UBS, subsequently dropped the name P&D. This episode illustrates only too clearly the dangers of selling too soon, both to an investment manager personally and to his or her firm.

10.3.7 Financial Bubbles

Occasionally something much more substantial than an upswing of a typical business cycle occurs. The invention of railways is an historical example. Another is an economy flooded with money because a new gold mine had been discovered. The invention of hire purchase in the US in the 1920s, which opened up a new reservoir of credit, is another. The revolution in information technology and financial innovation (for instance, the markets in financial futures and interest rate swaps) are the current examples.

A book that is essential reading about financial bubbles is *Manias, Panics and Crashes*, Charles P. Kindleberger, Macmillan. The 1978 edition analyses 29 market crashes, starting with the South Sea Bubble in England in 1720. The fundamental factors are different in each case but the monetary forces are similar. Each time the event is so significant that people carry on borrowing to acquire assets and the continuing monetary effects compound. Given the extremely favourable news about fundamentals, the monetary injection is like pouring gasoline on a bonfire that is already alight. Fuel is provided to inflate a financial bubble.

10.4 DEBT-DEFLATION

The effect of a financial bubble in the equity market is not merely financial. Wealth increases as a result of the rise in asset prices. Economic activity responds as people spend some of their increased wealth and as confidence improves. Part of the rise in the market is validated. The effects spiral upward. The bubble eventually bursts. Asset prices fall and a downward spiral starts.

The downward spiral starts symmetrically with the previous upward spiral. The earlier rise in asset prices, confidence, wealth and expenditure on goods and services is balanced by falls in the downswing. But there is a danger of asymmetry because of the gearing, and associated concentration of risk, inherent in the banking system's balance sheet.

The process becomes asymmetrical during the downswing when the value of asset prices falls to a level at which the value of collateral in general is no longer sufficient to cover the bank loans being secured. There are various stages to this process. In order of intensity they are:

(1) Borrowers become forced sellers of assets.
(2) People start to go bankrupt.
(3) Others retrench as they observe the pain of bankruptcy.
(4) Banks suffer from bad debts.
(5) Bankers become cautious about making new loans. They have more than enough trouble with bad debts on existing loans. The last thing they want is a bad debt on a new loan. Loan

officers become afraid of jeopardising their careers if they are not very cautious about new loans.
(6) Both the demand for and the supply of new loans subside.
(7) As bad debts multiply, banks may lack capital to make new loans.
(8) As bad debts multiply further, banks have to call in existing loans because they have insufficient capital to support their current business.
(9) Banks fail because the level of bad debts has wiped out their capital.
(10) Depositors lose money as banks fail.

Meanwhile, monetary growth has progressively collapsed; that is, monetary growth at first slowed, then declined sharply and finally turned negative. Economic activity and equity prices fall with it.[7] The whole process is called debt-deflation. The various stages of intensity should be noted. In the early 1930s, the US reached stage (10), whereas the UK only reached stage (6) in the early 1990s. Japan went beyond stage (7) in the early 2000s.

10.4.1   The cure for debt-deflation

Irving Fisher described debt-deflation and prescribed an essential part of its cure as long ago as 1932 (Fisher, 1933, pp. 337–357). The money supply must not be allowed to decline when prices are falling. Money-supply policy must be eased. But this advice needs interpreting for today's circumstances.

Some non-monetary economists are likely to misinterpret the advice. They will confuse money-supply policy with monetary policy. They will argue that reducing interest rates may be an insufficient stimulant because rates cannot fall below zero, which can be a high rate in real terms if retail prices are falling. Reducing interest rates has been likened to pushing on a string.

Money supply policy

It is correct to argue that growth of the money supply can become inadequate if the only action taken by the monetary authorities is to lower interest rates. It is nevertheless wholly within the power of a government to ensure adequate growth of broad money. The government can print money to offset any fall in fountain-pen money. A government can employ debt management to increase its borrowing from banks. Listed in order of aggressiveness, it can:

(1) reduce the sales of its own debt, below that needed to cover its net cash requirement;
(2) buy back bonds that it has previously issued;
(3) extend the range of bonds which it buys, to include, for example, corporate bonds;
(4) as a last resort, extend the type of security, to include, for example, common stocks.

It should be stressed that it is wholly within a government's power to stop the growth of broad money from undershooting.

Increasing printing-press money to offset a decline in fountain-pen money allows people to sell assets to repay a bank loan without the money supply falling. It slows the downward spiral at its origin. People do not have to either sell assets or reduce their expenditure on goods and

---

[7] There are real as well as monetary causes of depression. During the previous boom over exuberance leads to too much industrial investment, which leads to over capacity and excess supply.

services because they are unhappy about the amount of money in their bank account. Further, it helps directly to underpin asset prices and mutes the whole mechanism of debt-deflation.

Fiscal policy

Easing fiscal policy is another way of increasing government borrowing from banks and, therefore, boosting the money supply. This can be done by either cutting taxes or increasing public expenditure. This is the Keynesian remedy for debt-deflation.

The result of easing fiscal policy can, however, be an increase in the national debt to an unsustainable level and, in extreme cases, national debt compounding out of control, witness Japanese experience in the 1990s. The alternative of the government purchasing assets does not suffer from this disadvantage because the increase in the national debt is backed by holdings of assets. Indeed, there is a good chance that purchases of equities will turn out to be profitable in due course as capital profits are enjoyed when the stock market rebounds. The final result of the appropriate debt-management policy may thus be a fall in the national debt.

PART B: SHOULD A CENTRAL BANK TARGET ASSET PRICES?

Having outlined the monetary theory of asset prices, the obvious first question is how much attention should a central bank pay to asset prices? At a minimum, there is a clear case for monitoring them to obtain information.[8] In conditions of uncertainty, for example, the stance of monetary policy may be unclear and buoyant asset prices can be useful evidence that policy is easy.

There is also a clear case for a central bank to try to influence asset prices in special circumstances. A market can cease to function after an abrupt fall; for example, a new issue of a common stock or bond may become impossible. In such circumstances a central bank, for example, the Fed and the Bank of England in October 1987, gives priority to lender-of-last resort operations, lifeboats and other assistance, which may be designed in part to influence asset prices. A more extreme example is Irving Fisher's recommended cure for debt-deflation, when the case for the debt management policies described above is very strong.

More controversially, should action be taken to try to moderate a financial bubble when one appears to be developing? Even if debt-deflation is subsequently prevented by lender-of-last-resort operations, the disruption to the economy will be considerable. Resources will have been misallocated during the financial bubble. Balance sheets must be restored to health, which takes time. However, the cost of prevention might be greater than the disruption.

10.5 PREVENTING FINANCIAL BUBBLES

The first step in prevention is detection. A bubble must be distinguished from a rise in asset prices that is justified by real factors and genuinely optimistic expectations. A bubble almost certainly exists in the prices of some category of assets if money and credit have been growing for well over a year at a rate that is clearly much higher than normal, given the current growth of the economy and inflation. The category of assets depends on the favourable fundamental factors. The valuation of these assets will clearly exceed what has been normal in the past,

---

[8] For evidence of the impact of monetary growth in real terms on asset prices see Pepper and Oliver (2006, part IV), Pepper (1994, part II and ch. 1) and Pepper and Thomas (1973).

even allowing for the optimistic expectations. If the category of assets is equities, for example, dividend yields will be historically very low and price/earnings ratios will be historically very high, after adjustment for reasonable expectations of growth of dividends and earnings. The detection of a bubble is only the first step, however, and there might be several obstacles that impede action by policy-makers.

10.5.1   Political will

The first obstacle to early action is that the political will to stop a rapid rise in asset prices is unlikely to exist. Whereas people dislike product-price inflation, they enjoy asset-price inflation. With the latter, the more lenders lend on assets, the larger is the rise in asset prices and the greater is the collateral backing loans. Lenders are therefore content with a virtuous circle. Borrowers are happy too. They enjoy the increase in wealth as asset prices rise; borrowing to acquire assets is very profitable. A rise in house prices is popular with householders. Additional wealth also encourages higher consumer expenditure, which pleases industry. Politicians, for example, the Chancellor of the Exchequer, like basking in success.

10.5.2   Two basic problems

Apart from lack of political will, there are two basic difficulties with controlling bank lending to acquire assets. Firstly, experience has shown that changing short-term interest rates is a weak weapon once momentum has been allowed to develop. Secondly, the *real* rate of interest for financial transactions can diverge sharply from that for transactions in goods and services. The real rate is the nominal rate less expectations of inflation. Real rates diverge if expectations of asset-price inflation differ from expectations of product-price inflation. This will be the case when financial markets are rising at a time when product-price inflation is muted. Nominal interest rates set at a level appropriate for financial transactions will be very high in real terms for expenditure on goods and services. The result can easily be recession.

One solution is that it may be possible to solve the problem of real rates diverging by taking early action. The aim should be to arrest asset-prices inflation before expectations of rising asset prices have become ingrained. A rise in interest rates *that lasts for some time* affects expenditure on goods and services and raises industrial costs. A rise in rates *that is reversed quickly* has less effect on industry but, in contrast, it can have a substantial effect on confidence in financial markets.

A suggestion that was made in the US in the 1930s was that the Fed ought to have acted in the late 1920s to curb asset-price inflation by raising short-term interest rates until the equity market fell, where upon it should have raised them once more to ensure that equity prices fell sharply enough to rid the system of excessive exuberance, after which rates could be reduced permanently. Such a policy might, or might not, have worked.

10.5.3   Overfunding

Whereas it may not be possible to stop excessive borrowing to acquire assets, it is possible to neutralise the monetary effect of such borrowing. This was attempted in the UK after monetary targets were introduced in 1976. Private sector borrowing from banks continued to be strong. In an attempt to hit the published targets for the money supply the Bank of England sold more gilt-edged stock than was needed to finance the public sector. This policy was called 'overfunding'. Banks' holdings of government debt declined. Government borrowing from banks fell. Printing-press money declined and this offset excessive growth of fountain-pen money.

Overfunding is a well-designed weapon to combat asset-price inflation because it works on both supply and demand. Supply is increased and demand is reduced. The supply of assets is increased by additional issue of government bonds. The demand for assets is reduced as surplus money is mopped up and liquidity purchases decrease.

The position in the UK, however, became complicated because by 1981 banks' holdings of government debt had fallen to a level that was a working minimum. With few treasury bills remaining to purchase, the Bank of England started to buy commercial bills. By mid-1985 the Bank of England's holding of bills, its 'bill mountain', had become huge.

The policy was abolished in 1985 because it was considered that its effect was cosmetic. Lawson, Chancellor of the Exchequer between 1983 and 1989, states in his memoirs 'overfunding was essentially a way of massaging the money numbers to make it look as if monetary policy was tighter than it was' (Lawson 1992, pp. 449, 458). The mistake he and the others made was to concentrate on the effect of overfunding on credit and not on the fountain-pen money created by the credit. Whereas it was correct to argue that the effect on credit was cosmetic, because the Bank of England was itself providing the finance previously provided by banks, the effect on the money supply was not cosmetic. Lawson made the mistake committed by most non-monetary economists who focus on the economic decision associated with a credit transaction and ignore the continuing impact of any additional fountain-pen money that has been created.

Borrowing from a bank, issuing a corporate bond or issuing a commercial bill that is sold to the Bank of England are all ways in which a borrower can obtain credit. The trouble with a bank acting as the financial intermediary occurs because the funds for the credit come from an increase in fountain-pen money. If a corporate bond is issued the money for the credit comes from long-term savers. If a commercial bill is issued and sold to the Bank of England the money comes from the issue of gilt-edged stock by the Bank of England, that is, again from long-term savers. The difference is merely that the Bank of England rather than the borrower has issued the bond.

10.5.4 Official intervention in markets

Although overfunding is not cosmetic in the main, there are serious problems with very heavy intervention. Pepper must admit that he is implacably hostile to official intervention in markets as a result of personal experience. He started his career in the gilt-edged market in 1961. At that time there were three aims of debt management. First, to maximise investors' desire to hold gilt-edged stock in the long run. Second, to assist with monetary policy. Third, to minimise the cost of servicing the national debt.

During the Second World War there had been huge issues of gilt-edged stock. After the war large issues continued to pay for the nationalisation of the steel, coal, railway, gas and electricity industries, and so on. The result was that the Bank of England became worried about what might happen when very large issues came up for redemption and gave almost complete priority to maximising investors' desire to hold gilt-edged stock in the long run. One of the key attractions of gilt-edged stock was the size of the secondary market, the gilt-edged jobbers being prepared to undertake very large transactions by the standards of the time. The Bank thought that the crucial feature was investors having confidence that they would always be able to sell stock in quantity close to the prevailing price. The tactic was to preserve an orderly market. The Bank supported the market when there was selling. The Bank was also worried that a rapidly rising market was an indication of speculative activity, which could be troublesome in due course. Accordingly, it sold stock to moderate a rise when there was buying. The heavy official intervention lasted for more than two decades. The eventual result was exactly the opposite of what was intended. Very briefly, because the Bank would stop the market from rising rapidly, the reward for bargain hunting on a falling market was reduced. The risk/reward ratio was wrong and the Bank was eventually left to support a falling market on its own. When a clear turning point had been reached the Bank was very keen to sell stock and always allowed the speculators to get back in. The overall effect was that stabilising speculation ceased and de-stabilising speculation was encouraged. The result was a most disorderly market, in fact chaos.[9] There were similar episodes in the foreign exchange market.

In general, heavy official intervention in a market invariably causes problems in the longer run. Very often the long-run consequences are the opposite of what was originally intended. The experience of the 1980s indicated that overfunding was no exception. Sales of long-dated government bonds and purchases of short-dated bills by the Bank of England raised long-term rates relative to short-term rates of interest. This encouraged companies to borrow from a bank rather than raise funds by issuing bonds. A *persistent* policy of overfunding would lead in the long run to even greater reliance on bank lending, that is, to the problem becoming worse.[10]

The conclusion is that, although overfunding can be a useful weapon to employ in the short term, it is not suitable for general or long-run use.

10.5.5   Monetary Base Control

This chapter is not the time or place for a full description of Monetary Base Control (MBC).[11] Suffice to say that a central bank can control the total amount of reserves available to the banking system by controlling the size of its own balance sheet. Under the present system of monetary control in the UK the Bank of England stands ready to purchase whatever quantity of treasury bills banks wish to sell each day (albeit at a price of the Bank of England's own choosing). Such purchases increase banks' deposits with the Bank of England and, therefore, their reserves. Under the present system the Bank of England makes no attempt to control the supply of reserves available to banks. Under MBC the Bank of England would decide on how many bills it would purchase each day. It would control the growth of its own balance sheet and thereby the supply of reserves. Reserves would at times be less or greater than banks want.

---

[9] Elaboration is contained in two papers available at http://www.mjoliver.com/greenwell.html. The first is 'Official transactions in the gilt-edged market – a broker's view', March 1979, W. Greenwell & Co (Pepper's firm), which was not circulated to clients because the Bank of England deemed it to be 'unhelpful' but subsequently used by Pepper as the basis of a lecture to the Bank's biennial training courses. This paper gave estimates of sales of tap stocks superimposed on a graph of gilt-edged prices and showed that historically it had not paid to bargain-hunt on a falling market because the Bank had always allowed the 'bears to get back in' close to a trough of the market. The second paper is 'Official order: real chaos', 1990, commissioned originally by Frazer Green. This edition was circulated by the Crown Agents to their clients, including many central banks. It elaborated on how official intervention to maintain an orderly market had undermined the market's self-stabilisers, the result being the complete chaos of the 'Battle of Watling Street'. It also predicted that the Exchange Rate Mechanism of the European Monetary System would cause chaos, which happened in September 1992 when the UK was forced to leave the mechanism.

[10] Other problems with overfunding are described in Pepper and Oliver (2001).

[11] See Pepper and Oliver (2001, part III) for a discussion of the debate about MBC in 1979 in the UK.

Shortage of reserves

Under MBC, if banks as a whole were short of reserves, the Bank of England would not relieve the shortage and a bank that was short would initially borrow in the inter-bank market. This would merely pass the shortage to another bank, like the 'hot potato' of the children's game. Inter-bank rates would rise. This would continue until a bank decided that it would be better to sell an asset rather than borrow. There are two classes of assets that could be sold, namely public and private sector ones.

Public sector assets

The main public sector assets that banks hold are treasury bills and government bonds. Banks can influence the size of their balance sheet, and therefore the amount of reserves that they require, by purchases and sales of these holdings *providing the counterparty is not the government*. The money supply is reduced, and therefore banks' liabilities and assets, when someone in the non-bank private sector buys a gilt-edged stock from a bank. It should be noted that the Bank of England must not be the buyer of the stock if the money supply is to be reduced. Under MBC the Bank of England rather than banks decide on the amount of treasury bills that it purchases and, therefore, this condition is met.

Private sector assets

MBC also influences the total of bank lending to the private sector. This is in spite of banks not being able to control the total of their advances, at least in the short run. Whereas banks can control the total of overdraft limits and other credit facilities, borrowers and not banks determine how much of these facilities are actually used. Further, borrowing can be divided into voluntary and involuntary borrowing. The former occurs, for example, when an industrialist plans to build a new factory financed by a bank loan. The latter occurs when an industrialist is caught by surprise by a decline in demand for his products and experiences an unplanned rise in inventories of finished goods that has to be financed. Voluntary borrowing tends to fall when interest rates rise but involuntary borrowing may rise, and vice versa when rates fall. This is one reason why total borrowing may respond slowly to changes in interest rates.

Bank lending to the private sector does not, however, consist solely of advances. It includes holdings of commercial bills, corporate bonds and securitised loans. Banks can sell these and, thereby, influence the total of their lending in the short run.[12]

Non-deposit liabilities

Financial institutions are often called financial intermediaries. They provide a bridge between providers and users of funds. A life assurance company, for example, collects premiums and passes on the funds when it subscribes to new issues of bonds and stocks by industrial corporations. Banks are also financial intermediaries. They collect deposits and pass on the funds as loans. Intermediation by banks is different from that by other financial intermediaries if the

---

[12] Some will argue that a reduction in monetary growth because people are switching from CDs, for example, into treasury and commercial bills would be cosmetic. This argument might be right under the present system because the Bank of England stands ready to encash these bills, as explained. Under MBC, the Bank of England would not be prepared to purchase whatever quantity of bills the banks wanted to sell. The bills would not be so liquid as at present.

funds passed on are bank deposits. These deposits may be unintended savings that are subsequently spent on goods and services or financial assets. Funds lent to banks for a minimum of five years are genuine savings that cannot in the short run be spent. In the latter case banks are in the same position as the other financial intermediaries. Funds lent for five years are, accordingly, classified as 'non-deposit liabilities' and are excluded from the definition of the money supply. Banks do not need the same level of reserves as those for shorter-term deposits. A bank could, therefore, reduce its need for reserves by encouraging its customers to keep money on deposit for five years or longer.

10.5.6 MBC compared with overfunding

An advantage of MBC would be that some of the longer-term problems associated with overfunding would be avoided. Banks, acting in accordance with normal market criteria, rather than officials, would decide which assets to sell. Pressure would not be confined to the government bond market but would be spread across markets, including the money market. Comparing MBC with overfunding, banks rather than the Bank of England sell public sector debt. In other words overfunding would be privatised. MBC would also discourage banks from marketing and selling loans aggressively when reserves were in short supply.

10.6 CONCLUSIONS – AN ANSWER AND A QUESTION

In 1979, soon after she became Prime Minister, Mrs Thatcher commissioned an enquiry into Monetary Base Control. The Bank of England was totally against it (Pepper and Oliver 2001, pp. 74–76). Assuming that MBC is still ruled out, overfunding remains as a possible weapon for moderating a financial bubble. However, its long-run perverse effect and distortion to markets mean that the disadvantages of employing this weapon probably outweigh the advantages of moderating the bubble. The conclusion is that a central bank should not act to try to moderate financial bubbles.

10.6.1 The answer

The answer to the question 'Should a central bank target asset prices?' is that it should not, providing that it is confident that its lender-of-last-resort operations after a bubble has burst will prevent asset prices from falling to such an extent that there is a general problem of insufficient collateral.

10.6.2 The question

The question is 'have central banks been preventing debt-deflation or merely postponing it?'

There is a lurking fear that lender-of-last-resort operations by the Bank of England and the Fed during the last two decades have merely postponed the problem of debt-deflation and have not cured it. Only part of the necessary adjustment process after a bubble has burst – for example, the restructuring of balance sheets – has been completed. Some of the trends are becoming worse.

The crucial ratio is the personal sector's debt to income ratio, which has continued to rise. Not much comfort can be taken from the rise that has taken place in the wealth to income ratio because this is a symptom of asset price inflation, which will reverse when a bubble bursts.

The main threat is not from the cost of servicing debt, as long as interest rates remain low, but from the need to repay debt. Although the previous generation of borrowers in the UK paid high rates of interest on debt, inflation helped them to repay it. The debt was repaid with devalued pounds. The current generation will not be helped to anything like the same extent. As is widely known, the bonuses of with-profit assurance policies are lower than were predicted when the policies were taken out. The proceeds of many policies will be inadequate to repay the mortgages that they were designed to cover. This is merely one example of a repayment problem that is likely to become general.

ANNEX

Disequilibrium

Firstly, in the absence of monetary base control, short-term interest rates are not determined by the balance between supply and demand. They are set by the central bank.

Secondly, the real world is more complicated than many economic theories assume. A static system is the easiest to analyse. Then come dynamic systems that are in equilibrium. After that come dynamic systems that are out of equilibrium, which are moving from one state of equilibrium to another state of equilibrium. Finally come dynamic systems where disequilibrium is the normal state. The last is often the case in the market for money.

If the normal laws of supply and demand apply in a market, a rise in price discourages buyers and encourages sellers, and vice versa if prices fall. If either buyers or sellers respond quickly to a change in price intended buyers and sellers come quickly into line. Everyone who wishes to buy or sell at the new price will be able to do so. The market will clear quickly and a new equilibrium will have been reached.

If neither buyers nor sellers respond quickly to a change in price a market will not clear quickly. If intended buyers exceed intended sellers some potential buyers may, for example, be told that they must wait until more goods become available. If intended sellers exceed intended buyers, inventories of goods waiting to be sold will rise. It may take some time for the market to clear and for a new equilibrium to be reached.

The new equilibrium may not be reached. It will not be if an underlying factor affecting either supply or demand changes during the adjustment process. Indeed, if underlying factors are changing continuously equilibrium may never be reached. This is the state nearly all the time in the market for money.

Cash flow accounting

A corporation's annual accounts normally consist of a trading account, a balance sheet and a cash-flow statement. The trading account gives details of the corporation's income, expenditure and profit or loss during the corporation's financial year. The balance sheet gives details of its assets and liabilities at the end of the year. The cash-flow statement reconciles the changes in the balance sheet between the start and the end of the year.

In the UK the National Income Accounts are the trading accounts of the nation. Analysis of the economy as a whole (macroeconomic analysis) is based largely on this trading-account approach, although some balance sheet analysis is included, for example, a rise in wealth leads to additional consumption. Monetary analysis, in contrast, is based on cash-flow accounting plus balance sheet analysis.

Managers of small businesses, who may never produce a trading account or a balances sheet, understand the vital need to watch their cash flow. Individuals with bank accounts normally have a bank balance below which they are unhappy and have to take action, either by curtailing expenditure or selling something. Similarly, they have a maximum for a balance that is not expected to be temporary. If their current balance exceeds this amount either they will be tempted into incurring additional expenditure or they will take action to find a better medium of investment for their surplus funds. In each case they manage their cash. For non-accountants, cash-flow accounting is simpler than trading accounts and balance sheets. Even large firms monitor their cash. Budgets are prepared at the start of a financial year. The main elements of the trading account are predicted, together with certain key elements of the balance sheet. Emerging data are scrutinised, usually monthly (as part of the Management Information System) to detect how the year is progressing. Questions are immediately asked if cash or net liquid assets have done anything unexpected, especially if the company's balance sheet is not strong.

Expectations

When a financial bubble is building up, the expectations of some of the participants, but not those of monetary analysts who understand the behaviour of the market, may be adaptive or myopic. Adaptive means modified, in the light of recent experience. In contrast, monetary analysts will have expected the market to rise. Myopic means short-sighted, which is a defect that can be remedied. In the circumstances described monetary analysts correctly judge that the market will most probably continue to rise in the short-term. They are forced to give priority to these short-term expectations over their long-term ones because, if they act in accordance with their long-term expectations, the risk of loss in the short term and adverse consequences have become unacceptable. Short-term expectations are different from short-sighted ones.

REFERENCES

Bordo, M.D. and Jeanne, O. (2002) Monetary policy and asset prices: does 'benign neglect' make sense?, *International Finance*, **5**, 139–164.

Cecchetti, S.G. (*et al.*) (2000) *Asset prices and central bank policy*, Geneva: International Center for Monetary and Banking Studies.

Fisher, I. (1932) The debt-deflation theory of great depressions, *Econometrica*, **1**, 337–357.

Fisher, I. (1933) *Booms and depressions: some first principles*, New York: Adelphi.

Greenwell, W. & Co. (1979) Official transactions in the gilt-edged market – a broker's view, March. (http://www.mjoliver.com/greenwell.htmlhttp://www.mjoliver.com/).

Greenwell, W. & Co. (1990) Official order: real chaos, March. (http://www.mjoliver.com/greenwell.html).

Kindleberger, C.P. (1978) *Manias, panics, and crashes: a history of financial crises*, 2nd ed., London: Macmillan.

Lawson, N. (1992) The view from No. 11, London: Bantam.

Pepper, G.T. (1994) *Money, credit and asset prices*, London: Macmillan.

Pepper, G.T. and Oliver, M.J. (2001) *Monetarism under Thatcher: lessons for the future*, Cheltenham: Edward Elgar/IEA.

Pepper, G.T. and Oliver, M.J. (2004) The monetary theory of asset prices, module 3, *Practical History of Financial Markets*, Edinburgh Business School.

Pepper, G.T. and Oliver, M.J. (2006) *The liquidity theory of asset prices*, Chichester: John Wiley & Sons, Ltd.

Pepper, G.T. and Thomas, R.L. (1973) Cyclical changes in the level of the UK equity and gilt-edged markets, *Journal of the Institute of Actuaries*, **99**, 157–247.

Vickers, J. (1999) Monetary policy and asset prices, *Bank of England Quarterly Bulletin*, **34**, 428–435.

11

Monetary Policy and the Bank of Japan

John Greenwood

11.1 INTRODUCTION

This chapter examines the monetary aspects of Japan's economic problems during the 1990s. Booms often turn to bust, but in the Japanese case the aftermath of the bubble of the late 1980s persisted for an exceptionally long period. The downturn in the economy has been very prolonged, lasting more than a decade and a half, albeit punctuated with periodic but temporary export-led recoveries. The deflation of asset prices and consumer prices has been painful to businesses, homeowners and other borrowers alike. The decline in the nominal value of incomes and profits meant that tax revenues declined, causing huge government fiscal deficits, and generating an unprecedented level of government debt relative to GDP that will be a burden on Japanese taxpayers for generations to come. All these problems could have been either avoided or fixed much sooner with an appropriate set of expansionary monetary policies and an energetic set of restructuring policies. Unfortunately the Japanese authorities completely failed to devise strategies in either area that were appropriate to the task in hand, extending the misfortunes of the population far longer than necessary. The authorities' handling of monetary policy and bank and corporate restructuring policies during the 1990s was usually rationalised on the fallacious grounds that either they did not wish to repeat the mistakes of the preceding bubble period, or unorthodox measures were inappropriate. As we shall show, neither justification was valid.

In general the monetary and restructuring policies of the authorities have been too little too late. Following the election of Mr Koizumi to presidency of the LDP and hence Prime Minister of Japan in 2002, a start has been made on some restructuring policies. But since April 1999 the Bank of Japan has become more independent, and in some respects less responsive to Japan's political leadership. Nevertheless, after years of resistance, the Bank of Japan finally adopted some quantitative easing measures starting in March 2001 (under Governor Hayami, and boosted after March 2003 by Governor Fukui), but prior to this the approach taken by the leadership of the Bank was overly cautious, tentative and consensus-driven. Correcting the problems of the past 15 years now necessarily requires a larger dose of medicine (e.g. faster growth of money for longer), but implementing such a strategy is simply not part of the Japanese consensus, so no one should expect a quick solution. Given the unwillingness of the banks to lend the new funds created by the BOJ and the reluctance of corporate and household borrowers to take on additional debt in the current deflationary environment, it will require exceptional measures if any expansionary policy is to start to succeed within months or quarters rather than years.

Issues in Monetary Policy. Edited by K. Matthews and P. Booth.

11.2 JAPAN'S GOLDEN ERA IN MONETARY POLICY, 1975–85

To appreciate the catastrophic nature of Japan's monetary mistakes of the 1990s it is necessary to set out in brief the remarkable achievements of the Japanese authorities in the preceding decade, roughly 1975–85. Among the OECD economies it is no exaggeration to say that Japan went from having one of the best monetary policies (in the period up to1985) to having the most inept (in the 1990s).

Following the end of the Bretton Woods system of pegged but adjustable exchange rates in the early 1970s, Japan experienced a serious bout of inflation. The inflation was not the result of the OPEC-led increases in oil prices in 1973 (since the outbreak of serious price increases pre-dated the Arab-Israeli war), but followed from an exceptionally lax monetary policy in 1971–73. Some of the monetary easing in 1971 can be attributed to the authorities' deliberate attempt to offset the adverse impact of the initial effects of the 'Nixon Shock' or exchange rate appreciation after August 1971, but the export hiatus lasted for six months at most, and the remainder of the easy money policy should be viewed as part of a wider domestic economic strategy, launched by Prime Minister Tanaka in 1972 as a plan for the 'Remodelling of the Japanese Archipelago'. For 18 months between January 1972 and June 1973 Japan's money supply (M2+CDs) increased by an average of 26.5% p.a. compared with an average growth rate of 18.3% p.a. over the years 1960–71. Real and nominal spending soared, and inflation rose to peak at 25.1% year-on-year as measured by the CPI, while producer prices peaked at 38%, in February 1974. Faced with accelerating inflation the Bank of Japan raised interest rates steeply, and imposed strict 'window guidance' (or loan controls) on the commercial banks. Once the inflation had been brought down (in late 1975), and the exchange rate was floating (though not entirely freely), Japan's monetary policy underwent a thorough overhaul. The painful lessons of the inflation of 1973–75 prompted a revised modus operandi for the Bank of Japan (BOJ), the essence of which was to control broad money[1] growth, setting a target for the year-on-year changes in M2+CDs. (Suzuki, 1980).

In 1974 the Bank of Japan began to set monetary growth targets for M2+CDs, initially in the range 12–16%, later lowered to 8–10%. The targets were based on extensive research into the demand for money in Japan, and therefore took account of (i) the slower potential growth rate of the economy compared with the 1950s and 1960s, (ii) the expected increase in the demand for money, measured as the increase in the long-term ratio of money (M2+CDs) to nominal GDP, and (iii) a feasible target for the rate of inflation. A gradualist approach was adopted, with the result that the national CPI inflation rate more than halved from 8.8% in 1976–77 to 4.0% by 1978–79. After a brief interruption due to the impact of the second oil crisis in 1979–81, inflation declined further to a remarkable 2.2% in 1982–85. Throughout this period (1976–85) real GDP growth averaged a steady 3.7% p.a. with no recession, despite the second oil crisis of 1979–80 and the two American recessions of 1980 and 1981.

It is important to stress that throughout this period (1976–85) although there was intervention in the foreign exchange market, Japan's domestic monetary targeting was not compromised by the simultaneous pursuit of external objectives such as a particular exchange rate. As a legal matter the BOJ's interventions in the foreign exchange market are always conducted on behalf of the Ministry of Finance, and the MOF must pay for any additions of foreign currency to the

---

[1] Broad Money consists of M2+CDs plus the deposits and CDs of Post Offices, Shinkumi Federation Bank, Credit Coopera-tives, National Federation of Labor Credit Associations, Labor Credit Associations, Credit Federations of Agricultural Cooperatives, Agricultural Cooperatives, Credit Federations of Fishery Cooperatives, and Fishery Cooperatives plus money in trust of Domestically Licensed Banks (including Foreign Trust Banks).

Foreign Exchange Equalisation Account by issuing short term bills (in yen), and remitting the proceeds to the BOJ. Effectively this means that Japan's interventions in the foreign exchange market are always fully sterilised. However, the Bank of Japan could generally either counteract the intervention with open market operations or support them as it chose, subject to political constraints. The important point is that at this time the BOJ was left free to conduct its money market operations with the sole (intermediate) objective of meeting its monetary targets, which in turn would bring about the achievement of the broader (but unspecified) inflation target. As an early example of inflation control through monetary targeting, Japan's experience in 1976–85 was remarkably successful.

11.3   HOW MONETARY POLICY WENT OFF THE RAILS, 1985–89

In view of the achievement of stable monetary and economic growth combined with a low inflation rate during the decade 1976–85, it might seem strange that Japan's monetary policy should have been so drastically derailed in the subsequent five years. Yet this is exactly what happened. The misguided attempt to coordinate policy internationally in the years after 1985 and the abandonment of monetary targeting completely undermined the conduct of Japan's domestic monetary policy.

The US dollar had been immensely strong in the early years of the first Reagan administration (1980–84) appreciating by 64%, and by 1985 the US administration was very anxious about the consequences for employment (particularly in the auto industry) and economic growth. An international conference of the G-5 nations (France, West Germany, Japan, the United States and the United Kingdom) was convened at the Plaza Hotel in New York in September 1985 to resolve the problem. Under the resulting Plaza Agreement the G-5 countries decided to reduce the value of the US dollar in relation to the Japanese yen and German Deutsche Mark by intervening in currency markets. In the following two years the exchange value of the dollar declined 51% thanks in part to the US$10 billion spent during the coordinated interventions of the participating central banks.

For Japan, the interventions by the Bank of Japan in the foreign currency markets to sell the US dollar did not last very long. Japan's foreign exchange reserves were reduced from $28.45 billion in August 1985 to $26.3 billion in November, but from then onwards market participants switched from buying the dollar to selling it. Thereafter Japan's interventions were all on the other side, i.e. purchasing US dollars in an attempt to stop the yen rising too rapidly. From December 1985 foreign reserves increased continuously until April 1989 when they peaked temporarily at $100.36 billion. Such dollar purchases by the Bank of Japan had to be matched by the sale of an equivalent quantity (at the prevailing exchange rate) of newly created yen to the Japanese commercial banks. Since the Bank of Japan, now led by Governor Sumita, chose not to counteract these dollar purchases the Japanese monetary base inevitably accelerated, at first from 4% to 7%, and subsequently to 12% by late 1987, causing Japanese interest rates to decline sharply in 1985–86. For example, Japanese government bond yields fell from 6.4% prior to the Plaza Agreement to 4.5% by early 1986 and 3.2% by January 1987, while the official discount rate was cut from 5% in December 1985 to 2.5% by February 1987. The appreciation of the yen from 260 to almost 120 yen per US$ initially worried Japanese businesses, and the demand for loans remained sluggish. But once the demand for loans had recovered in late 1986, the money supply began to grow very rapidly, especially from 1987 onwards. Monetary growth accelerated from an average of 7.8% in 1983–85 to 9.5% in 1986–87 and then to12.3% by February 1988.

The extended monetary easing from 1985 onwards produced a host of symptoms of an asset bubble. First it produced a long and powerful bull market in equities that lasted, with only two brief corrections in September – October 1986 and October 1987, from early 1986 until December 1989. The Nikkei 225 index of stock prices more than trebled between January 1985 and December 1990, rising from 11 558 to 38 915. A flood of new share issues during these years meant that the stock market's capitalization increased even more, quadrupling over the same period. Land prices also soared. The Japan Real Estate Institute's index of overall land prices in Japan's six largest cities almost trebled between 1985 and 1990, while commercial property prices quadrupled. Together these upswings in Japanese asset prices constituted the largest asset bubble in recorded Japanese history.

The puzzle about this period is not so much the scale of the asset price inflation, but the relative lack of inflation at the CPI level. Despite vigorous real GDP growth throughout the years 1985–89 (averaging 4.1% per annum), and despite the acceleration in monetary growth after 1985, inflation of goods and service prices remained strangely subdued by comparison with previous Japanese post-war booms. At the end of 1989 CPI inflation was a modest 2.6%, less than half of the 6.2% recorded among other OECD member countries at the time. However, even this increase was mainly 'a one-time increase from the introduction of the 3% value added tax (in April 1989). The underlying inflation rate was close to zero'. (Kuroda, 2002) Two main explanations are first that the yen was also appreciating through much of this period (rising from 260 yen per US$ in early 1985 to 140 yen per US$ at the end of 1989), and second that Japan undertook extensive trade liberalisation measures during this period. Both factors helped to keep import prices and wholesale prices under control, and in turn contributed to the subdued pace of consumer price inflation despite 'the overheating of the economy' (Kuroda, 2002).

11.4   THE BURSTING OF THE BUBBLE, 1989–91

To prick the bubble the Japanese authorities started raising interest rates in May 1989. The official discount rate of the Bank of Japan was first raised from 2.5% to 3.25%, a jump of 75 basis points, and then in four further large successive hikes of 0.5% (twice), 1.0% and 0.75% until it reached 6.0% in August 1990. For a while credit and money growth actually accelerated as firms scrambled to secure credit lines ahead of the squeeze. Growth of M2+CDs peaked at 13.2% in May 1990, a whole year after the rates hikes had started, but thereafter monetary and credit growth collapsed, with M2+CDs slowing drastically until it recorded negative growth (-0.2%) on a year-on-year basis in September 1992.

The stock market peaked first – in December 1989 – and fell sharply in February, March and April 1990 before staging a brief summer rally and then falling steeply again in September and October. However, it was some months before real estate prices or the economy started to weaken. According to the Japan Real Estate Institute, an index of the level of land prices for six Major Cities peaked between April and September 1990, while an index of All Japan land prices peaked a year later in April-September 1991. The economy did not exhibit sustained weakness until mid-1991, a year after the peak in money growth, and the peak in urban real estate prices.

Not only did asset prices fall (as intended), but – and this had not been intended or expected – the economy also went into recession in 1993, recording three successive quarters of negative growth in Q2, Q3 and Q4. Further, because money growth remained so low for such an extended period, the economy began to experience deflation of goods and service prices on a year-on-year basis starting in 1994 and 1995 as well as asset prices. The authorities had taken the view that since the monetary easing after 1985 had created an asset bubble without significant impact on the real economic growth rate and without much impact on consumer prices, they could now unwind the asset bubble without adverse effects on the economy. As explained above, yen appreciation and trade liberalisation prior to 1990 had shielded the economy from consumer price inflation, concealing some of the possible adverse effects of the earlier monetary easing and this misled the authorities as to the likely impact of their monetary tightening.

11.5   ASSESSMENT OF POLICY RESPONSES

We now turn to an assessment of the policy responses by the Japanese authorities over the past 15 years. At different times during the past decade and a half a variety of strategies for an economic recovery and escape from deflation have been proposed or implemented, in part or in whole, mostly without success. In the remaining sections of this chapter these strategies are reviewed, and in each case I explain how and why the policy response failed, or how the policy might succeed if properly implemented.

11.5.1   Initial policy response – fiscal expansion

Initially the Japanese government addressed the twin problems of the economic downturn and the subsequent deflation by increasing government spending, not by raising overall domestic demand through quantitative or other monetary easing. A series of fiscal stimulus programmes was devised (see Table 11.1), which together had the effect of raising government expenditure as a fraction of GDP from 31.8% in 1990 to 38.3% in 2000, shifting the government budget from a surplus of 2.1% of GDP in 1990 to a deficit of 7.9% of GDP in 2002 (as tax revenues slumped due to the on-going deflation), and increasing government debt from 46.8% of GDP in 1990 to 138.7% of GDP by 2003 (Source, OECD).

As can be readily understood from the discrepancy between the cumulative percentages of GDP for the supplementary budgets shown in the table (26.6%) and the comparatively modest increase in GDP as a percentage of GDP (6.5 percentage points) over the period, the headline budget numbers exaggerated the true scale of the expenditures. The reason was that some of these expenditures were either already planned, or transferred (front-loaded) from another year. Even so, it would hard to find an example of a more egregious failure of Keynesian fiscal expansion. Year after year the government committed huge sums to little or no effect in terms of bringing about a sustainable economic recovery. Not only did the policy fail to restore economic growth, but it has also resulted in a legacy of government debt that will take

Table 11.1   Japanese government supplementary budgets, 1992–2002 Units: Yen trillion, (% of GDP).

August 1992	Feb 1994	April 1998	Sept 2000
Y10.7tr (2.2%)	Y15.3tr (3.1%)	Y16.7tr (3.2%)	Y5.0tr (0.9%)
April 1993	April 1995	Nov 1998	Nov 2002
Y13.2tr (2.7%)	Y4.6tr (0.9%)	Y23.9tr (4.6%)	Y6.2tr (1.2%)
Sept 1993	Sept 1995	Nov 1999	Total Y132.6tr
Y6.2tr (1.3%)	Y12.8tr (2.6%)	Y18.0tr (3.5%)	26.6% of 2002 (GDP)

Source: Solutions to a Liquidity Trap, p. 194.

several decades to reduce. Why was fiscal policy such a dismal failure? First, the government's expenditures were not monetised in any degree.[2]

Consequently, the increasing volume of borrowing conducted by the authorities to finance the growing budget deficits effectively crowded out any possible funding for a recovery by the private sector. In a situation where household and corporate balance sheets were already stretched due to the monetary squeeze and the subsequent recessions, the private sector needed some relief in the form of more funds at lower nominal and real interest rates to be able to start spending again, but the relentless spending by the authorities drained funds from the money markets, keeping money market rates higher than they otherwise would have been. Second, the expenditures were wasteful and misdirected.[3]

Finally in 2002 following public opposition to further public spending the incoming Prime Minister Koizumi decided to end the fiscal spending strategy and concentrate on restructuring the banks and their major corporate customers, downsizing government, privatising, and modernising the public sector. In effect the Japanese government had run out of ammunition. The failure of fiscal policy can be evidenced not only by the failure of the economy to recover, but also by the repeated downgrading of Japanese government debt (JGBs) by the rating agencies, and the public disillusionment about the effectiveness of government spending on projects with dubious rates of return. In effect the policy switch under Koizumi meant that the government was switching from Keynesian fiscal expansion to economic reform and restructuring.

Since the value of government debt is fixed in nominal terms, but nominal GDP and hence tax revenues have been declining, the value of the debt is rising faster than the country's capacity to service it. With the real interest rate on government debt exceeding the growth rate of the economy on a sustained basis, Japan is effectively in a debt trap. To escape the debt trap either the government must cut expenditure in order to run a primary budget surplus (i.e. before interest payments), or it must solve the deflation problem to enable revenues to start recovering. The only alternative is to raise taxes, which would be likely to depress the private sector even further. In short the budget deficit is largely a consequence of the deflation, and the authorities should focus on solving that problem first. If Japan were to resume positive real growth with a gently rising price level, the government (and private sector) debt problem would gradually be resolved.

11.5.2   Monetary policy – interest rate strategy, 1990–93

The Bank of Japan had aggressively raised the official discount rate by 350 basis points from 2.5% to 6.0% over a period of 16 months between May 1989 and August 1990. However, when it came to cutting rates, the Bank of Japan dragged its feet. For example, it took 19 months – from July 1991 until February 1993 – for the Bank to lower the official discount rate from 6.0% to the 2.5% level where the rate hikes had started. In September 1993 the official discount rate was cut again by 75 basis points to 1.75% and kept at this level until April 1995.

Why was the Bank of Japan so reluctant to cut rates in the first place, and so slow in implementing the rate cuts?

The Bank of Japan became significantly concerned about the asset bubble only in 1989, when Governor Sumita started to raise interest rates in May.

---

[2] There are also legal and constitutional reasons for this.
[3] Examples abound of bridges to nowhere, etc.

Yasushi Mieno took over the reins as Governor of the Bank of Japan from Governor Sumita on 17 December 1989. On 25 December the discount rate was hiked by a further 50 basis points from 3.75% to 4.25%. The Nikkei 225 index of equity prices peaked a few days later on 29 December 1989. Since it was under Mieno's leadership that the monetary squeeze was intensified and prolonged, a detailed examination of the next 18 months is required. The new Governor appeared to have a mission: he was deeply concerned that inflation might spread from asset prices to goods and services. When Iraq's invasion of Kuwait in August 1990 sent oil prices soaring, this added further to the Bank's anxieties about inflation. These wider concerns apparently made Mieno oblivious of, or at least unresponsive to, falling share prices. In addition, the Bank evidently did not pay adequate heed to the signals from the bond market. Ten-year government bond yields peaked at 8.03% in September 1990, but under the pressure of the Bank's continuing squeeze, the overnight call rate did not peak until March 1991 (at 8.25%). If bond and money market yields are viewed as a sensitive indicator of supply-demand conditions in the credit markets, the six-month interval between the peak in bond yields and the peaking of overnight rates demonstrates that the Bank of Japan was critically slow to change direction.

Was it possible that the economic signals were not clear enough that the economy had already turned down? The evidence from falling asset prices should have been incontrovertible. By the second half of 1990 the damage from falling share prices and falling land prices had already begun to percolate. Several major corporations and smaller financial institutions were hit by margin calls, by the widening bankruptcy of speculative investors and by the effects of falling land prices on leveraged property developers and finance companies. By yearend, consumer spending had started to weaken, and car sales had fallen sharply. In early 1991 falling property prices started to impact housing starts adversely. Inventories rose and investment spending started to fall. But still the Bank would not budge. Finally in July 1991, four months after overnight call rates in the money market had started to fall, ten months after bond yields had peaked, 19 months after the stock market had peaked, and long after land prices and economic activity had all clearly turned downwards, the Bank of Japan at last switched to cutting rates. It seems clear in retrospect that the BOJ had been determined all along to deflate asset prices to a point where all speculative activity was eliminated so that when rate cuts did come they would not generate any resurgence of the asset bubble.

However the Bank still dragged its feet. One key reason for the Bank's excessively long drawn out squeeze was that, in contrast to the close attention paid to monetary aggregates under Governors Morinaga (1974–79) and Mayekawa (1979–84), the Bank had abandoned this set of guidelines in 1985 under Governor Sumita (1984–89). The Bank of Japan under Governor Mieno (1989–94) was clearly not about to re-instate them. Indeed at times the Bank of Japan simply dismissed the dramatic deceleration in money growth rates as the inevitable consequence of the desirable ending of the bubble. The bursting of the bubble meant that it was no longer rational to borrow for speculative investment in real estate or equity, hence a slowdown in the growth of bank deposits and money supply was a natural corollary.

The reality is that the Bank kept rates too high for too long. In the three years 1988–90 bank reserve growth (adjusted for reserve requirement changes) had grown at an average growth rate of 17.8% p.a. However, between September 1990 and February 1991 the growth rate plummeted from 21.1% into negative territory (-2.2%). In terms of their level, unadjusted reserves fell from 5.17 trillion yen in September to 4.85 trillion yen in February, the only sustained period of weakness in this series that was not accompanied by reserve requirement changes since 1970. How could such an abrupt change occur? By holding rates above their equilibrium levels the BOJ was deliberately causing a decline in what the Bank viewed as speculative demand for borrowing, but this in turn was causing deposits and money supply to decline. In effect, the BOJ's high rates were draining reserves from the banking system, and this led directly to a contraction in the monetary base and the money supply.

However the data on reserves were not generally followed by economists or investors. Aside from the downturns in the equity and real estate markets, the first sign that interest rate policy had taken a seriously wrong turn was the abrupt reversal in the money supply figures. From a cycle-high growth rate of 13.2% in May 1990, M2+CDs plunged to 2.7% by August 1991 just a month after the Bank of Japan first cut the official discount rate, and a negative growth rate by September 1992. Similarly, the monetary base plunged from 13.3% in April 1990 to 0.4% in April of 1991 and -4.0% by March 1992.

An initial conclusion on this early phase of policy from the bursting of the bubble until February 1993 (when the official discount rate returned to 2.5%) is that the Bank's principal objective from late 1989 until mid-1991 was the deliberate deflation of asset prices in the mistaken belief that this could be achieved without precipitating recession and deflation in the wider economy. As far back as 1985 the Bank had taken its eye off the ball with respect to traditional indicators of domestic demand and inflation management (such as monetary growth). At that time international cooperation under the Plaza Agreement and later the Louvre Accord (February 1987) had displaced domestic priorities. In 1989–91 this mindset had been replaced with another quixotic objective – the reduction of asset prices to some appropriate yet undefined level.

11.5.3   Monetary policy – interest rate strategy, 1993–2001

Between February 1993 and March 2001 the Bank of Japan continued with interest rate policy as its primary modus operandi, lowering the official discount rate from 2.5% progressively to 0% in February 1999. (In early 1998 the Bank dropped the use of the official discount rate as its primary signalling mechanism and began announcing a target for the unsecured overnight call rate.) From 1999 until March 2001 the Bank effectively followed a zero interest rate policy (ZIRP), widening the range of instruments and maturities that it was willing to purchase in its open market operations, but resisting pressure from the government and elsewhere to take more aggressive expansionary actions. On 1 April 1999 the new Bank of Japan Law took effect, giving the Bank legal independence from the government. Despite the persistence of deflation, the Bank actually reversed course in August 2000, *raising* its target for rates to 0.25%. By February 2001 and in the face of intensifying recession and deflation the Bank acknowledged its error and began lowering rates again. Finally in March 2001 the Bank abandoned its interest rate strategy and formally adopted a policy of 'quantitative easing' and setting progressively higher targets for commercial banks' reserves.

Although the BOJ could argue that it was actively doing things to help the economy recover through most of this period, its stance was essentially passive and its senior officials resistant to any external pressure. This can be shown by reviewing the sources of the monetary base. As Figure 11.1 shows, even though the overall monetary base was growing at about 8% p.a., net domestic assets were *declining* through 1996 and 1997. The cautiousness of the BOJ under the last governor, Mr Hayami, is well illustrated in this figure which shows the sources of monetary base growth divided into its two main (asset-side) components: the purchase by the BOJ of domestic assets such as JGBs and financing bills, and the acquisition by the BOJ of

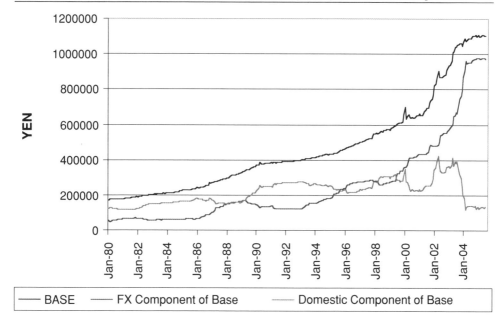

Figure 11.1   Sources of the Japanese monetary base

foreign assets. Viewed over the whole of the 1990s we can clearly see how most of the growth of the monetary base has been accounted for by acquisitions of foreign exchange.[4]

Why were the BOJ's interest strategies so unsuccessful? For a long time the problem was the Keynesian thinking of the BOJ economists and policy-makers who (1) equated low money market interest rates with an 'easy' monetary policy, and (2) considered that the primary or only transmission mechanism for monetary policy was from the interest rates on loans to corporate capital expenditure. For several years Bank of Japan staff therefore asserted that they had done enough because interest rates were already very low, and there were periodic signs of a revival in corporate capital expenditure. They ignored other transmission channels, continuing to model the economy according to the standard Keynesian tradition.

One problem with interest rates as a measure of the ease or tightness of policy is that they reflect both the supply of funds and the demand for funds, and whether rates are high or low depends on what is happening to supply *and* demand. In a typical case, easing monetary policy first leads to short rates falling as the supply of funds is raised relative to demand. However, as the economy recovers and monetary growth remains ample, the demand for funds rises relative to supply, and rates typically rise. Conversely, and this is the case for the last decade and a half in Japan, when monetary policy is tightened (as in 1989–91), the supply of funds is reduced as money growth slows and short term rates rise. But then as the economy weakens and goes into recession the demand for funds falls relative to supply, causing interest rates to fall even further. So the low level of rates in Japan in the 1990s reflected the weak demand for

---

[4] To compute the contribution of foreign assets to the base one should add the successive increases (or subtract decreases) to the monetary base in yen due to purchases (or sales) of total gold and foreign currency reserves, omitting interest earnings or changes due to valuation. This requires details of the composition of changes in Japan's foreign exchange reserves, which are unfortunately not available. Therefore total foreign exchange reserves have simply been translated at spot rates. This certainly overstates the contribution of foreign assets to the base. The domestic contribution to the base is obtained as a residual.

funds rather than any excess supply. Once deflation or the expectation of falling prices set in, far from falling, real rates started rising. By 1999 when nominal short term interest rates had reached virtually zero the BOJ's policy still could not revive the economy.

A further problem with this Keynesian theory of the interest rate transmission mechanism (as opposed to Keynes' own view of the transmission mechanism) was that the portfolio effect of monetary expansion on other assets was ignored. The result has been disastrous for Japan. One of the most important transmission channels for monetary policy (stressed by Keynes in the *Treatise on Money*) is through real, i.e. tangible asset prices (such as land, buildings, consumer durables, machinery and commodities) and their relation with financial asset prices, but this was omitted in the standard BOJ view. These assets comprise the majority of net worth in the economy, and represent the entire stock of collateral for the banking system. Their prices – and particularly their expected prices – have a huge influence on the capital markets and on economic activity. Based on expectations of the relative returns on financial and tangible assets, firms and households shift their entire portfolios. For example, the BOJ's monetary squeeze of 1989–91 (and subsequently) caused land prices to fall continuously during the 1990s, so total returns (capital returns plus rental yields, etc) from real estate and other tangible assets were negative. Not unnaturally, instead of buying real, tangible assets and promoting economic activity through these purchases, the Japanese have preferred to hold financial assets (bonds, deposits and cash). If the cost of loans (the long-term prime rate, as proxy for the return on financial assets) is compared with the change in land prices (as a proxy for total returns on tangibles) as in Figure 11.2, it is easy to see why Japanese companies have been struggling for the past decade.

L/T PRIME less CHANGE IN LAND PRICES
AVERAGE SPREAD
HIGH 25.07 14/8/92, LOW –29.91 14/8/87, LAST 5.44 15/2/05
HIGH 2.19 13/2/70, LOW 2.19 13/2/70, LAST 2.19 15/8/05

Figure 11.2   Japan: returns of financial assets (loans) and tangible (land prices)

Corporate assets are primarily tangibles while their liabilities are mainly bank borrowings and bonds. The average spread between the cost of borrowing and the return on land prices between 1990 and 2002 averaged 11.4% p.a. This is an enormously high cost when one considers that for capital market equilibrium the expected returns on tangibles and financial assets should be roughly equal. The high borrowing costs relative to the return on the tangibles not only undermined the incentive for Japanese companies to invest in new plant and equipment or hire new staff, but simultaneously discouraged investors from providing funds to the manufacturing sector because it inevitably implied a low return on equity. This was the main cause of Japan's high level of corporate failures, far more than any alleged need for restructuring.

Calculations of real interest rates based on nominal rates less the rate of change of the CPI or WPI massively understate the true cost of funds for Japan's battered corporate sector. Such rates fail to capture the debilitating effects of the BOJ's deflationary monetary policy on the expected returns from the whole range of tangible assets. Until the Bank of Japan once again makes it worthwhile to hold tangible assets, deflation will continue and Japanese companies and individuals will be reluctant to undertake spending on tangible assets that creates jobs, economic activity and returns to companies sufficient to drive the stock market up on a sustained basis. The only way to restore the relative expected returns on tangibles is for the Bank of Japan to reduce the relative expected returns on financial instruments. The only way to do that is to increase the supply of money on a sustained basis.

11.5.4   Monetary policy – quantitative expansion

After the Bank of Japan formally moved to zero interest rates combined with a quantitative expansion strategy in March 2001 its policies have essentially consisted of incremental increases in the monetary base, implemented by (1) regular monthly purchases of JGBs in the secondary market, or more variable purchases of (2) short-term financing bills, or (3) repos (repurchase arrangements which automatically unwind on expiry of each contract). When the BOJ buys any of these instruments the current accounts of commercial banks at the BOJ are credited by a corresponding amount, expanding the monetary base by a corresponding amount.

Under the quantitative easing phase of policy the monetary base initially increased rapidly. Between March 2001 and the end of April 2003 the monetary base (the sum of banknotes and banks' current account deposits (CADs) at the BOJ) increased from JPY60 trillion to JPY97 trillion, an increase of over 60%. The banknote component of the base grew more modestly, from JPY56 trillion to JPY69 trillion (+23%), while bankers' CADs increased sevenfold from JPY4 trillion to JPY28 trillion. More recently the growth of the base has slowed again as the BOJ ceased to push up the level of CADs. After the first phase of CAD expansion, the BOJs activism has dwindled, and policy has reverted from being pro-active to being incrementalist. Although at the time of writing the Japanese economy is experiencing a mild upswing, most of the upturn has been based on net export growth while domestic demand remains very weak. Deflation persists at the GDP deflator and CPI level.

Why has the quantitative expansion policy failed? What could have been done to enable it to succeed either earlier or now? In essence the BOJ could have moved much more assertively and consistently to expand reserves and hence money growth. Before the banking crisis of 1997 the scale of the expansionary measures required might have been within the normal parameters of measures taken in past deflations and recessions. After 1997 the magnitude of the problem became much greater as the money multiplier collapsed as a result of cash hoarding by the public and debt repayment by the corporate sector.

An alternative solution to Japan's deflation *would have been* for the Bank of Japan to engage in large-scale open market purchase operations (using JGBs or other instruments) just as the Federal Reserve did after 1933. US commercial bank reserves grew at 32% p.a. for the three years 1934–36, while M2 grew at 13.5% p.a. over the same period. If the BOJ had implemented such a policy from the early or mid-1990s it might have had some chance of success. The problem with this approach after 1997 was that by then the commercial banks' balance sheets were so impaired that the banks became reluctant either to lend to the private sector (for fear of further loan losses) or to lend to the government by buying JGBs (for fear that a successful reflation will push up bond yields and cause the banks capital losses on their bond portfolios). Consequently, even if the BOJ had injected substantial excess reserves into the banks' accounts at the BOJ by buying large amounts of JGBs, the excess current account balances would simply have remained in the banks' accounts at the BOJ and would not have been lent out.

Another way to say this is simply that the monetary multiplier (M2+CDs divided by the monetary base) halved from a range of 12–13 times at the beginning of the 1990s to just 6.4 times by the end of 2003. (The initial decline to below 10 occurred in the period up to 2001 and was driven by the actions of the banks and the non-bank public. After 2001 the BOJ-led increase in CADs pushed the multiplier down even more rapidly.) Consequently injections of base money by the BOJ were not being multiplied up into faster broad money growth. This was why, despite 30% growth of the monetary base in the year to March 2002, the money supply held by the public did not accelerate. As of March 2002, M2+CDs had increased just 3.8% year-on-year while broad money (M4) had grown by only 1.3% year-on-year.

The basic problem with the BOJ's quantitative strategy was that it was not aggressive enough, it was not sustained for long enough, and it completely failed to translate into any acceleration of the broader money supply, at least in the period 2001–04. As shown in Figure 11.3, following the disastrous move into negative growth in 1992–93, M2+CD growth has remained in the 2–5% range since 1994, and has recently shifted towards the bottom end of the range. Bank lending has been steadily falling since 1998. As a consequence it has been quite impossible for nominal GDP to grow at anything like a normal rate of about 5% p.a. (i.e. allowing 2–3% for real growth, with the balance permitting a low positive inflation rate, and some accumulation of money balances per unit of income). At the time of writing (in May 2005), M2+CDs had grown only 1.5% over the year while broad money (M4) had increased just 2.7%. Bank lending is still declining.

On a simple view one might have expected the Japanese economy eventually to adjust to mild deflation, and for the economy to start growing again in real terms at something close to its long run potential, just as the US did in the last quarter of the nineteenth century, or as the US and Japan did in the 1920's. However, because so much of the Japanese commercial banks' assets were collateralised against real estate and real estate prices kept falling, deflation has had a corrosive effect on the soundness of the banks' balance sheets, generating massive non-performing loans (NPLs) and making the banks unwilling to expand their lending to private sector borrowers.

A further key point that Japanese policy-makers overlooked was that monetary growth must not simply return to a *normal* growth rate (perhaps 6% p.a.), but initially there must be much

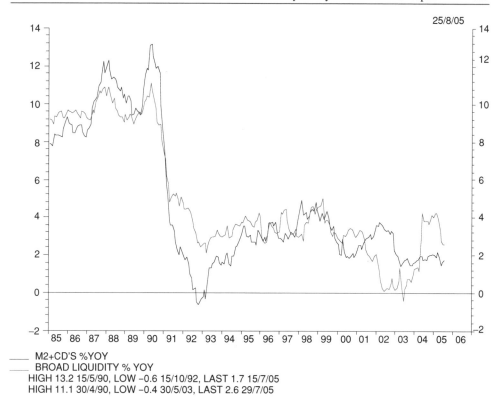

25/8/05

M2+CD'S %YOY
BROAD LIQUIDITY % YOY
HIGH 13.2 15/5/90, LOW −0.6 15/10/92, LAST 1.7 15/7/05
HIGH 11.1 30/4/90, LOW −0.4 30/5/03, LAST 2.6 29/7/05

Figure 11.3   Japan: M2+CDS and broad liquidity % YOY

faster money growth. The reason is that just as hyperinflation *lowers* the demand for real money balances, intensifying the inflation as people try to spend their depreciating money balances, so deflation *raises* the demand for real money balances, intensifying the deflation as firms and individuals hoard appreciating cash (instead of spending it) in anticipation of lower prices later. To overcome this inertia, the Bank of Japan needs to increase money growth at a much faster rate initially, but there has been a marked unwillingness to undertake such fundamental measures. Invariably such proposals are dismissed as unorthodox, and therefore inapplicable. In reality they are only a logical and necessary response to the underlying conditions in Japan. Consequently Japan continues to muddle along with sub-par growth rates and continuing deflation, interrupted only by the temporary impact of occasional government spending programmes and periodic upturns in the global business cycle. Until Japan adopts and succeeds in enforcing a more vigorous programme of quantitative monetary expansion it is unlikely that we shall see a full-fledged recovery of the Japanese economy.

Maybe, just maybe there are starting to be signs that current monetary policy is starting to succeed (e.g. land prices are reported to be recovering in some parts of Tokyo), but as the example of the US in the 1930s shows (see below, Alternative Monetary Solutions), the policy will need to be in place for several years before full-fledged recovery can reasonably be expected.

11.6   MONETARY POLICY – DELIBERATE YEN DEPRECIATION

We now turn to cover two monetary solutions to Japan's deflation which were either categorically rejected by the Japanese authorities or never even contemplated.

Throughout the period 1990–95 the yen was appreciating, exacerbating the effects of the downturn in domestic demand by making any export-led recovery more problematic. From a level of 160 yen per US$ the currency appreciated continuously until it hit 83 in April 1995. To begin with the Japanese authorities did not intervene to prevent or slow the appreciation. However, from early 1993 dollar purchases increased sharply, taking Japan's foreign exchange reserves from US$69 billion at the start of 1993 to US$153 billion in April 1995, and US$220 billion by the end of 1997. As explained above (Section 11.2) it was normal in Japan for all these purchases to be automatically sterilized. But as in the period 1985–89 it should have been possible for the BOJ to pursue an expansionary policy. Instead the BOJ allowed the low rate of money growth to persist, and, despite their scale, the BOJ's foreign currency purchases failed to prevent the yen appreciating. In addition, from 1994 onwards the on-going deflation was continuously making Japan more competitive on a purchasing power parity basis at any given exchange rate.

However, from April 1995 the yen abruptly weakened from its peak of 83, falling to 147 yen per US$ in mid-1998. This could have been taken as a heaven-sent opportunity to promote an export-led recovery, but 1997–98 saw the onset of the Asian financial crisis when numerous smaller Asian economies devalued their currencies, and the Japanese authorities were anxious not to be seen to allow their currency to be involved in a competitive spiral of devaluations. Indeed, in April 1998 the authorities intervened on the other side of the market, selling dollars and buying yen to prevent further depreciation.

In the second half of 1998 the yen recovered and continued appreciating through most of 1999 to a level approaching 100 yen per US$. Apart from one further episode of yen weakness in late 2001 and early 2002 when the yen reached 133 per US$, subsequent fluctuations (up to 2005) have been more modest and the Japanese authorities have shown a tendency to intervene decisively only if the currency has threatened to move outside the range 120–100. For example during the yen appreciation of 2002–04 the authorities intervened strongly, taking Japan's foreign exchange reserves from $400 billion in January 2004 to $840 billion by the end of 2004. In effect the yen is now free to float but only within limits (which may be altered from time to time).

One solution to Japan's monetary deflation would be for the BOJ to buy foreign exchange in very large quantities, driving down the yen in the process. I have long favoured this proposal for unsterilised intervention (Greenwood, 2000) and it has more recently been advocated by Professor Lars Svennson (2003) but unfortunately it stands almost no prospect of being implemented on account of the huge opposition it would provoke from other governments and central banks, particularly in Asia and in Washington. It is possible that the excess reserves of the banks resulting from the purchases of dollars and sale of yen by the BOJ might not be lent out. Nevertheless, there can be little doubt that any large-scale yen depreciation, by reinvigorating Japan's export sector, would provide attractive lending opportunities for Japan's banks. This would have enhanced profitability in the exporting sector, encouraged bank lending to exporters, and gradually this lending would have percolated through the economy until the growth of the quantity of money in Japan was sufficient to stimulate domestic demand. Moreover, once the economy had started to recover, the yen would surely appreciate again. The choice here is between a temporarily weak yen with a recovering

Japanese economy, and a permanently strong yen with a permanently stagnant Japanese economy.

The policy would also necessitate the Bank of Japan and the Ministry of Finance abandoning their standard practice of sterilising foreign exchange purchases. In this context it needs to be emphasised that although the Bank of Japan gained nominal independence in April 1999, that independence is essentially meaningless. In reality the fact that foreign exchange policy remains in the hands of the Ministry of Finance means that if the MOF's desired trading range for the currency is not compatible with an easy domestic monetary policy, it is domestic monetary policy that will ultimately be sacrificed. 'For fiat money systems the relevant analytical point is that, from a long-run perspective money stock and exchange rate paths cannot be independently controlled or managed, as a consequence of the neutrality of money' (McCallum, 2001).

11.7 MONETARY POLICY – GOVERNMENT BORROWING FROM THE BANKS

The other option that has never really been contemplated by the Japanese authorities would have been to increase the money supply directly by changing the government's funding strategy. Instead of issuing JGBs, the government could have borrowed directly from the commercial banks. This would have had the advantage of putting on the books of the banks assets that were not subject to a capital risk (like JGBs), and from the banks' point of view the borrower was creditworthy. With the proceeds the government could have purchased JGBs from the secondary market (i.e. from insurance companies and pension funds etc.), thus putting deposits (= money supply) into the hands of institutional investors who in turn would have been induced at some point to spend the money on higher-earning assets such as bonds, equities or real estate. In time the normal effects of faster money growth would have resulted in faster spending growth on goods and services. From the government's point of view total government debt would not have been increased because the stock of JGBs would have declined while loans from banks would have seen a matching increase. For historical and constitutional reasons however, there would no doubt have been huge opposition to this proposal in Japan, so we should not count on its early adoption. (The immediate post war hyperinflation of 1945–49 is widely associated with direct government borrowing – in that case from the BOJ – and although the Bank of Japan Law prohibits such government borrowing from the BOJ, there seems no reason in principle why the government should not borrow from the commercial banks in the form of loans rather than JGBs.)

By borrowing from the banks, the government achieves an expansion of banks' balance sheets. In turn the government could use the proceeds of its borrowing to buy back JGB's in the market (from insurance companies, pension funds and others), thus transferring the funds raised by the government's borrowing into private hands, and hence increasing the money supply. From the banks' viewpoint, they would have a safe, but low-yielding asset. From the government's viewpoint there would be no increase in the total amount of government borrowing, only a change in the composition of its borrowing as total JGB's outstanding would decline but total government debt (including borrowing from the banks) would be unchanged. And the non-bank public would now own deposits (that are part of the money supply), which they would want to invest in bonds or equities or other assets (to raise returns), thus triggering an initial round of portfolio adjustment as part of the standard monetary transmission process.

In the simplified, consolidated balance sheet below (Step 1), the government borrows JPY50 trillion and acquires a deposit of JPY50 trillion. At this point the money supply has not increased because government deposits are not part of the money supply. The deposits of JPY519 trillion constitute 90% of M2+CDs.

Japanese Commercial Bank Balance
Sheets (Proposed Step 1) Yen tn.

• Deposits at BOJ	27	• Deposits of non-bank	
• Loans to firms &		public	519
individuals	447	• **Government**	
• **Loans to**		**Deposits**	**50**
Government	**50**		
• JGB's	77		
• Other securities	94	• Other liabilities	239
• Other assets	113	• Total Liabilities & Net	
• Total Assets	808	Worth	808

In Step 2 the government has used its JPY50 trillion of deposits to buy back or redeem JGB's from the market. To pay for these securities, it draws down its newly acquired bank deposits (from Step 1), making payments to the sellers of JGB's (mainly Life Insurance Companies, Pension Funds and the like). Collectively non-bank institutions or individuals now hold Y569 tn, or an additional JPY50 trillion of deposits. Not only are these new deposits in excess of the desired holdings of individuals and institutions, but the deposits are likely to have very low or near-zero yields. This calls for a process of portfolio rebalancing, and would trigger spending on portfolio investments or new lending by those individuals, firms or institutions. (Insurance companies are substantial lenders of funds in the Japanese market.) Such portfolio shifts would surely bring about the renewed spending on securities, real estate, durables or other assets that would in time raise overall spending on goods and services, or nominal and real GDP.

Japanese Commercial Bank Balance
Sheets (Proposed Step 2) Yen tn.

• Deposits at BOJ	27	• **Deposits of non-bank**	
• Loans to firms &		**public**	**519**
individuals	447	• **Government**	
• **Loans to**		**Deposits**	0
Government	**50**		
• JGB's	77		
• Other securities	94	• Other liabilities	239
• Other assets	113	• Total Liabilities & Net	
• Total Assets	808	Worth	808

What rate of monetary growth is required to restore Japanese economic growth and end deflation of asset prices or goods and service prices?

Just as it required both devaluation *and* substantial acceleration of monetary growth to revive the US, the UK and Japanese economies from their depressions in the early 1930's, it probably requires the same combination of medicine to overcome Japan's deflation today. One reason is that not only must the authorities create enough money for normal growth with low positive inflation plus an amount to compensate for annual declines in velocity, but in addition an extra boost is required to overcome the tendency (explained above) to accumulate excess money balances under deflation. Initially double digit money growth may be necessary for two or three years.

Without this extra monetary growth Japan continues to muddle along with sub-par growth rates and continuing deflation, relieved only by the temporary impact of fiscal spending programmes or export booms. Until Japan adopts a more vigorous programme of quantitative monetary expansion it is unlikely that we shall see a full-fledged recovery of the Japanese economy.

11.8   RESTRUCTURING POLICIES

Once Japan had lapsed into recession and deflation in the mid 1990s there was a constant debate among the Japanese authorities on whether to implement structural reforms first or monetary expansion first.

Many criticisms can be directed at the Japanese authorities for their failure at different times to implement meaningful reform and restructuring programmes. To take just one example, in resolving the bad loan problem of the banks there are various models that could have been followed, such as the creation of the Resolution Trust Corporation (RTC) in the US in the wake of the savings and loan crisis in the late 1980s. This system saw the vigorous acquisition and disposal of the bad debts of the S&Ls together with any underlying collateral by the RTC. The bad loans were then securitised and sold into the market, as was the underlying collateral – mainly real estate – which ended up in the hands of new, solvent owners. The losses were absorbed – ultimately – by taxpayers. The crux of this programme was the creation of a liquid market in former S&L assets, and a liquid market in the underlying real estate. But in Japan there was huge opposition to forcing companies and individuals into bankruptcy; the development of the capital market instruments needed to create such liquid markets in securitised bank loans was slow to take off; few Japanese were willing to acknowledge and crystallise the loss on their real estate; and there was widespread opposition to the idea that taxpayers should bail out banks and their shareholders.

Until the appointment of Mr Takenaka as head of the Financial Services Agency by Mr Koizumi in October 2002 the Japanese government has consistently backed away from such a radical restructuring programme. Weak attempts were made to try to reform Japan's banking system over the past decade, but until recently with little impact on management practices, on lending policies, or return on equity. The resistance is deeply ingrained and could take years – if not decades – to overcome. The major problems are both cultural (such as the unwillingness to enforce bankruptcy and a reluctance to curtail lending to a long-standing customer) and technical (such as the unwillingness to recognise non-performing loans). Takenaka has addressed the regulatory forbearance by tightening the rules on loan loss recognition and encouraging consolidation in the banking sector, but the political climate may not long support such changes if a monetary expansion that eases many of these problems is not forthcoming.

As land and stock prices fell further and further the extent of the bad debt problems worsened and the apparent need for structural reforms became more urgent, but the implementation of such reforms has also become more difficult. Insofar as the bad debt problems of the banks, the bankruptcies in the corporate and personal sector, the continued weakness of consumption and investment spending and falling land and equity prices are all *symptoms* of monetary deflation caused by a growth rate of money which is too slow for Japan's economy, the obvious solution is to reflate the economy. But the impaired state of bank and corporate balance sheets has made this simple prescription unworkable, particularly after 1997. It was not simply that interest rates had reached the zero bound. The problems of indebtedness and the unwillingness of households and firms to take on any additional debt meant that the normal transmission mechanism of monetary policy had become inoperable. As explained above, the continuing decline in bank lending, the reluctance of the banks to buy long-term government debt and the collapse of the monetary multiplier all meant that even very large injections of base money could not be guaranteed to produce a resurgence of monetary growth. The banks need to be confident that there are solvent borrowers who can repay their loans. This is the basis of the proposals outlined in section 11.6 (deliberately depreciating the yen) and section 11.7 (replacing lending to the private sector with lending to the government).

11.9 CONCLUSION

The broad conclusion is that Japan requires first and foremost monetary reflation. Structural reforms are secondary to the need for eliminating deflation. However, given the breakdown of the normal transmission mechanism (through additional bank lending to the private sector or bank purchases of government bonds), exceptional measures will still be needed to achieve a sustained recovery and an end to deflation. Those exceptional monetary measures discussed in sections 11.6 (deliberate depreciation of the yen) and 11.7 (government funding by direct borrowing from the commercial banks) of this chapter are straightforward to describe, but are likely to encounter widespread opposition both abroad (in the first case) and at home (in the second case). However, in the absence of such measures being adopted there can be no guarantee – on Japan's current course – that monetary growth will recover sufficiently to put an end to deflation.

REFERENCES

Greenwood, J. (2000) No, the BOJ Shouldn't Raise Rates, *The Asian Wall Street Journal*, July 17.
Keynes, J.M. (1930) *A Treatise on Money*, London: Macmillan.
Kuroda, H. (2002). Japan in the Global Economy, speech at Chatham House, London, June.
McCallum, B.T. (2001) Japanese Monetary Policy Again, Shadow Open Market Committee website, October.
Suzuki, Y. (1980) *Money and Banking in Contemporary Japan* New Haven: Yale University Press.
Svensson, L.E.O. (2003) Escaping from a Liquidity Trap and Deflation: The Foolproof Way and Others, *Journal of Economic Perspectives*, **17(4)**, 145–166.

Appendix 1
Unemployment versus Inflation? An Evaluation of the Phillips Curve

Milton Friedman[1]

FISHER AND PHILLIPS

The discussion of the Phillips curve started with truth in 1926, proceeded through error some 30 years later, and by now has returned back to 1926 and to the original truth. That is about 50 years for a complete circuit. You can see how technological development has speeded up the process of both producing and dissipating ignorance.

I choose the year 1926 not at random but because in that year Irving Fisher published an article in the *International Labour Review* under the title 'A Statistical Relation between Unemployment and Price Changes'.[2]

The Fisher approach

Fisher's article dealt with precisely the same empirical phenomenon that Professor A.W. Phillips analysed in his celebrated article in *Economica* some 32 years later.[3] Both were impressed with the empirical observation that inflation tended to be associated with low levels of unemployment and deflation with high levels. One amusing item in Fisher's article from a very different point of view is that he starts out by saying that he has been so deeply interested in this subject that 'during the last three years in particular I have had at least one computer in my office almost constantly at work on this project'[4] Of course what he meant was a human being operating a calculating machine.

There was, however, a crucial difference between Fisher's analysis and Phillips', between the truth of 1926 and the error of 1958, which had to do with the direction of causation. Fisher took *the rate of change of prices* to be the independent variable that set the process going. In his words,

> When the dollar is losing value, or in other words when the price level is rising, a business man finds his receipts rising as fast, on the average, as this general rise of prices, but not his expenses, because his expenses consist, to a large extent, of things which are contractually fixed . . . Employment is then stimulated – for a time at least.[5]

---

[1] This paper was first published by the IEA as Occasional Paper 44 in 1975. Reproduced with permission of the IEA.
[2] June 1926, pp. 785–92. It was reprinted in the *Journal of Political Economy*, March/April, 1973, pp. 496–502.
[3] 'The Relation between Unemployment and the Rate of Change of Money Wage Rates in the United Kingdom, 1861–1957', *Economica*, November 1958, pp. 283–99.
[4] Fisher, *op. cit.*, p. 786.
[5] *Ibid.*, p. 787.

Issues in Monetary Policy. Edited by K. Matthews and P. Booth.
© 2006 John Wiley & Sons, Ltd.

To elaborate his analysis and express it in more modern terms, let anything occur that produces a higher level of spending – or, more precisely, a higher rate of increase in spending than was anticipated. Producers would at first interpret the faster rate of increase in spending as an increase in real demand for their product. The producers of shoes, hats, or coats would discover that apparently there was an increase in the amount of goods they could sell at pre-existing prices. No one of them would know at first whether the change was affecting him in particular or whether it was general. In the first instance, each producer would be tempted to expand output, as Fisher states, and also to allow prices to rise. But at first much or most of the unanticipated increase in nominal demand (i.e. demand expressed in £s) would be absorbed by increases (or faster increases) in employment and output rather than by increases (or faster increases) in prices. Conversely, for whatever reason, let the rate of spending slow down, or rise less rapidly than was anticipated, and each individual producer would in the first instance interpret the slow-down at least partly as reflecting something peculiar to him. The result would be partly a slow-down in output and a rise in unemployment and partly a slow-down in prices.

Fisher was describing a *dynamic* process arising out of fluctuations in the rate of spending about some average trend or norm. He went out of his way to emphasise the importance of distinguishing between 'high and low prices on the one hand and the rise and fall of prices on the other'.[6] He put it that way because he was writing at a time when a stable level of prices was taken to be the norm. Were he writing today, he would emphasise the distinction between the rate of inflation and changes in the rate of inflation. (And perhaps some future writer will have to emphasise the difference between the second and the third derivatives!) The important distinction – and it is quite clear that this is what Fisher had in mind – is between *anticipated* and *unanticipated* changes.

The Phillips approach

Professor Phillips' approach was from exactly the opposite direction. He took the level of *employment* to be the independent variable that set the process going. He treated the rate of change of wages as the dependent variable. His argument was a very simple analysis – I hesitate to say simple-minded, but so it has proved – in terms of *static supply* and demand conditions. He said:

> When the demand for a commodity or service is high relatively to the supply of it we expect the price to rise, the rate of rise being greater the greater the excess demand . . . It seems plausible that this principle should operate as one of the factors determining the rate of change of money wage rates, which are the price of labour services.[7]

Phillips' approach is based on the usual (*static*) demand and supply curves as illustrated in Figure A.1. At the point of intersection, 0, the market is in equilibrium at the wage rate W_0, with the amount of labour employed E_0 equal to the amount of labour demanded. Unemployment is zero – which is to say, as measured, equal to 'frictional' or 'transitional' unemployment, or to use the terminology I adopted some years ago from Wicksell, at its 'natural' rate. At this point, says Phillips, there is no upward pressure on wages. Consider instead the point F, where the quantity of labour demanded is higher than the quantity supplied. There is over-employment, wages at W_F are below the equilibrium level, and there will be upward pressure on them. At

---

[6] *Ibid.*, p. 788.
[7] Phillips, op. cit., p. 283.

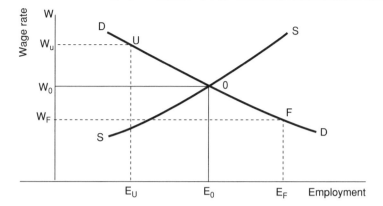

Figure A.1

point U, there is unemployment, W_U is above the equilibrium wage rate and there is downward pressure. The larger the discrepancy between the quantity of labour demanded and the quantity supplied, the stronger the pressure and hence the more rapidly wages will rise or fall.

Phillips translated this analysis into an observable relation by plotting the level of unemployment on one axis, and the rate of change of wages over time on the other, as in Figure A.2. Point E_0 corresponds to point 0 in Figure A.1. Unemployment is at its 'natural' rate so wages are stable (or in a growing economy, rising at a rate equal to the rate of productivity growth). Point F corresponds to 'over-full' employment, so wages are rising; point U to unemployment, so wages are falling.

Fisher talked about price changes, Phillips about wage changes, but I believe that for our purpose that is not an important distinction. Both Fisher and Phillips took it for granted that wages are a major component of total cost and that prices and wages would tend to move together. So both of them tended to go very readily from rates of wage change to rates of price change and I shall do so as well.

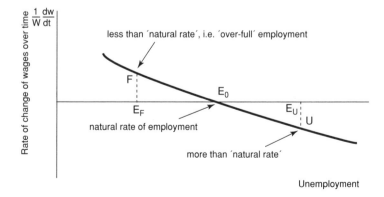

Figure A.2

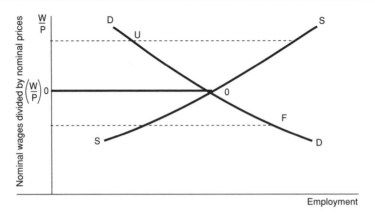

Figure A.3

The fallacy in Phillips

Phillips' analysis seems very persuasive and obvious, yet it is utterly fallacious. It is fallacious because no economic theorist has ever asserted that the demand and supply of labour were functions of the *nominal* wage rate (i.e. wage rate expressed in £s). Every economic theorist from Adam Smith to the present would have told you that the vertical axis in Figure A.1 should refer not to the *nominal* wage rate but to the *real* wage rate.

But once you label the vertical axis $\frac{W}{P}$ as in Figure A.3, the graph has nothing to say about what is going to happen to *nominal wages* or prices. There is not even any *prima facie* presumption that it has anything to say. For example, consider point 0 in Figure A.3. At that level of employment, there is neither upward nor downward pressure on the real wage. But that real wage can remain constant with W and P separately *constant*, or with W and P each *rising* at the rate of 10 per cent a year, or *falling* at the rate of 10 per cent a year, or doing anything else, provided both change at the *same* rate.

THE KEYNESIAN CONFUSION BETWEEN NOMINAL AND REAL WAGES

How did a sophisticated mind like Phillips' – and he was certainly a highly sophisticated and subtle economist – come to confuse nominal wages with real wages? He was led to do so by the general intellectual climate that had been engendered by the Keynesian revolution. From this point of view, the essential element of the Keynesian revolution was the assumption that prices are highly rigid relative to output so that a change in demand of the kind considered by Fisher would be reflected almost entirely in *output* and very little in prices. The price level could be regarded as an institutional datum. The simple way to interpret Phillips is that he was therefore assuming the change in nominal wages to be equal to the change in real wages.

But that is not really what he was saying. What he was saying was slightly more sophisticated. It was that changes in *anticipated* nominal wages were equal to changes in *anticipated* real wages. There were two components of the Keynesian system that were essential to his construction: first, the notion that prices are rigid in the sense that people in planning their behaviour do not allow for the possibility that the price level might change, and hence regard a change in nominal wages or nominal prices as a change in real wages and real prices; second, that real wages *ex post* could be altered by *unanticipated* inflation. Indeed the whole Keynesian argument for the possibility of a full employment policy arose out of the supposition that it was possible to get workers (at least in the 1930s when Keynes wrote *The General Theory*) to accept lower real wages produced by inflation that they would not have accepted in the direct form of a reduction in nominal wages.[8]

These two components imply a sharp distinction between *anticipated* nominal and real wages and *actual* nominal and real wages. In the Keynesian climate of the time, it was natural for Phillips to take this distinction for granted, and to regard anticipated nominal and real wages as moving together.

I do not criticise Phillips for doing this. Science is possible only because at any one time there is a body of conventions or views or ideas that are taken for granted and on which scientists build. If each individual writer were to go back and question all the premises that underlie what he is doing, nobody would ever get anywhere. I believe that some of the people who have followed in his footsteps deserve much more criticism than he does for not noting the importance of this theoretical point once it was pointed out to them.

At any rate, it was this general intellectual climate that led Phillips to think in terms of nominal rather than real wages. The intellectual climate was also important in another direction. The Keynesian system, as everybody knows, is incomplete. It lacks an equation. A major reason for the prompt and rapid acceptance of the Phillips curve approach was the widespread belief that it provided the missing equation that connected the real system with the monetary system. In my opinion, this belief is false. What is needed to complete the Keynesian system is an equation that determines the equilibrium price level. But the Phillips curve deals with the relation between a rate of change of prices or wages and the level of unemployment. It does not determine an equilibrium price level. At any rate, the Phillips curve was widely accepted and was seized on immediately for policy purposes.[9] It is still widely used for this purpose as supposedly describing a 'trade-off', from a policy point of view, between inflation and unemployment.

It was said that what the Phillips curve means is that we are faced with a choice. If we choose a low level of inflation, say, stable prices, we shall have to reconcile ourselves to a high level of unemployment. If we choose a low level of unemployment, we shall have to reconcile ourselves to a high rate of inflation.

REACTION AGAINST THE KEYNESIAN SYSTEM

Three developments came along in this historical account to change attitudes and to raise some questions.

One was the general theoretical reaction against the Keynesian system which brought out into the open the fallacy in the original Phillips curve approach of identifying nominal with real wages.

---

[8] J.M. Keynes, *The General Theory of Employment, Interest, and Money* (Macmillan, 1936): 'Whilst workers will usually resist a reduction of money wages, it is not their practice to withdraw their labour whenever there is a rise in the price of wage-goods' (p. 9). '...The workers, though unconsciously, are instinctively more reasonable economists than the classical school...They resist reductions of money-wages...whereas they do not resist reductions of real wages' (p. 14). '...Since no trade union would dream of striking on every occasion of a rise in the cost of living, they do not raise the obstacle to any increase in aggregate employment attributed to them by the classical school' (p. 15).

[9] For example, Albert Rees, 'The Phillips Curve as a Menu for Policy Choices', *Economica*, August 1970, pp. 227–38, explicitly considers the objections to a stable Phillips curve outlined below, yet concludes that there remains a trade-off that should be exploited. He writes: 'The strongest policy conclusion I can draw from the expectations literature is that the policy makers should not attempt to operate at a single point on the Phillips curve...Rather, they should permit fluctuations in unemployment within a band' (p. 238).

The second development was the failure of the Phillips curve relation to hold for other bodies of data. Fisher had found it to hold for the United States for the period before 1925; Phillips had found it to hold for Britain for a long period. But, lo and behold, when people tried it for any other place they never obtained good results. Nobody was able to construct a decent empirical Phillips curve for other circumstances. I may be exaggerating a bit – no doubt there are other successful cases; but certainly a large number of attempts were unsuccessful.

The third and most recent development is the emergence of 'stagflation', which rendered somewhat ludicrous the confident statements that many economists had made about 'trade-offs', based on empirically-fitted Phillips curves.

Short- and long-run Phillips curves

The empirical failures and the theoretical reaction produced an attempt to rescue the Phillips curve approach by distinguishing a short-run from a long-run Phillips curve. Because both potential employers and potential employees envisage an implicit or explicit employment contract covering a fairly long period, both must guess in advance what real wage will correspond to a given nominal wage. Both therefore must form anticipations about the future price level. The real wage rate that is plotted on the vertical axis of the demand and supply curve diagram is thus not the *current* real wage but the *anticipated* real wage. If we suppose that anticipations about the price level are slow to change, while the nominal wage can change rapidly and is known with little time-lag, we can, for *short* periods, revert essentially to Phillips' original formulation, except that the equilibrium position is no longer a constant nominal wage, but a nominal wage changing at the same rate as the anticipated rate of change in prices (plus, for a growing economy, the anticipated rate of change in productivity). Changes in demand and supply will then show up first in a changed rate of change of nominal wages, which will mean also in anticipated real wages. Current prices may adjust as rapidly as or more rapidly than wages, so real wages *actually* received may move in the opposite direction from nominal wages, but *anticipated* real wages will move in the same direction.

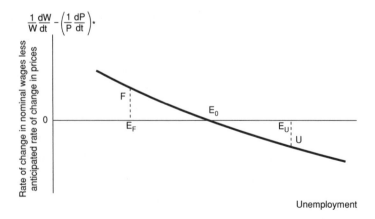

Figure A.2   revised

One way to put this in terms of the Phillips curve is to plot on the vertical axis not the change in nominal wages but that change minus the anticipated rate of change in prices, as in the revised Figure A.2, where $(\frac{1}{P}\frac{dP}{dt})^*$, standing for the anticipated rate of change in prices, is subtracted from $\frac{1}{W}\frac{dW}{dt}$. This curve now tells a story much more like Fisher's original story than Phillips'. Suppose, to start with, the economy is at point E_0, with both prices and wages stable (abstracting from growth). Suppose something, say, a monetary expansion, starts nominal aggregate demand growing, which in turn produces a rise in prices and wages at the rate of, say, 2 per cent per year. Workers will initially interpret this as a rise in their real wage – because they still anticipate constant prices – and so will be willing to offer more labour (move up their supply curve), i.e. employment grows and unemployment falls. Employers may have the same anticipations as workers about the general price level, but they are more directly concerned about the price of the products they are producing and far better informed about that. They will initially interpret a rise in the demand for and price of their product as a rise in its relative price and as implying a fall in the real wage rate they must pay measured in terms of their product. They will therefore be willing to hire more labour (move down their demand curve). The combined result is a movement, say, to point F, which corresponds with 'over-full' employment, with nominal wages rising at 2 per cent per year.

But, as time passes, both employers and employees come to recognise that prices *in general* are rising. As Abraham Lincoln said, 'You can fool all of the people some of the time, you can fool some of the people all of the time, but you can't fool all of the people all of the time.' As a result, they raise their estimate of the anticipated rate of inflation, which reduces the rate of rise of anticipated real wages, and leads you to slide down the curve back ultimately to the point E_0. There is thus a *short-run* 'trade-off' between inflation and unemployment, but *no long-run* 'trade-off'.

By incorporating price anticipations into the Phillips curve as I have just done, I have implicitly begged one of the main issues in the recent controversy about the Phillips curve. Thanks to recent experience of 'stagflation' plus theoretical analysis, everyone now admits that the apparent short-run Phillips curve is misleading and seriously overstates the *short*-run trade-off, but many are not willing to accept the view that the *long*-run trade-off is *zero*.

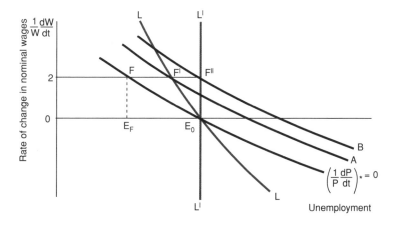

Figure A.4

We can examine this issue by using a different way of incorporating price anticipations into the Phillips curve. Figure 4 keeps the rate of change of nominal wages on the vertical axis but contains a series of different curves, one for each anticipated rate of growth of wages. To put it algebraically, instead of writing the Phillips curve relation as

$$\frac{1}{W}\frac{dW}{dt} - \left(\frac{1}{P}\frac{dP}{dt}\right)^* = f(U), \tag{A1.1}$$

where U is unemployment, we can write it in more general form as

$$\frac{1}{W}\frac{dW}{dt} = f\left[U, \left(\frac{1}{P}\frac{dP}{dt}\right)^*\right] \tag{A1.2}$$

Now suppose something occurs to put the economy at point F at which wages are rising at 2 per cent a year and unemployment is less than the natural rate. Then, as people adjust their expectations of inflation, the short-run Phillips curve will shift upwards and the final resting place would be on that short-run Phillips curve at which the anticipated rate of inflation equals the current rate. The issue now becomes whether that Phillips curve is like A, so that the long-run curve is negatively sloping, like LL, in which case an anticipated rate of inflation of 2 per cent will still reduce the level of unemployment, though not by as much as an unanticipated rate of 2 per cent, or whether it is like B, so that the long-run curve is *vertical*, that is, unemployment is the *same* at a 2 per cent anticipated rate of inflation as at a zero per cent anticipated rate.

NO LONG-RUN MONEY ILLUSION

In my Presidential Address to the American Economic Association seven years ago, I argued that the long-run Phillips curve was vertical, largely on the grounds I have already sketched here: in effect, the absence of any long-run money illusion.[10] At about the same time, Professor E.S. Phelps, now of Columbia University, offered the same hypothesis, on different though related grounds.[11] This hypothesis has come to be called the 'accelerationist' hypothesis or the 'natural rate' hypothesis. It has been called accelerationist because a policy of trying to hold unemployment below the horizontal intercept of the long-run vertical Phillips curve must lead to an *accelerated* inflation.

Suppose, beginning at point E_0, on Figure A.4, when nobody anticipated any inflation, it is decided to aim at a lower unemployment level, say E_F. This can be done initially by producing an inflation of 2 per cent, as shown by moving along the Phillips curve corresponding to anticipations of no inflation. But, as we have seen, the economy will not stay at F because people's anticipations will shift, and if the rate of inflation were kept at 2 per cent, the economy would be driven back to the level of unemployment it started with. The only way unemployment can be kept below the 'natural rate' is by an *ever-accelerating* inflation, which always keeps current inflation ahead of anticipated inflation. Any resemblance between that analysis and what you in Britain have been observing in practice is not coincidental: what recent British governments have tried to do is to keep unemployment below the natural rate, and to do so they

---

[10] 'The Role of Monetary Policy', *American Economic Review*, March 1968, pp. 1–17.
[11] 'Money Wage Dynamics and Labour Market Equilibrium', in E.S. Phelps (ed.), *Microeconomic Foundations of Employment and Inflation Theory*, Norton Press, New York, 1970.

have had to accelerate inflation – from 3.9 per cent in 1964 to 16.0 per cent in 1974, according to your official statistics.[12, 13]

Misunderstandings about the 'natural rate' of unemployment

The hypothesis came to be termed the 'natural rate' hypothesis because of the emphasis on the natural rate of unemployment. The term 'the natural rate' has been misunderstood. It does not refer to some *irreducible minimum* of unemployment. It refers rather to that rate of employment which is consistent with the *existing* real *conditions* in the labour market. It can be lowered by removing obstacles in the labour market, by reducing friction. It can be raised by introducing additional obstacles. The purpose of the concept is to separate the monetary from the non-monetary aspects of the employment situation – precisely the same purpose that Wicksell had in using the word 'natural' in connection with the rate of interest.

In the past few years, a large number of statistical studies have investigated the question of whether the long-run Phillips curve is or is not vertical. That dispute is still in train.

Most of the statistical tests were undertaken by rewriting Equation (A1.2) in the form:

$$\frac{1}{W}\frac{dW}{dt} = a + b\left(\frac{1}{p}\frac{dP}{dt}\right)^{*} + f(U) \qquad\qquad (A1.3)$$

or

$$\frac{1}{P}\frac{dP}{dt} = a + b\left(\frac{1}{p}\frac{dP}{dt}\right)^{*} + f(U),$$

where the left-hand side was either the rate of change of wages or the rate of change of prices. The question then asked was what is the value of b.[14] The original Phillips curve essentially assumed b = 0; the acceleration hypothesis set b equal to 1. The authors of the various tests I am referring to used observed data, mostly time-series data, to estimate the numerical value of b.[15] Almost every such test has come out with a numerical value of b less than 1, implying that there is a long-run 'trade-off'.[16] However, there are a number of difficulties with these tests, some on a rather superficial level, others on a much more fundamental level.

One obvious statistical problem is that the statistically fitted curves have not been the same for different periods of fit and have produced very unreliable extrapolations for periods subsequent to the period of fit. So it looks very much as if the statistical results are really measuring a short-term relationship despite the objective. The key problem here is that, in order to make the statistical test, it is necessary to have some measure of the anticipated rate of inflation. Hence,

---

[12] United Kingdom General Index of Retail Prices, *Department of Employment Gazette.*

[13] It is worth noting that the annual rate of inflation peaked at over 26 per cent and the annualised monthly rate at over 66 per cent after this paper was originally published.

[14] This is the coefficient on the anticipated rate of inflation, that is, the percentage point change in the current rate of change in wages or in prices that would result from a 1 percentage point change in the anticipated rate of inflation.

[15] I might note as an aside that one much-noticed attempt along these lines was contained in lectures given in Britain by Robert Solow a few years ago (*Price Expectations and the Behaviour of the Price Level*, Manchester University Press, 1969). Unfortunately, his test has a fatal flaw which renders it irrelevant to the current issue. In order to allow for costs as well as demand, he included on the right-hand side of an equation like Equation (3) the rate of change of wages, and, on the left-hand side, the rate of change of prices. In such an equation, there is no reason to expect b to be unity even on the strictest acceleration hypothesis, because the equation is then an equation to determine what happens to the margin between prices and wages. Let the anticipated rate of inflation rise by one percentage point, but the rate of change of wages be held constant, and any resulting rise in prices raises the excess of prices over costs and so stimulates output. Hence, in Solow's equation, the strict acceleration hypothesis would imply that b was less than 1.

[16] A succinct summary of these studies is in S.J. Turnovsky, 'On the Role of Inflationary Expectations in a Short-Run Macro-Economic Model', *Economic Journal*, June 1974, pp. 317–37, especially pp. 326–27.

every such test is a joint test of the accelerationist hypothesis and a particular hypothesis about the formation of anticipations.

THE ADAPTIVE EXPECTATIONS HYPOTHESIS

Most of these statistical tests embody the so-called adaptive expectations hypothesis, which has worked well in many problems. It states that anticipations are revised on the basis of the difference between the current rate of inflation and the anticipated rate. If the anticipated rate was, say, 5 per cent but the current rate 10 per cent, the anticipated rate will be revised upward by some fraction of the difference between 10 and 5. As is well known, this implies that the anticipated rate of inflation is an exponentially weighted average of past rates of inflation, the weights declining as one goes back in time.

Even on their own terms, then, these results are capable of two different interpretations. One is that the long-run Phillips curve is not vertical but has a negative slope. The other is that this has not been a satisfactory method of evaluating people's expectations for this purpose.

A somewhat more subtle statistical problem with these equations is that, if the accelerationist hypothesis is correct, the results are either estimates of a short-run curve or are statistically unstable. Suppose the true value of b is unity. Then when current inflation equals anticipated inflation, which is the definition of a long-run curve, we have that

$$f(U) = -a. \tag{A1.4}$$

This is the vertical long-run Phillips curve with the value of U that satisfies it being the natural rate of unemployment. Any other values of U reflect either short-term equilibrium positions or a stochastic component in the natural rate. But the estimation process used, with $\frac{1}{P}\frac{dP}{dt}$ on the left-hand side, treats different observed rates of unemployment as if they were exogenous, as if they could persist indefinitely. There is simply no way of deriving Equation (A1.4) from such an approach. In effect, the implicit assumption that unemployment can take different values begs the whole question raised by the accelerationist hypothesis. On a statistical level, this approach requires putting U, or a function of U, on the left-hand side, not $\frac{1}{p}\frac{dP}{dt}$.

RATIONAL EXPECTATIONS

A still more fundamental criticism has recently been made by a number of economists in the United States. This criticism has its origin in an important article by John Muth on rational expectations. The rational expectations approach has been applied to the problem in recent articles by Robert Lucas of Carnegie-Mellon (later Chicago), Tom Sargent of the University of Minnesota, and a number of others.[17]

This criticism is that you cannot take seriously the notion that people form anticipations on the basis of a weighted average of past experience with fixed weights – or any other scheme that is inconsistent with the way inflation is really being generated. For example, let us suppose that

---

[17] John Muth, 'Rational Expectations and the Theory of Price Movements', *Econometrica, July* 1961, pp. 315–35; Robert E. Lucas, 'Econometric Testing of the Natural Rate Hypothesis', in Otto Eckstein (ed.), *The Econometrics of Price Determination Conference*, Board of Governors of the Federal Reserve System and Social Science Research Council, Washington, 1972, 'Econometric Policy Evaluation: A Critique', Carnegie-Mellon University Working Paper, 1973. 'Some International Evidence on Output-Inflation Tradeoffs', *American Economic Review*, June 1973, pp. 326–34; Thomas J. Sargent, 'Rational Expectations, the Real Rate of Interest, and the "Natural" Rate of Unemployment', *Brookings Papers on Economic Activity*, Vol. 2, 1973, pp. 429–72; and Thomas J. Sargent and Neil Wallace, '"Rational" Expectations, the Optimal Money Instrument and the Optimal Money Supply Rule', *Journal of Political Economy*, April 1974.

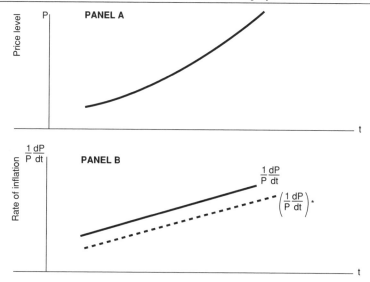

Figure A.5

the current course of the price level is the one drawn on panel A of Figure A.5, that inflation is accelerating. With a fixed exponential weighting pattern (with weights summing to unity) the anticipated rate of inflation will always be lagging behind, as in Panel B. But people who are forming anticipations are not fools – or at least some of them are not. They are not going to *persist* in being wrong. And more generally they are not going to base their anticipations solely on the past history of prices. Is there anybody in this room whose anticipation of inflation next year will be independent of the result of the coming British elections? That is not reported in the past record of prices. Will it be independent of policies announced by the parties that come into power, and so on? Therefore, said Muth, we should assume that people form their anticipations on the basis of a correct economic theory: not that they are right in *each individual* case but that over any long period they *will on the average* be right. Sometimes this will lead to the formation of anticipations on the basis of adaptive expectations, but by no means always.

If you apply that idea to the present problem it turns out that, if the true world is one in which people form expectations on a rational basis so that on the average they are right, then assuming that they form expectations by averaging the past with fixed weights will yield a value of b in equation (3) less than unity even though the true value is unity.

Consider a world in which there is a vertical long-run Phillips curve and in which people form their expectations rationally, so that on the average, over a long period, their expectations are equal to what happens. In such a world, the statistician comes along and estimates equation (A1.3) on the assumption that people form their anticipations by averaging past experience with fixed weights. What will he find? It turns out that he will find that b is less than 1. Of course, this possibility does not prove that the statistical tests incorporating adaptive expectations are wrong but only provides an alternative interpretation of their results.

In a series of very interesting and important papers, Lucas and Sargent[18] have explored the implication of the rational expectations hypothesis and have tried to derive empirical tests of

---

[18] See reference in footnote 17.

the slope of the long-run Phillips curve without the possibly misleading assumption of adaptive expectations.

Their empirical tests use a different kind of information. For example, one implication of a rational expectations hypothesis is that, in a country in which prices have fluctuated a great deal, expectations will respond to changes in the current rate of inflation much more rapidly than in a country in which prices have been relatively stable. It follows that the observed short-run Phillips curve will be steeper in the first country than in the second. Comparisons among countries in this way, as well as other tests, seem so far entirely consistent with what any reasonable man must surely expect: which is that, *since you can't fool all the people all the time, the true long-run Phillips curve is vertical.*

IMPLICATIONS FOR THEORY AND POLICY

It is worth noting how far-reaching are the implications of this view not only for the Phillips curve problem but also for policy.

One very strong and very important implication for policy is that, if you treat people as forming expectations on a rational basis, no fixed rule of monetary or fiscal policy will enable you to achieve anything other than the natural rate of unemployment. And you can see why. Because – to go back to my initial Phillips curve analysis – the only way in which you ever get a reduction of unemployment is through *unanticipated* inflation.

If the government follows any fixed rule whatsoever, *so long as the people know it*, they will be able to take it into account. And consequently you cannot achieve an unemployment target other than the natural rate by any fixed rule. The only way you can do so is by continually being cleverer than all the people, by continually making up *new* rules and using them for a while until people catch up with them. Then you must invent a new set of rules. That is not a very promising possibility.

This analysis provides a different sort of intellectual background for a view that some of us have held for a long time: that it is a better approach to policy to say that you are going to co-operate with the people and inform them of what you are doing, so giving them a basis for their judgements, rather than trying to fool them. What the Sargent/Lucas argument and analysis really suggests is that you are fooling yourself if you think that you can fool them.

That is about where the present state of the argument is. I might summarise by saying that there is essentially no economist any longer who believes in the naive Phillips curve of the kind originally proposed. The argument has shifted now to a second level, where everybody agrees that the long-run Phillips curve is steeper than the short-run Phillips curve. The only argument is whether it is vertical or not quite so vertical. And here the evidence is not quite all in. But there is a line of approach in analysis and reasoning which enables you to interpret, so far as I know, all the existing evidence consistently on the hypothesis of a long-run vertical Phillips curve.

Appendix 2
The Counter-Revolution in Monetary Theory[1]

Milton Friedman

INTRODUCTION

It is a great pleasure to be with you today, partly because I am honoured at being the first of the Harold Wincott lecturers,[2] partly because economics owes so much to the work that has been done on this island. Coming back to Britain, as I am fortunate enough to be able to do from time to time, always means coming back to a warm circle of friends or friendly enemies.

I am going to talk this afternoon primarily about a scientific development that has little ideological or political content. This development nonetheless has great relevance to governmental policy because it bears on the likely effects of particular kinds of governmental policy regardless of what party conducts the policy and for what purpose.

A counter-revolution must be preceded by two stages: an initial position from which there was a revolution, and the revolution. In order to set the stage, I would like first to make a few remarks about the initial position and the revolution.

It is convenient to have names to describe these positions. The initial position I shall call the quantity theory of money and associate it largely with the name of an American economist, Irving Fisher, although it is a doctrine to which many prominent English economists also made contributions. The revolution, as you all know, was made by Keynes in the 1930s. Keynes himself was a quantity theorist, so that his revolution was from, as it were, within the governing body. Keynes's name is the obvious name to attach to the revolution. The counter-revolution also needs a name, and perhaps the one most widely used in referring to it is 'the Chicago School'. More recently, however, it has been given a name which is less lovely but which has become so attached to it that I find it hard to avoid using it. That name is 'monetarism' because of the renewed emphasis on the role of the quantity of money.

A counter-revolution, whether in politics or in science, never restores the initial situation. It always produces a situation that has some similarity to the initial one but is also strongly influenced by the intervening revolution. That is certainly true of monetarism, which has benefited much from Keynes's work. Indeed I may say, as have so many others since there is no way of contradicting it, that if Keynes were alive today he would no doubt be at the forefront of the counter-revolution. You must never judge a master by his disciples.

---

[1] I chose this title because I used it about a dozen years ago for a talk at the London School of Economics. At that time, I was predicting. Now, I am reporting.

[2] The first impression of this paper was the first Wincott Memorial Lecture in 1970 published as IEA Occasional Paper 33 by the IEA in 1970. Reproduced with permission of the Wincott Foundation.

Issues in Monetary Policy. Edited by K. Matthews and P. Booth.

IRVING FISHER AND THE QUANTITY THEORY

Let me then start briefly to set the stage with the initial position, the quantity theory of money as developed primarily by Irving Fisher, who is to my mind by far the greatest American economist. He was also an extraordinarily interesting and eccentric man. Indeed, I suspect that his professional reputation suffered during his life because he was not only an economist but also involved in many other activities, including being one of the leading members of the American prohibitionist party. He interviewed all potential presidential candidates for something like 30 years to find out what their position was on the subject of alcohol. His best-selling book, which has been translated into the largest number of languages, is not about economics at all but about health. It is about how to eat and keep healthy and is entitled *How to Live* (written jointly with Dr E.L. Fisk). But even that book is a tribute to his science. When he was a young man in his early thirties, he contracted tuberculosis, was given a year to live by his physicians, went out to the Far West where the air was good and proceeded to immerse himself in the study of health and methods of eating and so on. If we may judge the success of his scientific work by its results, he lived to the age of 80. As you may know, he was also a leading statistician, developed the theory of index numbers, worked in mathematics, economics and utility theory and had time enough besides to invent the Kar-dex filing system, the familiar system in which one little envelope flaps on another, so you can pull out a flat drawer to see what is in it. He founded what is now Remington-Rand Corporation in order to produce and distribute his invention. As you can see, he was a man of very wide interests and ability.

MV = PT

The basic idea of the quantity theory, that there is a relation between the quantity of money on the one hand and prices on the other, is surely one of the oldest ideas in economics. It goes back thousands of years. But it is one thing to express this idea in general terms. It is another thing to introduce system into the relation between money on the one hand and prices and other magnitudes on the other. What Irving Fisher did was to analyse the relationship in far greater detail than had ever been done earlier. He developed and popularised what has come to be known as the quantity equation: $MV = PT$, money multiplied by velocity equals prices multiplied by the volume of transactions. This is an equation that every college student of economics used to have to learn, then for a time did not, and now, as the counter-revolution has progressed, must again learn. Fisher not only presented this equation, he also applied it in a variety of contexts. He once wrote a famous article interpreting the business cycle as the 'dance of the dollar', in which he argued that fluctuations in economic activity were primarily a reflection of changes in the quantity of money. Perhaps even more pertinent to the present day, he analysed in detail the relation between inflation on the one hand and interest rates on the other. His first book on this subject, *Appreciation and Interest*, published in 1896, can be read today with profit and is immediately applicable to today's conditions.

In that work, Fisher made a distinction which again is something that went out of favour and has now come back into common use, namely the distinction between the nominal interest rate in pounds per year per hundred pounds and the real interest rate, i.e., corrected for the effect of changing prices. If you lend someone £100 today and in 12 months receive back £106, and if in the meantime prices rise by 6 per cent then your £106 will be worth no more than your £100 today. The nominal interest rate is 6 per cent, but the real interest rate is zero.

This distinction between the nominal interest rate and the real interest rate is of the utmost importance in understanding the effects of monetary policy as well as the behaviour of interest rates. Fisher also distinguished sharply between the actual real rate, the rate realised after the event, and the anticipated real rate that lenders expected to receive or borrowers expected to pay. No one would lend money at 6 per cent if he expected prices to rise by 6 per cent during the year. If he did lend at 6 per cent, it must have been because he expected prices to rise by less than 6 per cent: the realised real rate was less than the anticipated real rate. This distinction between the actual real rate and the anticipated real rate is of the greatest importance today in understanding the course of events. It explains why inflation is so stubborn once it has become imbedded, because as inflation accelerates, people come to expect it. They come to build the expected inflation into the interest rates that they are willing to pay as borrowers or that they demand as lenders.

Wide consensus

Up to, let us say, the year 1930, Irving Fisher's analysis was widely accepted. In monetary theory, that analysis was taken to mean that in the quantity equation $MV = PT$ the term for velocity could be regarded as highly stable, that it could be taken as determined independently of the other terms in the equation, and that as a result changes in the quantity of money would be reflected either in prices or in output. It was also widely taken for granted that short-term fluctuations in the economy reflected changes in the quantity of money, or in the terms and conditions under which credit was available. It was taken for granted that the trend of prices over any considerable period reflected the behaviour of the quantity of money over that period.

In economic policy, it was widely accepted that monetary policy was the primary instrument available for stabilising the economy. Moreover, it was accepted that monetary policy should be operated largely through a combination of two blades of a scissors, the one blade being what we in the USA call 'discount rate' and you in Britain call 'Bank rate', the other blade being open-market operations, the purchase and sale of government securities.

That was more or less the initial doctrinal position prior to the Keynesian revolution. It was a position that was widely shared. Keynes's *A Tract on Monetary Reform*[3] which I believe remains to this day one of his best books, reflects the consensus just described.

THE KEYNESIAN REVOLUTION

Then came the Keynesian revolution. What produced that revolution was the course of events. My colleague, George Stigler, in discussing the history of thought, has often argued that major changes within a discipline come from inside the discipline and are not produced by the impact of outside events. He may well be right in general. But in this particular instance I believe the basic source of the revolution and of the reaction against the quantity theory of money was a historical event, namely the great contraction or depression. In the United Kingdom, the contraction started in 1925 when Britain went back on gold at the pre-war parity and ended in 1931 when Britain went off gold. In the United States, the contraction started in 1929 and ended when the USA went off gold in early 1933. In both countries, economic conditions were depressed for years after the contraction itself had ended and an expansion had begun.

---

[3] Macmillan, 1923.

Wrong lessons from the Great Depression

The Great Depression shattered the acceptance of the quantity theory of money because it was widely interpreted as demonstrating that monetary policy was ineffective, at least against a decline in business. All sorts of aphorisms were coined that are still with us, to indicate why it was that providing monetary ease would not necessarily lead to economic expansion, such as 'You can lead a horse to water but you can't make him drink' or 'Monetary policy is like a string: you can pull on it but you can't push on it', and doubtless there are many more.

As it happens, this interpretation of the depression was completely wrong. It turns out, as I shall point out more fully below, that on re-examination, the depression is a tragic testament to the effectiveness of monetary policy, not a demonstration of its impotence. But what mattered for the world of ideas was not what was true but what was believed to be true. And it was believed at the time that monetary policy had been tried and had been found wanting.

In part that view reflected the natural tendency for the monetary authorities to blame other forces for the terrible economic events that were occurring. The people who run monetary policy are human beings, even as you and I, and a common human characteristic is that if anything bad happens it is somebody else's fault. In the course of collaborating on a book on the monetary history of the United States, I had the dismal task of reading through 50 years of annual reports of the Federal Reserve Board. The only element that lightened that dreary task was the cyclical oscillation in the power attributed to monetary policy by the system. In good years the report would read 'Thanks to the excellent monetary policy of the Federal Reserve . . . ' In bad years the report would read 'Despite the excellent policy of the Federal Reserve . . . ', and it would go on to point out that monetary policy really was, after all, very weak and other forces so much stronger.

The monetary authorities proclaimed that they were pursuing easy money policies when in fact they were not, and their protestations were largely accepted. Hence Keynes, along with many others, concluded that monetary policy had been tried and found wanting. In contrast to most others, he offered an alternative analysis to explain why the depression had occurred and to indicate a way of ameliorating the situation.

Keynes's critique of the quantity theory

Keynes did not deny Irving Fisher's quantity equation. What Keynes said was something different. He said that, while of course MV equals PT, velocity, instead of being highly stable, is highly adaptable. If the quantity of money goes up, he said, what will happen is simply that the velocity of circulation of money will go down and nothing will happen on the other side of the equation to either prices or output. Correspondingly, if something pushes the right-hand side of the equation, PT or income, up without an increase in the quantity of money, all that will happen will be that velocity will rise. In other words, he said, velocity is a will-of-the-wisp. It can move one way or the other in response to changes either in the quantity of money or in income. The quantity of money is therefore of minor importance. (Since I am trying to cover highly technical material very briefly, I am leaving out many qualifications that are required for a full understanding of either Fisher or Keynes. I do want to stress that the statements I am making are simplifications and are not to be taken as a full exposition of any of the theories.)

What matters, said Keynes, is not the quantity of money. What matters is the part of total spending which is independent of current income, what has come to be called autonomous spending and to be identified in practice largely with investment by business and expenditures by government.

Keynes thereby directed attention away from the role of money and its relation to the flow of income and toward the relation between two flows of income, that which corresponds to autonomous spending and that which corresponds to induced spending. Moreover, he said, in the modern world, prices are highly rigid while quantities can change readily. When for whatever reason autonomous spending changes, the resulting change in income will manifest itself primarily in output and only secondarily and only after long lags in prices. Prices are determined by costs consisting mostly of wages, and wages are determined by the accident of past history.

The great contraction, he said, was the result of a collapse of demand for investment which in turn reflected a collapse of productive opportunities to use capital. Thus the engine and the motor of the great contraction was a collapse of investment transformed into a collapse of income by the multiplier process.

The implications for policy

This doctrine had far-reaching implications for economic policy. It meant that monetary policy was of little importance. Its only role was to keep interest rates down, both to reduce the pressure on the government budget in paying interest on its debts, and also because it might have a tiny bit of stimulating effect on investment. From this implication of the doctrine came the cheap money policy which was tried in country after country following World War II.

A second implication of the doctrine was that the major reliance for economic stabilisation could not be on monetary policy, as the quantity theorists had thought, but must be on fiscal policy, that is, on varying the rate of government spending and taxing.

A third implication was that inflation is largely to be interpreted as a cost-push phenomenon. It follows, although Keynes himself did not draw this conclusion from his doctrine, that the way to counteract inflation is through an incomes policy. If costs determine prices and costs are historically determined, then the way to stop any rise in prices is to stop the rise in costs.

These views became widely accepted by economists at large both as theory and as implications for policy. It is hard now at this distance in time to recognise how widely they were accepted. Let me just give you one quotation which could be multiplied many-fold, to give you the flavour of the views at the end of World War II. Parenthetically, acceptance of these views continued until more recently in Britain than in the United States, so it may be easier for you to recognise the picture I have been painting than it would be now for people in the United States. I quote from John H. Williams, who was a Professor of Economics at Harvard University, a principal adviser to the Federal Reserve Bank of New York, and widely regarded as an anti-Keynesian. In 1945 he wrote: 'I have long believed that the quantity of money by itself has a permissive rather than a positive effect on prices and production'. And in the sentence I want to stress he wrote: 'I can see no prospect of a revival of general monetary control in the post-war period'. That was a sweeping statement, and one that obviously proved very far indeed from the mark.

The high point in the United States of the application of Keynesian ideas to economic policy probably came with the new economists of the Kennedy administration. Their finest hour was the tax cut of 1964 which was premised entirely on the principles that I have been describing.

Having sketched briefly the initial stage of the quantity theory, and the revolutionary stage of the Keynesian theory, I come now to the monetarist counter-revolution.

THE COUNTER-REVOLUTION

As so often happens, just about the time that Keynes's ideas were being triumphant in practice, they were losing their hold on the minds of scholars in the academies. A number of factors contributed to a change of attitude towards the Keynesian doctrine. One was the experience immediately after World War II. On the basis of the Keynesian analysis, economists and others expected the war to be followed by another great depression. With our present experience of over two decades of inflation behind us it is hard to recognise that this was the sentiment of the times. But alike in the United States, in Great Britain and in many other countries, the dominant view was that, once World War II ended, once the pump-priming and government spending for military purposes ended, there would be an enormous economic collapse because of the scarcity of investment opportunities that had been given the blame for the Great Depression. Massive unemployment and massive deflation were the bugaboos of the time. As you all know, that did not happen. The problem after the war turned out to be inflation rather than deflation.

A second post-war experience that was important was the failure of cheap money policies. In Britain, Chancellor Dalton tried to follow the Keynesian policy of keeping interest rates very low. As you all know, he was unable to do so and had to give up. The same thing happened in the United States. The Federal Reserve System followed a policy of pegging bond prices, trying to keep interest rates down. It finally gave up in 1953 after the Treasury-Federal Reserve Accord of 1951 laid the groundwork for setting interest rates free. In country after country, wherever the cheap money policy was tried, it led to inflation and had to be abandoned. In no country was inflation contained until orthodox monetary policy was employed. Germany was one example in 1948; Italy shortly after; Britain and the United States later yet.

Reconsideration of the Great Depression

Another important element that contributed to a questioning of the Keynesian doctrine was a re-examination of monetary history and particularly of the Great Depression. When the evidence was examined in detail it turned out that bad monetary policy had to be given a very large share of the blame. In the United States, there was a reduction in the quantity of money by a third from 1929 to 1933. This reduction in the quantity of money clearly made the depression much longer and more severe than it otherwise would have been. Moreover, and equally important, it turned out that the reduction in the quantity of money was not a consequence of the unwillingness of horses to drink. It was not a consequence of being unable to push on a string. It was a direct consequence of the policies followed by the Federal Reserve system.

From 1930 to 1933, a series of bank runs and bank failures were permitted to run their course because the Federal Reserve failed to provide liquidity for the banking system, which was one of the main functions the designers of the Federal Reserve system intended it to perform. Banks failed because the public at large, fearful for the safety of their deposits, tried to convert their deposits into currency. In a fractional reserve system, it is literally impossible for all depositors to do that unless there is some source of additional currency. The Federal Reserve system was established in 1913 in response to the banking panic of 1907 primarily to provide additional liquidity at a time of pressure on banks. In 1930–33, the system failed to do so and it failed to do so despite the fact that there were many people in the system who were calling upon it to do so and who recognised that this was its correct function.

It was widely asserted at the time that the decline in the quantity of money was a consequence of the lack of willing borrowers. Perhaps the most decisive bit of evidence against
that interpretation is that many banks failed because of a decline in the price of government
securities. Indeed, it turned out that many banks that had made bad private loans came through
much better than banks that had been cautious and had bought large amounts of Treasury and
municipal securities for secondary liquidity. The reason was that there was a market for the
government securities and hence when bank examiners came around to check on the banks,
they had to mark down the price of the government's debt to the market value. However, there
was no market for bad loans, and therefore they were carried on the books at face value. As a
result, many careful, conservative banks failed.

The quantity of money fell by a third and roughly a third of all banks failed. This is itself a
fascinating story and one that I can only touch on. The important point for our purposes is that
it is crystal clear that at all times during the contraction, the Federal Reserve had it within its
power to prevent the decline in the quantity of money and to produce an increase. Monetary
policy had not been tried and found wanting. It had not been tried. Or, alternatively, it had been
tried perversely. It had been used to force an incredible deflation on the American economy
and on the rest of the world. If Keynes – and this is the main reason why I said what I did at
the beginning – if Keynes had known the facts about the Great Depression as we now know
them, he could not have interpreted that episode as he did.

Wider evidence

Another scholarly element that contributed to a reaction against the Keynesian doctrine and to
the emergence of the new doctrine was extensive empirical analysis of the relation between the
quantity of money on the one hand, and income, prices and interest rates on the other. Perhaps
the simplest way for me to suggest why this was relevant is to recall that an essential element
of the Keynesian doctrine was the passivity of velocity. If money rose, velocity would decline.
Empirically, however, it turns out that the movements of velocity tend to reinforce those of
money instead of to offset them. When the quantity of money declined by a third from 1929
to 1933 in the United States, velocity declined also. When the quantity of money rises rapidly
in almost any country, velocity also rises rapidly. Far from velocity offsetting the movements
of the quantity of money, it reinforces them.

I cannot go into the whole body of scientific work that has been done. I can only say
that there has arisen an extensive literature concerned with exploring these relations which
has demonstrated very clearly the existence of a consistent relation between changes in the
quantity of money and changes in other economic magnitudes of a very different kind from
that which Keynes assumed to exist.

The final blow, at least in the United States, to the Keynesian orthodoxy was a number of
dramatic episodes in our recent domestic experience. These episodes centred around two key
issues. The first was whether the behaviour of the quantity of money or rates of interest is a
better criterion to use in conducting monetary policy. You have had a curious combination in
this area of central bankers harking back to the real bills doctrine of the early 18th century on the
one hand, and Keynesians on the other, who alike agreed that the behaviour of interest rates was
the relevant criterion for the conduct of monetary policy. By contrast, the new interpretation is
that interest rates are a misleading index of policy and that central bankers should look rather
at the quantity of money. The second key issue was the relative role of fiscal policy and of
monetary policy. By fiscal policy, I mean changes in government spending and taxing, holding

the quantity of money constant. By monetary policy, I mean changes in the quantity of money, holding government spending and taxing constant.

Fiscal versus Monetary Policy

The problem in discussing the relative roles of fiscal policy and monetary policy is primarily to keep them separate, because in practice they operate jointly most of the time. Ordinarily if a government raises its spending without raising taxes, that is if it incurs a deficit in order to be expansionary, it will finance some of the deficit by printing money. Conversely if it runs a surplus, it will use part of that surplus to retire money. But from an analytical point of view, and from the point of view of getting at the issue that concerns the counter-revolution, it is important to consider fiscal policy and monetary policy separately, to consider each operating by itself. The Keynesians regarded as a clear implication of their position the proposition that fiscal policy by itself is important in affecting the level of income, that a large deficit would have essentially the same expansionary influence on the economy whether it was financed by borrowing from the public or by printing money.

The 'monetarists' rejected this proposition and maintained that fiscal policy by itself is largely ineffective, that what matters is what happens to the quantity of money. Off-hand that seems like an utterly silly idea. It seems absurd to say that if the government increases its expenditures without increasing taxes, that may not by itself be expansionary. Such a policy obviously puts income into the hands of the people to whom the government pays out its expenditures without taking any extra funds out of the hands of the taxpayers. Is that not obviously expansionary or inflationary? Up to that point, yes, but that is only half the story. We have to ask where the government gets the extra funds it spends. If the government prints money to meet its bills, that is monetary policy and we are trying to look at fiscal policy by itself. If the government gets the funds by borrowing from the public, then those people who lend the funds to the government have less to spend or to lend to others. The effect of the higher government expenditures may simply be higher spending by government and those who receive government funds and lower spending by those who lend to government or by those to whom lenders would have loaned the money instead. To discover any net effect on total spending, one must go to a more sophisticated level – to differences in the behaviour of the two groups of people or to effects of government borrowing on interest rates. There is no first-order effect.

Evidence from US 'experiments'

The critical first test on both these key issues came in the USA in 1966. There was fear of developing inflation and in the spring of 1966 the Federal Reserve Board, belatedly, stepped very hard on the brake. I say 'stepped very hard' because the record of the Federal Reserve over 50 years is that it has almost invariably acted too much too late. Almost always it has waited too long before acting and then acted too strongly. In 1966, the result was a combination of a very tight monetary policy, under which the quantity of money did not grow at all during the final nine months of the year, and a very expansive fiscal policy. So you had a nice experiment. Which was going to dominate? The tight money policy or the easy fiscal policy? The Keynesians in general argued that the easy fiscal policy was going to dominate and therefore predicted continued rapid expansion in 1967. The monetarists argued that monetary policy would dominate, and so it turned out. There was a definite slowing down in the rate of growth of economic activity in the first half of 1967, following the tight money policy of 1966. When, in early 1967, the Federal Reserve reversed its policy and started to print money like mad, about six or nine months later, after the usual lag, income recovered and a rapid expansion in economic activity followed. Quite clearly, monetary policy had dominated fiscal policy in that encounter.

A still more dramatic example came in 1968 and from 1968 to 1970. In the summer of 1968, under the influence of the Council of Economic Advisers and at the recommendation of President Johnson, Congress enacted a surtax of 10 per cent on income. It was enacted in order to fight the inflation which was then accelerating. The believers in the Keynesian view were so persuaded of the potency of this weapon that they were afraid of 'overkill'. They thought the tax increase might be too much and might stop the economy in its tracks. They persuaded the Federal Reserve system, or I should rather say that the Federal Reserve system was of the same view. Unfortunately for the United States, but fortunately for scientific knowledge, the Federal Reserve accordingly decided that it had best offset the overkill effects of fiscal policy by expanding the quantity of money rapidly. Once again, we had a beautiful controlled experiment with fiscal policy extremely tight and monetary policy extremely easy. Once again, there was a contrast between two sets of predictions. The Keynesians or fiscalists argued that the surtax would produce a sharp slow-down in the first half of 1969 at the latest while the monetarists argued that the rapid growth in the quantity of money would more than offset the fiscal effects, so that there would be a continued inflationary boom in the first half of 1969. Again, the monetarists proved correct. Then, in December 1968, the Federal Reserve Board did move to tighten money in the sense of slowing down the rate of growth of the quantity of money and that was followed after the appropriate interval by a slow-down in the economy. This test, I may say, is still in process at the time of this lecture, but up to now it again seems to be confirming the greater importance of the monetary than of the fiscal effect.

'This is Where I came in'

One swallow does not make a spring. My own belief in the greater importance of monetary policy does not rest on these dramatic episodes. It rests on the experience of hundreds of years and of many countries. These episodes of the past few years illustrate that effect; they do not demonstrate it. Nonetheless, the public at large cannot be expected to follow the great masses of statistics. One dramatic episode is far more potent in influencing public opinion than a pile of well-digested, but less dramatic, episodes. The result in the USA at any rate has been a drastic shift in opinion, both professional and lay.

This shift, so far as I can detect, has been greater in the United States than in the United Kingdom. As a result, I have had in the UK the sensation that I am sure all of you have had in a continuous cinema when you come to the point where you say, 'Oh, this is where I came in.' The debate about monetary effects in Britain is pursuing the identical course that it pursued in the United States about five or so years ago. I am sure that the same thing must have happened in the 1930s. When the British economists wandered over to the farther shores among their less cultivated American brethren, bringing to them the message of Keynes, they must have felt, as I have felt coming to these shores in the opposite direction, that this was where they came in. I am sure they then encountered the same objections that they had encountered in Britain five years earlier. And so it is today. Criticism of the monetary doctrines in this country today is at the naive, unsophisticated level we encountered in the USA about five or more years ago.

Thanks to the very able and active group of economists in this country who are currently working on the monetary statistics, and perhaps even more to the effect which the course of events will have, I suspect that the developments in this country will continue to imitate those in the United States. Not only in this area, but in other areas as well, I have had the experience of initially being in a small minority and have had the opportunity to observe the scenario that unfolds as an idea gains wider acceptance. There is a standard pattern. When anybody threatens an orthodox position, the first reaction is to ignore the interloper. The less said about him the better. But if he begins to win a hearing and gets annoying, the second reaction is to ridicule him, make fun of him as an extremist, a foolish fellow who has these silly ideas. After that stage passes the next, and the most important, stage is to put on his clothes. You adopt for your own his views, and then attribute to him a caricature of those views saying, 'He's an extremist, one of those fellows who says only money matters – everybody knows that sort. Of course money does matter, but . . . '

KEY PROPOSITIONS OF MONETARISM

Let me finally describe the state to which the counter-revolution has come by listing system-atically the central propositions of monetarism.

1. There is a consistent though not precise relation between the rate of growth of the quantity of money and the rate of growth of nominal income. (By nominal income, I mean income measured in pounds sterling or in dollars or in francs, not real income, income measured in real goods.) That is, whether the amount of money in existence is growing by 3 per cent a year, 5 per cent a year or 10 per cent a year will have a significant effect on how fast nominal income grows. If the quantity of money grows rapidly, so will nominal income; and conversely.

2. This relation is not obvious to the naked eye largely because it takes time for changes in monetary growth to affect income and how long it takes is itself variable. The rate of monetary growth today is not very closely related to the rate of income growth today. Today's income growth depends on what has been happening to money in the past. What happens to money today affects what is going to happen to income in the future.

3. On the average, a change in the rate of monetary growth produces a change in the rate of growth of nominal income about six to nine months later. This is an average that does not hold in every individual case. Sometimes the delay is longer, sometimes shorter. But I have been astounded at how regularly an average delay of six to nine months is found under widely different conditions. I have studied the data for Japan, for India, for Israel, for the United States. Some of our students have studied it for Canada and for a number of South American countries. Whichever country you take, you generally get a delay of around six to nine months. How clear-cut the evidence for the delay is depends on how much variation there is in the quantity of money. The Japanese data have been particularly valuable because the Bank of Japan was very obliging for some 15 years from 1948 to 1963 and produced very wide movements in the rate of change in the quantity of money. As a result, there is no ambiguity in dating when it reached the top and when it reached the bottom. Unfortunately for science, in 1963 they discovered monetarism and they started to increase the quantity of money at a fairly stable rate and now we are not able to get much more information from the Japanese experience.

4. The changed rate of growth of nominal income typically shows up first in output and hardly at all in prices. If the rate of monetary growth is reduced then about six to nine months later, the rate of growth of nominal income and also of physical output will decline. However,

the rate of price rise will be affected very little. There will be downward pressure on prices only as a gap emerges between actual and potential output.

5. On the average, the effect on prices comes about six to nine months after the effect on income and output, so the total delay between a change in monetary growth and a change in the rate of inflation averages something like 12–18 months. That is why it is a long road to hoe to stop an inflation that has been allowed to start. It cannot be stopped overnight.

6. Even after allowance for the delay in the effect of monetary growth, the relation is far from perfect. There's many a slip 'twixt the monetary change and the income change.

7. In the short run, which may be as much as five or ten years, monetary changes affect primarily output. Over decades, on the other hand, the rate of monetary growth affects primarily prices. What happens to output depends on real factors: the enterprise, ingenuity and industry of the people; the extent of thrift; the structure of industry and government; the relations among nations, and so on.

8. It follows from the propositions I have so far stated that *inflation is always and everywhere a monetary phenomenon* in the sense that it is and can be produced only by a more rapid increase in the quantity of money than in output. However, there are many different possible reasons for monetary growth, including gold discoveries, financing of government spending, and financing of private spending.

9. Government spending may or may not be inflationary. It clearly will be inflationary if it is financed by creating money, that is, by printing currency or creating bank deposits. If it is financed by taxes or by borrowing from the public, the main effect is that the government spends the funds instead of the taxpayer or instead of the lender or instead of the person who would otherwise have borrowed the funds. Fiscal policy is extremely important in determining what fraction of total national income is spent by government and who bears the burden of that expenditure. By itself, it is not important for inflation. (This is the proposition about fiscal and monetary policy that I discussed earlier.)

10. One of the most difficult things to explain in simple fashion is the way in which a change in the quantity of money affects income. Generally, the initial effect is not on income at all, but on the prices of existing assets, bonds, equities, houses, and other physical capital. This effect, the liquidity effect stressed by Keynes, is an effect on the balance-sheet, not on the income account. An increased rate of monetary growth, whether produced through open-market operations or in other ways, raises the amount of cash that people and businesses have relative to other assets. The holders of the now excess cash will try to adjust their portfolios by buying other assets. But one man's spending is another man's receipts. All the people together cannot change the amount of cash all hold—only the monetary authorities can do that. However, as people *attempt* to change their cash balances, the effect spreads from one asset to another. This tends to raise the prices of assets and to reduce interest rates, which encourages spending to produce new assets and also encourages spending on current services rather than on purchasing existing assets. That is how the initial effect on balance-sheets gets translated into an effect on income and spending. The difference in this area between the monetarists and the Keynesians is not on the nature of the process, but on the range of assets considered. The Keynesians tend to concentrate on a narrow range of marketable assets and recorded interest rates. The monetarists insist that a far wider range of assets and of interest rates must be taken into account. They give importance to such assets as durable and even semi-durable consumer goods, structures and other real property. As a result, they regard the market interest rates stressed by the Keynesians as only a small part of the total spectrum of rates that are relevant.

11. One important feature of this mechanism is that a change in monetary growth affects interest rates in one direction at first but in the opposite direction later on. More rapid monetary growth at first tends to lower interest rates. But later on, as it raises spending and stimulates price inflation, it also produces a rise in the demand for loans which will tend to raise interest rates. In addition, rising prices introduce a discrepancy between real and nominal interest rates. That is why world-wide interest rates are highest in the countries that have had the most rapid rise in the quantity of money and also in prices – countries like Brazil, Chile or Korea. In the opposite direction, a slower rate of monetary growth at first raises interest rates but later on, as it reduces spending and price inflation, lowers interest rates. That is why world-wide interest rates are lowest in countries that *have had* the slowest rate of growth in the quantity of money – countries like Switzerland and Germany.

This two-edged relation between money and interest rates explains why monetarists insist that interest rates are a highly misleading guide to monetary policy. This is one respect in which the monetarist doctrines have already had a significant effect on US policy. The Federal Reserve in January 1970 shifted from primary reliance on 'money market conditions' (i.e., interest rates) as a criterion of policy to primary reliance on 'monetary aggregates' (i.e., the quantity of money).

The relations between money and yields on assets (interest rates and stock market earnings-price ratios) are even lower than between money and nominal income. Apparently, factors other than monetary growth play an extremely important part. Needless to say, we do not know in detail what they are, but that they are important we know from the many movements in interest rates and stock market prices which cannot readily be connected with movements in the quantity of money.

CONCLUDING CAUTIONS

These propositions clearly imply both that monetary policy is important and that the important feature of monetary policy is its effect on the quantity of money rather than on bank credit or total credit or interest rates. They also imply that wide swings in the rate of change of the quantity of money are destabilising and should be avoided. But beyond this, differing implications are drawn.

Some monetarists conclude that deliberate changes in the rate of monetary growth by the authorities can be useful to offset other forces making for instability, provided they are gradual and take into account the lags involved. They favour fine tuning, using changes in the quantity of money as the instrument of policy. Other monetarists, including myself, conclude that our present understanding of the relation between money, prices and output is so meagre, that there is so much leeway in these relations, that such discretionary changes do more harm than good. We believe that an automatic policy under which the quantity of money would grow at a steady rate – month-in, month-out, year-in, year-out – would provide a stable monetary framework for economic growth without itself being a source of instability and disturbance.

One of the most widespread misunderstandings of the monetarist position is the belief that this prescription of a stable rate of growth in the quantity of money derives from our confidence in a rigid connection between monetary change and economic change. The situation is quite the opposite. If I really believed in a precise, rigid, mechanical connection between money and income, if also I thought that I knew what it was and if I thought that the central bank shared that knowledge with me, which is an even larger 'if', I would then say that we should use the knowledge to offset other forces making for instability. However, I do not believe any of these 'ifs' to be true. On the average, there is a close relation between changes in the quantity of money and the subsequent course of national income. But economic policy must deal with the individual case, not the average. In any one case, there is much slippage. It is precisely this leeway, this looseness in the relation, this lack of a mechanical one-to-one correspondence between changes in money and in income that is the primary reason why I have long favoured for the USA a quasi-automatic monetary policy under which the quantity of money would grow at a steady rate of 4 or 5 per cent per year, month-in, month-out. (The desirable rate of growth will differ from country to country depending on the trends in output and money-holding propensities.)

There is a great deal of evidence from the past of attempts by monetary authorities to do better. The verdict is very clear. The attempts by monetary authorities to do better have done far more harm than good. The actions by the monetary authorities have been an important source of instability. As I have already indicated, the actions of the US monetary authorities were responsible for the 1929–33 catastrophe. They were responsible equally for the recent acceleration of inflation in the USA. That is why I have been and remain strongly opposed to discretionary monetary policy – at least until such time as we demonstrably know enough to limit discretion by more sophisticated rules than the steady-rate-of-growth rule I have suggested. That is why I have come to stress the danger of assigning too much weight to monetary policy. Just as I believe that Keynes's disciples went further than he himself would have gone, so I think there is a danger that people who find that a few good predictions have been made by using monetary aggregates will try to carry that relationship further than it can go. Three years ago I wrote:

> We are in danger of assigning to monetary policy a larger role than it can perform, in danger of asking it to accomplish tasks that it cannot achieve and, as a result, in danger of preventing it from making the contribution that it is capable of making.[4]

A steady rate of monetary growth at a moderate level can provide a framework under which a country can have little inflation and much growth. It will not produce perfect stability; it will not produce heaven on earth; but it can make an important contribution to a stable economic society.

---

[4] Milton Friedman, "The Role of Monetary Policy", Presidential Address to the American Economic Assoclation, 29 December 1967: *American Sconomic Review*, March 1968 (reprinted in *The Optimum Quantity of Money and Other Essays*, Aldine Publishing, 1969, pp. 95–110 – quotation from p. 99).

Index